Law and Economic Policy in America

Law and Economic Policy in America

The Evolution of the Sherman Antitrust Act

William Letwin

The University of Chicago Press
Chicago and London

The University of Chicago Press, Chicago 60637
The University of Chicago Press, Ltd., London

Phoenix edition 1981
Printed in the United States of America

88 87 86 85 84 83 82 81 1 2 3 4 5

Library of Congress Cataloging in Publication Data

Letwin, William.
Law and economic policy in America.

Originally published: New York: Random House.
Bibliography: p.
Includes index.
1. Antitrust law—United States. I. Title.
KF1649.L4 1981 343.73′072 81-7551
ISBN 0-226-47353-8 347.30372 AACR2

CONTENTS

PREFACE

"There ought to be a law against it." The American Dream, that special optimism which marks Americans off from other people, nowhere expresses itself better than in the belief that every new social disorder can be remedied by adding another statute to the books. Legislation, in that view, moves directly and by simple steps. The public sees that something is wrong. It protests, and its representatives dutifully pass a law. The law eliminates the problem. All is well until another evil arises and is disposed of in the same way.

This view of government, echoing the aspiration that every wrong should have a legal remedy, is venerable, noble, and ambitious. Declining to acknowledge that any problem is insoluble, and thus avoiding the crippling fatalism of some other societies, it is one of the great faiths that moves American civilization. At the same time, however, this optimism has a darker aspect. It encourages those outbursts of political passion that have marked great crises in American history; for men who strongly believe that every problem is soluble also believe that any problem which long continues unsolved must owe its persistence to frightful inefficiency or willful malice. Nevertheless, the benefits conferred by a passionate desire for justice served with undisillusioned energy seem to have exceeded the disadvantages of cynicism, irresponsibility, and violence; thus, one might conclude that, on balance, the common American view of law is socially wholesome.

It would still be subject to one other criticism. It is totally inaccurate.

Contrary to its premises, the public does not easily recognize wrongs. Especially in the domain of economic policy, what people eventually come to regard as wrong is often an inevitable by-product of arrangements they regard as good and desirable.

Contrary to its premises, the legislature does not always execute the will of the people, even when it would like to, because it cannot tell exactly what that will is or exactly how to translate that will into statutes.

And finally, statutes do not eliminate all problems. A statute cannot prevent violations; it can only teach, persuade, or penalize. More precisely, it can only penalize men if other men have first accused them and then found them guilty.

A law, therefore, never produces exactly the results that anyone would have desired. It falls short, overshoots, or goes clean off in some other direction.

This somewhat somber view of law as an instrument of economic policy is illustrated in the history of the Sherman Antitrust Act. My account of it will show why so big but apparently simple a problem as monopoly cannot be solved neatly or conclusively, and why so short and apparently simple a statute as the Sherman Act cannot be made to yield comfortably certain results. The essential difficulties are described in the opening chapter, and the story of how they affected the making and using of the law is then told in detail.

In telling a story that illustrates the insolubility of fundamental economic problems and the inevitable uncertainty of law, I do not mean to suggest that nothing can ever be done to ameliorate such problems or that no law is worth passing. Neither, on the other hand, do I tell the story as though it were a parable tending to promote any particular solution of the problem or revision of existing laws. I disclaim any purpose other than the recounting of a piece of history whose consequences are very much alive, though I would not be sorry if the telling suggested that tidiness is less desirable in a great society than in a tiny cottage.

ACKNOWLEDGMENTS

It is difficult to express adequately and accurately my gratitude to Dean Edward H. Levi and Professor Aaron Director, who administered the Antitrust Research Project at the University of Chicago Law School, under whose auspices the earlier parts of this work were done. They took great pains to teach me; but as I cannot affirm that what I learned was in all particulars what they meant to be teaching, I wish to thank them and at the same time to exonerate them.

I acknowledge generous aid during a number of years from the Sloan Research Fund at the Sloan School of Industrial Management of the Massachusetts Institute of Technology.

The editors of the *University of Chicago Law Review* and of the *Yale Law Journal* have kindly given permission to use materials originally published in my articles: "The English Common Law Concerning Monopolies," 21 *U. Chi. L. Rev.* 355 (1954); "Congress and the Sherman Antitrust Law," 23 *U. Chi. L. Rev.* 221 (1956); "The First Decade of the Sherman Act: Early Administration," 68 *Yale L. J.* 464 (1959); "The First Decade of the Sherman Act: Judicial Interpretation," 68 *Yale L. J.* 900 (1959).

Law and Economic Policy in America

CHAPTER ONE

INTRODUCTION: HAZARDS OF ECONOMIC POLICY AND OF LAW

The Sherman Act stands at the crossroads of economic policy and law. It declares the rules of the game for the American economy, and endows the government with broad authority to control private economic power. It is a peculiarly American institution, emerging from a legal tradition which, though not unique in the United States, is one of the great foundations of American civilization, and expressing a policy that has nowhere been followed so long and consistently as in the United States. If not the most powerful instrument of economic policy in the United States, the Sherman Act is the most characteristic.

Much economic policy today, far more than in the past, is made by discretionary acts of officials or by political acts of the legislature. The President adjusts tariff rates within broad statutory limits. The Federal Reserve Board alters rediscount rates at will. Congress passes a budget each year that registers hosts of fresh policy decisions. All such discretionary and political actions take place within the framework of Constitution and statutes; though discretionary, they are not arbitrary. Yet, though lawful, they resemble rule by fiat more than they do rule by law.

By contrast, the Sherman Act is the best example of an economic policy imposed by a general law. It lays down a far-reaching principle of policy—that the American economy shall continue competitive, or to put it more finely, that private efforts to eliminate competition shall be prohibited. The specific, concrete effects of the Act flow from this principle more or less "automatically," neither requiring nor permitting the sort of personal choice that enters every discretionary or political decision. The specific effects of the Act are produced in the first place by citizens who trim their behavior so as to conform to its commands, and otherwise by prosecutors and judges, who, though they cannot fail to exercise some personal judgment and some discretion, properly regard themselves as mere servants of the statutes and pupils of the precedent interpretations laid down by former judges. It is always men rather than laws that govern; but the Sherman Act comes as close as can be to establishing the rule of law within its own domain.

Since antitrust policy—or, more broadly, the policy governing the structure of the American economy—is fixed by statute and cannot be modified from moment to moment by discretionary or political action, it might be supposed to confer on the community one of the great benefits of law, which is certainty. Under the governance of law the citizen is supposed to be immune to the whims of those in power, knowing always the rules to which he is subject and will continue subject until due notice is given. And he is supposed to know, or be able to know, not only the words of the rules but also their real meaning, so that he can utterly avoid colliding with them.

But it is visionary to expect that the certainty of effect which every general law should aim at can ever be achieved absolutely. It is especially so in the case of the Sherman Act. From the beginning many men have criticized the Act as vague, its meaning as elusive, its commands as ambiguous. So it was and is. But these defects did not result, as many have supposed, from failings in the men who devised it and executed it. On the contrary, the defects resulted, almost inevitably, from two causes: the subtlety of the economic objectives that the Act was desired to achieve and the complexity of the political and legal process of which it is part.

Complexities of Economic Policy

To speak of the subtlety of the Sherman Act's economic objectives may seem extravagant. Need there be anything subtle about a statute that outlaws monopoly? Leaving the Sherman Act aside, why could not a statute declare in starkest simplicity: "Every monopoly is prohibited." The economic objective at which such a statute aimed would be as direct and uncomplicated as its language. The community, recognizing that a monopoly gives its owner the power to charge a higher price than he could were he exposed to competition, and regarding that power as unwarranted, destroys it. Stated in the converse, the community, recognizing the benefits of competition, prohibits the existence of noncompetitive firms. However stated, the objective would be single and simple. Where then does subtlety enter?

No doubt in a simple economy such a simple law might work well. In a very primitive economy, where everyone earned his living by farming his own farm, a simple law to preserve competition would be practicable and, moreover, redundant. However, in a very simple market economy, where each farmer worked his own farm and each city-dweller kept his own shop, a simple law to preserve competition would be both practicable and pertinent. It might, for instance, prevent any one man from buying up all existing cloth shops and becoming the only seller of cloth. It would enforce an unqualified rule of policy against monopoly.

Even in such a simple economy, of course, the simple law could not operate without raising desperate difficulties of judgment. For instance, suppose the community contained only one tradesman of a certain sort—say, a mapmaker. Suppose, moreover, that he were the only mapmaker for no reason other than that he made as many maps as anyone cared to buy. He would be, in fact, an unmistakable monopolist; he would enjoy the power to set a price on maps greater than he could have charged had there been competitors. Yet, on the other hand, even if he made the most of his power he might still earn a very meager income; and he might be universally acknowledged to be a man of impeccable innocence. Nevertheless, the simple law declaring "every monopoly" to be unlawful, if that law were applied even-handedly, would necessarily condemn him. He would then be forced either to quit his trade, thus depriving himself of work and the community of maps, or to bribe someone else to set up as a fictitious competitor, thus depriving himself of income and saddling the community with a redundant and costly service. No community that cared for justice would tolerate such a result. Its judges or legislators would invent a distinction between a "monopolist" and a "monopolizer," between one who inadvertently controls the whole of his trade and another who controls it as a result of deliberate efforts to acquire and retain that control. This distinction once invented, the law would have lost some of its pristine simplicity, for now the state's prosecutors and the judges would have to use judgment in determining whether any given monopoly was achieved with innocent or guilty intent.

Furthermore, even in the simple economy many other problems would arise in interpreting the simple antimonopoly law. Granted that if any one man quickly bought up all ten of the community's cloth shops he would obviously have violated the law—that is, the intent to monopolize might fairly be inferred from his behavior, unless he could prove some other intent—still, what if some man acquired only five of the ten? Judges might then reasonably disagree as to how the law should apply, some saying that in prohibiting an end result the law implicitly prohibits steps toward it, others holding that if the law implicitly prohibited any act that *might* lead to an unlawful result the laws would be safeguarding the public at the cost of paralyzing it. If a man known to hate his mother-in-law buys a rope, has he or has he not gone far enough on the road to murder so that the law should stop him? Has the buyer of five of the ten cloth shops come close enough to monopolizing to be stopped by the law?

If the citizens of the community loved competition to the exclusion of all other rights and values, they might readily answer that even if buying half the cloth shops did not confer monopolistic power on their owner, he ought to be prevented from buying them because he could have no acceptable justification for owning more than one shop. They would in effect urge judges to interpret the law that *said* "Every monopoly is prohibited" as *meaning* "Every diminution of competition is prohibited." If, however, the citizens of the community were not so single-minded, if they believed that not only is competition good but also that every man's right to buy and sell is good, then they would be deeply perplexed by the case of the five-shop buyer. They would be perplexed also by a two-shop buyer. After all, a man's right to buy and sell ought to stretch far enough to let him buy a second shop; and if anyone wondered why he needed to buy a second cloth shop rather than a second shop selling some other sort of goods, he might justifiably answer that he neither understood nor enjoyed any trade but his own. Yet on the other hand, the exercise of this admired right to buy and sell shops would clash sooner or later with the equally admired principle of maintaining competition. Where to draw the line would be a problem for any conscientious citizen of that community.

It is clear, therefore, that even in a very simple economy possessing the simplest conceivable antimonopoly law, subtlety would inevitably appear if the community prized as few as two principles that might on occasion clash. The economic policy of that law would be complex rather than simple: it would be to prevent men from monopolizing, but to prevent them in a manner that did not excessively interfere with their freedom to transfer property. Needless to say, if the economy were as simple as may be, but the community's system of ideals rich and complex, the economic policy implicit in that law would necessarily be complex and subtle as well. And it would be still more so if the community did not have a uniform system of ideals and aspirations, but its various members disagreed about the weights that ought to be attached to various of the commonly held values.

No minute demonstration is needed to establish that the American economy and the American system of values were quite complex by the 1880's, when the Sherman Act was first considered. Both, indeed, were so complex that they cannot be described fully, but can only be represented in drastically simplified outline.

The fraction of the American system of values which immediately touches on economic policy can be summarized by the label "capitalist," though the label is dangerously close to a caricature. A slightly fuller, and therefore safer, statement is that American economic policy has always rested on two principles: (1) government should play a fairly confined role in economic life, and (2) private economic activities should be controlled largely by competition. The first of these propositions is regularly misrepresented in the phrase *laissez faire*. If *laissez faire* means that government should keep its hands off private economic matters, neither helping nor hindering citizens in any of their undertakings, then government in the United States has never practiced *laissez faire*. On the contrary, governments in the United States—Federal and state alike—have always intervened in economic matters, sometimes more and sometimes less, sometimes to aid and encourage certain private efforts and sometimes to repress others, sometimes indirectly and sometimes directly.[1] Nevertheless, while all this went on, the doctrine prevailed, so universally and unquestionably as to call forth little comment, that the government should not carry on very much economic activity of its own accord (in the form, say, of nationalized industries) nor direct in any great detail the economic activities of private citizens.

Private enterprises, it was felt with equally implicit faith, would be sufficiently controlled and correlated by their interplay in free competitive markets. Buying cheap and selling dear, private men would be moved by private incentives to produce what was wanted and consume what they could. And each man's desire to make a good thing of his own business would prevent anyone from getting or keeping a profitable monopoly.

Behind these principles of economic policy, needless to say, stood a large number of ethical and political preconceptions. Two of them may be mentioned as having more universal and undoubted acceptance than others in the United States: wealth is highly desirable; no free man should be subject to the commands of any private person, nor subject to very many commands even of government.

In the field of antitrust law, the principles of limited interference by government and control of private enterprise by competition, otherwise so compatible in American economic policy, clashed. They did so because of the complexity of the American economy, or, more precisely, because the American economy changed markedly in one important respect during the half-century before 1890. The change was a substantial increase in the efficient scale of manufacturing enterprises. To choose one broad example from many, in 1840 iron was produced by hundreds of small foundries, each employing at most a few score men; in 1890 most of the nation's iron was being produced by a few dozen plants, some employing thousands of men. The larger plants could produce iron more cheaply than most of the remaining small ones. Growth in size and improvement in efficiency took place for many reasons. Increasing density of population, rising personal incomes, and reduced costs of transportation all contributed to widen the extent

[1] Cf. Letwin, *Documentary History of American Economic Policy* (1961).

of the market. The introduction of steam power, invention and diffusion of technology, and a rapidly growing supply of capital served to reduce the costs of production. These changes affected various occupations at different times and in different degrees, but throughout the American economy they had the same effect of more or less sharply increasing the optimal size and general efficiency of manufacturing firms. Whether or not the change was in fact sudden is immaterial; it was perceived suddenly, and during the 1880's it impressed itself on the consciousness of the American public.

Simultaneously the public became aware that many of the old, small firms were vanishing in the process. In many instances the most convenient way for a firm to expand quickly to a larger and more efficient scale was to buy out another firm or to merge with it. Much of the expansion in scale throughout American industry did occur in this manner of "combination." Much of it, on the other hand, took place by the expansion of existing firms, expansion financed by borrowing, sale of capital stock, and reinvestment of profits. But, by analogy, the term "combination" slipped over to cover growth by the second method as well as by the first, it being clear that any business, and especially any incorporated business, consisted of a "combination" of many owners of capital, many managers and officers, and multitudinous employees.

Most of this expansion in size of firms, one may guess, was undertaken without any thought or prospect of monopolizing. Nevertheless each expansion by merger undeniably reduced the number of competitors in its industry, certainly for the time being and possibly forever. If in an industry consisting of one thousand firms, each firm coupled off with another, it could not be denied that five hundred competitors had disappeared. And in some notorious instances, the twenty or thirty competitors in an industry were all, or nearly all, swallowed up by one single firm, which thereby became an undeniable monopolist. Since "combinations" reduced the number of competitors and sometimes produced monopolies, Americans in the 1880's fell into the habit of contrasting "combination" and "competition" as though they were direct opposites.

It seemed to follow that each act of "combination" led to a proportional decline in competition. In discussions of the question during the 1880's nobody much noticed that an industry containing ninety-nine firms was likely to be as competitive as an industry with one hundred, or that an industry with one giant firm amidst one hundred little ones would be less competitive than an industry with only thirty firms but those of equal size, or that the competitiveness of an industry might depend much more on the spirit of entrepreneurs than on their number. Instead, the disappearance of any erstwhile competitor was reckoned a perceptible move toward monopoly.

And here the quandary of policy entered. Combination must be good because it permitted enterprises to become more efficient, and efficiency was good because it reduced the cost of goods, which was equivalent to raising people's incomes. Competition must be good because it kept down the prices of goods and prevented any seller from lording it over his customers. But, unhappily, combination and competition, both good, were opposites, and every increase in one necessarily, so it seemed, meant a decrease in the other.

The outline of the policy desired became clear after 1888. Combination, whenever it went as far as monopoly, must be prohibited. It must be prohibited, indeed, whenever it went at all close to monopoly. On the other hand, combination should not be suppressed—so many insisted—when it left adequate room for competition.

It was with this quandary of economic policy that Congress dealt, as well as it could, in drafting the Sherman Act.

It is, in fact, an unresolvable dilemma. It is as live now as it ever was, and will continue so long as people place a high value on both economic efficiency and competition. In many industries the most efficient scale of firms is such that only one or very few firms will exist if the operation of the market is the only controlling force. But if only one or very few firms exist, competition is effectively ruled out in that industry, since each firm can influence the price of goods by altering the quantity it produces. Indeed, in such a situation of monopoly or oligopoly, each firm not only can but inevitably does exercise private economic power. On the other hand, its scale makes it a highly efficient producer.

Many remedies can be conceived, but each is costly in the sense that it militates against some principle that is fundamental in traditional and current American economic policy. The prices of the few, large, naturally efficient producers can be regulated in the public interest—but this means foregoing competition and bringing government very directly into economic intervention. The large firms can forcibly be broken into enough smaller firms to restore competition—but this means foregoing in some measure economic efficiency and making the nation to that extent poorer. And so it is with every remedy that has been suggested.

Given this inescapable dilemma, it is not surprising that antitrust cases are often difficult to resolve. It is not surprising that the decision in one antitrust case cannot always be easily reconciled with others, or that the personal views of judges sometimes color their opinions slightly. There is no reason to expect simple certainty from a statute that maps the way through so awkward a terrain.

Intricacies of Legal Processes

Certainty and exact predictability are ruled out not only by the multiplicity of ends that the Sherman Act must serve but equally by the indirectness of the political and legal process that determines its means.

The process of making and then enforcing a law in America creates a strong likelihood that those who wanted the law will be less than satisfied with its effects. It would be different if the wishes of some could by fiat instantly force others to do this or that. A representative democracy whose legal order stems from the common-law tradition is exactly the opposite. The will of the people is first narrowed to a focus, slowly, by successive stages of abstraction; at the focus stands the statute, a number of words printed on paper; and then the words are laboriously translated, case by case, into rules of action, which after some long time spread their influence over the actions or lives of all the people. It is a process, one might say, shaped like an hourglass.

The process begins when many citizens become perturbed about something, perhaps without being able clearly to identify the cause of their irritation, or, having identified it, advocating no cure more concrete than "a law against it." To be able to identify exactly where the rub comes is one function of the professional politician; if he lacks the necessary sensitivity he cannot succeed in a vigorously democratic community; but if he is skillful he will be able to point out more sharply than the citizens themselves have ever conceived it the sources of their concern. The politician's first task, then, is to begin arranging and bringing toward convergence the loose, shapeless, spread-out grains of public sentiment. In time, enough of this may have been done so that the party, the administration, or—as often happens—one or two congressmen feel that they have a clear commission to prepare a statute. A bill is introduced in Congress. Most bills are stillborn, because they deal with evils felt and remedies welcomed by none but their sponsors. If, however, the bill is of some general interest, it is considered by a standing committee, which may at its discretion report the bill to the house. The house may then debate the bill—members extolling, criticizing, and offering amendments—during sittings spread out over weeks or months, or during one hectic hour, after which the bill may, if it has attracted sufficiently strong sponsorship, be brought to a vote. If it passes, it is then sent to the other house, where it goes through a similar process of scrutiny by committee, debate, and vote. But even after both houses have voted favorably, the bill may yet be far from law, for the two houses may have passed bills which are nearly the same but not exactly the same. The discrepant bills are now delivered to a conference committee, charged with inventing a compromise draft. The bill, in its new version, is reconsigned to each house for further action. If passed by both houses, and if signed by the President, the bill finally becomes law.

In this, the first political chapter of law, a great work of condensation has taken place. The diverse and inchoate sentiments that make up public opinion in its early unformed stage have been marshalled into the conflicting positions of congressmen; these in turn are reduced to order by debate and negotiation—that is, by persuasion, bargaining, hectoring, charming, and voting; and finally all is crystallized in a few abstract words.

In the course of producing the Sherman Act by this procedure, the Iowa farmer who felt that it cost too much to ship his corn to Chicago lent his sovereign power to a statute; but the statute did not command the Burlington railroad to lower its freight charges; instead, it prohibited "contracts in restraint of trade" and other equally abstract actions. Those words were also the intermediate product of a Boston matron's outrage at the noisy spending of August Belmont, a Southern preacher's conviction that Mammon had settled in Memphis, and an immigrant mineworker's certainty that he was being exploited by the Reading Coal Company. They were the product also of congressmen, some of whom believed that competition was overrated, others that the real cause of trusts was the tariff, still others that it was better to do something than nothing, and some—who may or may not have been a large fraction—that the statute was the best that could be devised, that is, the most likely to accomplish roughly what many of their constituents most wanted.

A statute will accomplish very little, of course, so long as it remains words in a book. It must be put into action; that is, from being a compact verbal formula, it must now be spread until it alters the behavior of many citizens. But the process of enforcement, like the process of enactment, does much to guarantee that the law's results will differ from those that any citizen would have chosen.

The first step in enforcing a statute like the Sherman Act waits on a decision of the public prosecutor, the Attorney General. Whom should he sue or prosecute? Obviously, a violater. But if there are many, which one, or which first? Obviously, one whom he should and can defeat. But just there the public prosecutor is perplexed, for without knowing what the statute means he cannot know which violater would be most vulnerable to attack, nor whether any potential defendant is indeed a violater. And to know what the statute means is not a question of knowing what the statute says but of anticipating how the courts will read it. It is not a mere guess, for he knows how the courts have decided related questions. More important, he knows he can go to court, where his job is to persuade judges, if he can, to interpret the statute in his way. His decision, then, is based on an informed estimate of how much he can affect the court, but he can never be assured of the outcome beforehand.

The prosecutor's estimate is tied up not only with the merits of the case and the meaning of the statute but also with technicalities of law. Is it better to indict the defendant on charges of criminally violating the Sherman Act or to sue for an injunction to stop him from further violations? The criminal proceeding requires a more rigorous standard of proof, but a jail sentence may do more than an injunction to dissuade others from disobeying the law. Should he plan to have the case tried on the allegations of his bill in equity and the defendant's answer, which is risky, or must he make the effort to collect proof, which is costly? If he sues in equity, what relief should he ask for? If the remedy he proposes is too broad, he may end with nothing, but if it is too narrow, he may get nothing that is worth having. Nowhere in the case is there any certainty on which he can rest, unless the case is utterly hackneyed. In a case of any complexity, under a law new or old, the prosecutor finds himself in an intrinsically dubious situation, calling for discretionary and arbitrary decisions at every turn. He is a teacher who sets out to instruct the judge, but the defendant's attorney is another and opposite teacher, and the judge enjoys the power to decide which of the adversary teachers is better.

The judge, for his part, can rest his decision on no certainties except in small and hackneyed cases. But in all courts of appeal —and especially in the Supreme Court, which admits only such appeals as present difficult problems of judgment—judges know that each party before them has a good deal to be said for his side of the question. Where the rights and wrongs of the matter are more or less evenly balanced, judges can and must decide for one side or the other, but their decision partakes of no automatic certainty or utter predictability.

Judges in a common-law system do not act on arbitrary whim. Like the attorneys, they guide themselves and justify themselves by precedent. But it is of the essence of concrete happenings and particular cases that none is *exactly* like any other. The parties, times, and places are always different, as is an infinity of surrounding facts; when the judge likens one case to another, therefore, he is asserting that they are alike in the most important respects though obviously not in all respects. But in the application of precedents, the judge's work of weighing the likenesses and differences, in order to decide which is greater, though it involves reasoning cannot rest exclusively on demonstrative reasoning. He must somewhere make use of judgment—personal, inexplicable, and partly incommunicable.

Decisions in particular cases, the ultimate legal product of the private and inchoate views from which the statute was distilled, therefore unavoidably depart from the decisions that any given citizen would have reached had he been given power to enforce his own wishes directly. The indirectness of the political and legal process, together with the multiplicity of ends desired, could not have resulted in an antimonopoly law that was anything but uncertain and somewhat unpredictable in its effects. The hope of eradicating *all* uncertainty in such a domain is chimerical; the criticism that *all* uncertainty has not been eradicated is puerile.

History of the Sherman Act

The difficulties that arise in making and applying a statutory instrument of economic policy are vividly represented in the history of the Sherman Act.

The Act was fashioned of materials borrowed from the common law, and some people have concluded that the Act does nothing more than to declare principles of policy and rules of law that have been observed continuously during six or seven centuries of Anglo-American legal tradition. In reality the common-law material was much less tractable than that. Of the four branches of English common law that had any bearing on the problem, two had been terminated by statute and the remaining two very much weakened by decisions of English courts during the nineteenth century. American common law, having sharply though never completely diverged from the mother lineage after 1776, contained precedents in which the framers of the Sherman Act could find a certain amount of hope. Nevertheless, the common law was very unwieldy material from which to have constructed a law to control modern corporations and big businesses; the most that could be said for it was that nothing better was available.

The Sherman Act was passed in response to public demand. The American public, schooled in a long tradition of opposing special privileges of every sort and in an old habit of calling all such privileges "monopoly," began to protest sharply against the "trusts" that grew steadily more numerous after 1885. This public opposition to trusts was not, however, expressed in the form of any specific proposals for remedies. Two bodies of professional experts, the economists and the lawyers, though much more ready to propose remedies could only reach an approximate consensus on a loose principle of policy, that whatever was done about the trusts ought to be such as to leave ample room for both competition and combination. A similar view was held by Congress, which after much debate and shifting passed the Sherman Act as a tentative experimental effort to express such a policy with the use of common-law categories.

A statute whose policy was somewhat vague and whose words drew their meaning from a long and sometimes diffuse tradition was not easy to interpret. When set the task of enforcing the Sherman Act, the Attorneys General of the United States were forced to engage in a slow process of exploration by hits and misses. Their exploration was impeded by lack of funds, discouraged by doubts as to the legal meaning of the Act, and occasionally colored by the political cast of the administrations they served.

In dealing with the succession of cases that the Department of Justice brought before them, judges were forced to resolve the ambiguities that had been, as it were, necessarily written into the Sherman Act. Extremes of interpretation gave rise at first to sharply divergent rules of law. Yet within a decade, a fairly coherent doctrine about the Act's intent and scope had become acceptable to most judges, including those who strongly preferred their own way of summarizing that doctrine to any other judge's.

By the beginning of the twentieth century, the executive and the judiciary branches had both become quite proficient in the uses of the Sherman Act. But, as the Northern Securities case showed (see Chapter 6), the essential difficulties created by the Act's policy—to stop excessive concentration of private economic power without unduly constraining private economic action—and by its legal mechanics—the mixture of common-law and constitutional terms, and the mixture of criminal, penal, and civil remedies—remained unsolved.

Many misinterpreted these difficulties as arising from defects in the drafting of the Sherman Act, defects that they thought might easily have been avoided or could now easily be remedied; some believed that they flowed from the willfulness of prosecutors and judges. Dissatisfied with some effects of the Sherman Act, and hoping to modify it so as to offend nobody, they pressed for establishment of a regulatory system in which continuous and expert administration would replace the sporadic and unpredictable rulings of courts. These desires, forwarded by the proclamation of the Rule of Reason and the powerful leadership of President Wilson, brought forth the Clayton Antitrust Act and the Federal Trade Commission Act. Thus it was hoped that twenty-five years of growth would be capped by one brilliant and final invention.

How the Sherman Act was fashioned out of a legal tradition and a traditional economic policy, how the government's attorneys learned to use the Act and judges decided what it must mean in practice, how the Act was used with great effect and how it was then augmented in the hope of making it still more effective—it is along these lines that the history of the first twenty-five years of antitrust law moves.

CHAPTER TWO

LEGAL FOUNDATIONS OF THE SHERMAN ACT

The Sherman Act was founded on the common law, the body of judicial decisions that the United States inherited from England. The common law, it has been widely believed, always favored freedom of trade. When English and American judges during the eighteenth and nineteenth centuries decided cases against monopolists, engrossers, or restrainers of trade, they thought they were continuing a tradition that reached back into "time of which no man hath memory." The congressmen who drafted and passed the Sherman Antitrust Law thought they were merely declaring the illegality of offenses that the common law had always prohibited. Those judges and legislators, like other lawyers, must have known, or at least would not have doubted, that the common law rules on these subjects had changed in the course of time, for it is taken as axiomatic that the common law "grows." But it is not always recognized that the common law can change its direction, and without much warning begin to prohibit practices it had formerly endorsed, or to protect arrangements it had earlier condemned. Lawyers do not so readily see that the common law at any given time reflects the economic theories and policies then favored by the community, and may change as radically as those theories and policies. As a result they have too easily accepted the mistaken view that the attitude of the common law toward freedom of trade was essentially the same throughout its history.

The common law did not always defend freedom of trade and abhor monopoly. For a long time it did quite the opposite: it supported an economic order in which the individual's getting and spending were closely controlled by kings, parliaments, and mayors, statutes and customs, and his opportunities limited by the exclusive powers of guilds, chartered companies, and patentees. The common law first began to oppose this system of regulation and privilege at the end of the sixteenth century; it did not do so wholeheartedly until the eighteenth century; and by the middle of the nineteenth century, it had again lost its enthusiasm for the task. It would have been surprising if the pattern of development had been different. Changes in the common law are changes in the attitudes of judges and of lawyers; it would have been remarkable if they had persistently opposed monopoly when the rest of the community did not know the word and considered the phenomenon natural or desirable. It would have been strange if lawyers had upheld *laissez-faire* policies centuries before any statesman or economist had advocated or stated them, and had continued following them long after they had been abandoned or denied by the rest of the community. In fact, English laws governing monopoly and English policies for the economic organization of society changed together, except for minor differences in timing. The English law of monopoly traditionally includes four branches: the law on monopoly proper, whether by patent, charter, or custom; on forestalling, engrossing, and regrating; on contracts in restraint of trade; and on combinations in restraint of trade. These branches, distinct in form and based on more or less independent bodies of precedent, nevertheless show the same development from an active support of monopolies in the earliest period, through active opposition during an interlude of less than two centuries, to the leniency and indifference which characterized them in 1890.

English Common Law on Monopolies

The idea that the common law opposed monopolies from the earliest time onward was invented largely by Sir Edward Coke, who argued that monopoly was forbidden by the Civil Law, and implicitly by Magna Carta as well as by certain statutes of Edward III's reign.[1] The earliest common-law precedent he could mention

[1] Wagner, "Coke and the Rise of Economic Liberalism," *Econ. Hist. Rev.*, VI, 30 (1935). See Coke's argument in Davenant v. Hurdis, Moore 576, 580 (K.B., 1599). Coke, *Institutes*, II, 47, 62 f.; III, at c. 85. See the admirable

was a case that arose during the fourteenth century, and the modern lawyers and historians who follow his authority continue to cite that case as evidence of the ancient antagonism of common law to monopolies.[2] Yet the case gives at least equally good evidence to the contrary. One John Pecche had a patent giving him the exclusive right to sell sweet wines at retail in London, and the Parliament of 1376 petitioned that he be punished for the flagrant use he had made of his privilege, "to the great damage and oppression of the people." [3] Had this been an action to suppress and punish monopoly, it would tend to justify the theory that Coke put forward. But the fact that Pecche, who had a monopoly, was punished, does not mean that he was punished for having the monopoly.

Pecche came by his patent during the last years of Edward III's reign, when the King was too old to rule actively, and his heir, the Black Prince, was too ill. Another son, John of Gaunt, Duke of Lancaster, was therefore virtual ruler of England from about 1370 to 1377. He hoped to succeed his father, but until that happy time came he intended to make the best of his position, and so he set out to increase his fortune. His chief agent in this venture was Richard Lyons, a merchant and alderman of London, who apparently financed Gaunt, in return for which the Duke gave economic privileges to him and to his associates.[4] John Pecche, merchant, alderman, and once mayor of London,[5] was among the associates favored. In 1373, "by the assent and aid of Richard Lyons," [6] he was given letters-patent permitting him to sell sweet wines at retail in London, notwithstanding an ordinance of Parliament prohibiting retail sale of sweet wines throughout the

---

analysis of the common-law tradition in Dewey, *Monopoly in Economics and Law,* chaps. IX, X (1959).

[2] Coke, *Institutes,* III, 181; 11 Co. Rep. 53, 88a,b. Cf. Holdsworth, *History,* IV, 344 n. 6 (1924). The case was cited in the same sense by Laurence Hyde during the parliamentary debate on monopolies in 1601; Tawney and Power, *Tudor Economic Documents,* II, 275 (1924).

[3] *Rotuli Parliamentorum, 50 Edw. III,* No. 33 (1376).

[4] Trevelyan, *England in the Age of Wycliffe* 10-12 (1915 ed.). For details on Lyons, see Sargeant, "The Wine Trade with Gascony," in Unwin (ed.), *Finance and Trade under Edward III,* 297-98 (1918).

[5] Riley, *Memorials of London,* I, 308; II, 390 (1868).

[6] *Rot. Parl., 50 Edw. III,* No. 33 (1376).

realm.[7] In return for this exclusive privilege,[8] he was to pay the King a fee of 10 shillings on each pipe of wine he sold.[9] The King further endorsed the grant by sending writs to the Mayor and Sheriffs of London commanding them to give Pecche every assistance in exercising his monopoly, and ordering the Mayor to set a reasonable price for the wine.[1] Nor did the Mayor and Aldermen of London seem to object in principle to the monopoly; in fact Pecche asserted that they had approved it before he put it in practice.[2] Needless to say, they denied it in Parliament, but however they may have felt about Pecche's privilege, they were not generally averse to monopoly: only a few years earlier they had leased to Lyons the three taverns reserved for the sale of sweet wines, at an annual rent of £200,[3]—which suggests that they did not object to monopolies that paid them good returns.

For three years Pecche worked his monopoly in peace. But John of Gaunt became less popular than ever, encountering increased opposition from those who preferred that the Black Prince's son, Richard, should succeed Edward; from the Church, because he sponsored Wycliffe; and from the Londoners, who hated his arrogance and showed it by burning his palace during the Rebellion of 1381. When Parliament met in 1376, it therefore attacked Gaunt, though indirectly, by accusing his associates. It attainted Lyons for engrossing and raising the prices of "all the merchandise that came into England," William Lord Latimer for taking bribes and misappropriating funds, Alice Perrers, the King's mistress, for obstructing justice,[4] and Pecche, for having fraudulently obtained and excessively exploited his patent, and for having failed to pay the

[7] The patent is missing from the *Calendar of Patent Rolls,* but is given in the *Calendar of Letter Books of the City of London, Letter Book G,* 318 (Nov. 30, 1373). The prohibitory ordinance of Parliament seems to be missing both from *Rot. Parl.* and *Statutes of the Realm,* but is referred to in *Rot. Parl.* when repealed (cf. note 9 below) as well as in the patent.

[8] Exclusive only in London; John Beverle had a similar license for Boston, Lincoln, Staunford, and Grantham. *C.P.R., 48 Edw. III,* 414 (March 5, 1374).

[9] *Rot. Parl., 50 Edw. III,* No. 33 (1376).

[1] *Letter Book G,* 318 (Dec. 13, 1373); 320 (Dec. 11, 1373).

[2] *Rot. Parl., 50 Edw. III,* No. 33 (1376). *Letter Book H,* 38-40 (Aug. 1, 1376).

[3] *Letter Book G,* 199 (Aug. 26, 1365).

[4] Longman, *Life and Times of Edward III,* II, 251-54 (1869).

King the required fees. Pecche was sentenced "to be imprisoned, to make fine and ransom to the King, and also to give satisfaction to the parties complaining of his extortionate prices." [5] He spent only a short while in prison,[6] and was soon after given a pardon excusing him from all further penalties and from paying any outstanding license fees.[7] Although his patent was not revoked,[8] it lost its value when Parliament repealed the former prohibition so that thereafter anyone could sell sweet wine at retail.[9]

Pecche's case was an accident of contemporary politics rather than part of an already developed common-law tradition against monopolies. The ultimate object of the attack was Gaunt; his various agents were assailed on the most plausible pretexts available. Parliament could find no other form in which to accuse Pecche except that he had defrauded the King and charged the public unreasonable prices. The word "monopoly" was not even mentioned in the accusation; it was unknown in England until over a century later.[1] The legal concept then existing which came closest to the notion of monopoly was "engrossing"; Lyons was accused of engrossing, but Pecche could not be accused of it because he had acted under royal license. Parliament did not question the King's right to grant such patents; indeed a judge during the same reign declared that the King might grant privileges "even though, prima facie, they appear absolutely against common right." [2] There was as yet no basis at common law for holding a grant void because it created a monopoly.

The great movement against the granting of monopolies by letter-patent began only at the end of the sixteenth century, although it

[5] *Rot. Parl., 50 Edw. III,* No. 33 (1376).

[6] It cannot have been long, for Parliament met on April 24, 1376 and Pecche was released from the Tower on an order of mainprise dated July 26; *Calendar of Close Rolls, 50 Edw. III,* 437 (1376).

[7] *C.P.R., 51 Edw. III,* 448, 457 (April 10, 1377).

[8] As Wagner (*Econ. Hist. Rev.,* VI, 41) points out, following Gordon, *Monopolies by Patents* 231, n. (1897). Both, however, overlooked the condition that made revocation unnecessary.

[9] *Rot. Parl., 50 Edw. III,* No. 14 (1376). Cf. *C.C.R., 51 Edw. III,* 529 (Feb. 18, 1377).

[1] It was first used, according to Fox, *Monopolies and Patents* 24 (1947), by Thomas More in 1516.

[2] *Year-Book, 40 Edw. III,* Pasch., pl. 8 (ff. 17-18).

was so strongly supported that within less than a hundred years the principle had been established that Parliament alone could grant a monopoly, and that generally even it could not, as the King had regularly done, sell a patent or award it on a whim or as a friendly gesture. By the end of the seventeenth century the royal letter-patent had been converted into a more or less modern version of the patent, justifiable only by a solid contribution to economic development. The process was not, however, moved by coherent opposition to monopoly; it was brought about mainly by disturbances within the monopolistic system administered largely by the guilds, and by objections not to the broad economic effect of monopolies but to the political power which the crown exercised in granting them.

The first recorded case on monopolies was *Davenant v. Hurdis,* or *The Merchant Tailors'* case decided in 1599,[3] which shows not only the extent of monopolistic control that the guilds exercised, but also the ends that such controls were supposed to serve, and the collisions that were taking place between several guilds as each tried to maintain intact its power over a trade. The case arose under a by-law passed by the London tailors' guild in 1571, titled "An Ordinance for Nourishing and Relieving the Poor Members of the Merchant Tailors Company." The ordinance begins with a noble preamble, "Forasmuch as it is the duty of every Christian society to help and relieve every willing labouring brother in the Commonwealth, and especially such as are incorporated, grafted, and knit together in brotherly society . . . ,"[4] and goes on to require every merchant who belongs to the guild and sends cloth to be finished by outside labor to have at least half the work done by fellow members of his guild.

The ordinance is a sign that the Merchant Tailors Company had lost control of the cloth-finishing trade. Its members, according to the charter of 1502, were permitted to practice any art connected with the making of men's apparel, but the members of the Clothworkers Guild, incorporated about 1530, had overlapping rights.[5] It therefore became a constant question whether any fuller or

[3] Moore 576 (K.B., 1599).

[4] Clode, *Merchant Taylors,* I, 393-94 (1888).

[5] Clode, *Merchant Taylors,* I, 198; Unwin, *Industrial Organization in the 16th and 17th Centuries* 40-45 (1904).

shearman was to belong to the Tailors or Clothworkers, whether his work was to be approved, his prices set, and the number of his apprentices regulated by the one company or the other. The dispute led to rioting in the streets of London, litigation, and requests that Parliament settle the matter by legislation.[6] It led also to the Tailors' by-law, the need for which reflected the Tailors' weakness and also the decay of the entire system of guild regulation. The system presumed that each trade would be regulated by its own guild, but with increasing specialization of labor it became more and more difficult to define the limits of a trade or to keep the guilds from splitting into smaller units. There were disputes within disputes: at the very moment that the Tailors were fighting the Clothworkers, the fullers and shearmen who made up the latter company were quarreling over the power to set the price of "rowing" (the process of putting a nap on cloth)—the fullers insisting that it should be theirs alone, while the shearmen claimed it as theirs by custom.[7] The conflicting interests of related but distinct trades led the Feltmakers to separate from the Haberdashers, and the Glovers from the Leather-sellers. Competition between the guilds led fourteen smaller guilds to petition the government of London to restore the old system whereby "in ancient times the company of artificers or handicraftsmen of the city had reserved the *only* use, trade, or exercise of their several arts and handicrafts," [8] but the petition was never granted because the Aldermen of London could not restore the economic conditions that had made the guild system possible. One by-product of this general decay was the ordinance in which the Tailors, with a disarming appearance of fairness, decreed that half of the cloth-finishing done for its members must be done by its members.

The by-law was tested in *Davenant v. Hurdis.*[9] Davenant, a clothmerchant of the Tailors' company, had sent out twenty cloths to be finished, but refused to give an equal number to members of his guild, and was assessed a fine of 10 shillings per cloth, as

[6] Clode, *Merchant Taylors,* I, 199-203.

[7] Clothworkers' Court Book, April 8, 1567, in Unwin, *Industrial Organization,* 231.

[8] Unwin, *The Gilds and Companies of London* 262 (1938 ed.).

[9] Moore 576 (K.B., 1599).

the by-law provided. He refused to pay, whereupon the Company instructed Hurdis, its beadle,[1] to take from Davenant goods equal in value to the fine. Davenant brought an action of trespass, and Edward Coke, then Attorney General, appeared for him. Coke questioned the authority of the Tailors to make such a by-law or to distrain for the fine, but his principal arguments were that the by-law was unreasonable and contrary to law. It was unreasonable, he maintained, because it absolutely required the merchants of the company to give their business to the clothworkers who belonged to the company, but did not require the latter to provide quick service, good workmanship, or reasonable prices for this business; as a result the merchants might be "utterly impoverished and forced to deceive their customers." [2] It was illegal because it made a monopoly: the same authority that gave the Tailors' Company power to make by-laws keeping half of cloth-dressing to their members would justify them in gradually appropriating the whole of the trade to their own sole use, until finally there would be no cloth-dressing except at their pleasure, and all other clothworkers would be unemployed and live on relief.[3] Coke concluded that a by-law which might create such monopoly powers must be against the public good, and cited precedents to prove that it must therefore be void. But the curious collection of authorities to which he appealed demonstrates how difficult it was to find a traditional basis in common law for the position he was taking. He could merely cite a number of cases in which by-laws or patents were held valid because they were for the public good: a regulation that all ships must harbor in one port and no other, a grant by the King giving a skilled foreigner the sole right to make sailing canvas, and another giving a skilled projector exclusive right to drain lands, a by-law that all cloth sold in London must first be inspected and passed at Blackwell Hall, a by-law of St. Albans requiring each inhabitant to pay a contribution toward cleaning the town, and by-laws for the maintenance of bridges, walls, and similar public works. From these instances, Coke concluded: "but by-laws that establish monopolies are against common law and void." Yet the

[1] Clode, *Merchant Taylors,* I, 81.
[2] Moore 576, 580-81 (K.B., 1599).
[3] Moore 576, 579-80.

only direct authority that he offered for this rule was a text from the Civil Law,[4] though he himself maintained that the Civil Law was not authoritative in English courts.[5]

It was against just this weakness in Coke's argument that Francis Moore, attorney for Hurdis, made his principal attack. He conceded that laws ought to be for the public good and that the by-law in question would be void if it created a monopoly. But he denied that it did so, for the by-law did not prohibit any clothworker from using his trade since it regulated the disposal of only a fraction of the business. Moreover, he continued, "if this by-law were really a monopoly, then all the privileges and customs of cities and boroughs, tending to exclude foreigners and to give the sole trading within the city or borough to its own freemen, could be called monopolies and illegal; from which would ensue the decay of all cities and boroughs in the realm . . . which until this day have never been disallowed as monopolies against law and common right."[6] This argument, telling as it was against Coke's assertion that restrictive ordinances were bad at law, failed to convince the judges, who unanimously held that "a rule of such nature as to bring all trade or traffic into the hands of one company, or one person, and to exclude all others, is illegal."[7]

The decision represented an innovation in the law as much as in economic policy. There is no reported common-law case on monopoly prior to *Davenant v. Hurdis;* Coke later mentioned in Parliament some unreported cases,[8] but their precise content is unknown. The willingness of Francis Moore, Hurdis' attorney, to concede that a monopoly would be void at common law does not

[4] Moore, 576, 580.

[5] Coke, *Institutes,* II, 98 (1797). See Wagner, "The Common Law and Free Enterprise: An Early Case of Monopoly," *Econ. Hist. Rev.,* VII, 217, 218 (1936).

[6] Moore 576, 587 (K.B., 1599).

[7] Moore 576, 591: "prescription de tiel nature de inducer sole trade. . . ." "Prescription" does not seem to be used here in its specific technical sense.

[8] 1 *House of Commons Journal* 555 (March 15, 1621), 606 (May 3, 1621). Fox, *Monopolies and Patents,* 119, cites three cases before Davenant v. Hurdis "in which monopoly grants were considered by the courts of common law." Of these, the case of John the Dyer did not concern a grant of monopoly (see pages 39-40 below) and Hasting's case, Noy 182, and Humphrey's case, Noy 183, [both mentioned in Darcy v. Allen, Moore 673 (1603)], were tried in the Exchequer.

necessarily indicate that the legal principle was well established; it may, rather, show the intensity of public opposition to monopolies, in which Moore shared.[9] A number of prior cases are known, but these were heard in the Star Chamber, Privy Council, and other prerogative courts, which generally defended such monopolies as proper exercises of the King's power.[1] The law was still so divided on the validity of monopolies as late as 1624 that Parliament felt it necessary to include in the Statute of Monopolies a provision that "all monopolies . . . and the force and validity of them and of every of them, ought to be and shall be forever hereafter examined, heard, tried and determined by and according to the common laws of this Realm and not otherwise." [2]

The next step, and perhaps the greatest single one, in creating the modern common law on monopolies was *Darcy v. Allen,* or *The Case of Monopolies,*[3] decided in 1603. Where *Davenant v. Hurdis* established that a corporate by-law was invalid if it created a monopoly, *Darcy v. Allen* went further, laying down the principle that even a royal grant by patent would be invalid if it did so. Queen Elizabeth granted Darcy, her groom, a patent for a monopoly of the manufacture and importing of playing cards.[4] In 1601, soon after Elizabeth issued her proclamation on monopolies, Allen, a London haberdasher, made and sold some playing cards, and Darcy brought an action of infringement. The Court of King's Bench unanimously held the patent void.

They held it void as a "dangerous" and "unprecedented" innovation, apparently because no other patent of this sort had previously been issued under the Great Seal. They held it void although it had undoubtedly been granted by the Queen, but in order not to attack royal prerogative directly, they adopted the

[9] In 1597 Moore introduced a motion in Parliament against monopolies and was chairman of the committee to which the motion was referred; Cheyney, *History of England,* II, 296 (1926). He also participated in the debates of 1601; Tawney and Power, *Tudor Economic Documents,* II, 274 (1924).

[1] Fox, *Monopolies and Patents,* 119 ff.

[2] 21 Jac. I, c. 3 (1624).

[3] 11 Co. Rep. 84, Moore 671 (K.B., 1599), Noy 173. These reports are collated in Gordon, *Monopolies by Patent,* 193-232.

[4] The patent was originally awarded in 1578, passed through several hands, and was granted to Darcy in 1598. Cheyney, *History of England,* II, 307-8.

fiction that "[t]he Queen was deceived in her grant; for the Queen, as by the preamble appears, intended it to be for the weal public, and it will be employed for the private gain of the patentee, and for the prejudice of the weal public." It prejudiced the public good by raising the price and lowering the quality of playing cards, but even more by depriving various workmen of a living. In explaining this main objection, the court said that

> All trades, as well mechanical as others, which prevent idleness (the bane of the commonwealth) and exercise men and youth in labour for the maintenance of themselves and their families, and for the increase of their substance, to serve the Queen when occasion shall require, are profitable for the commonwealth and therefore the grant to the plaintiff to have the sole making of them is against the common law and the benefit and liberty of the subject.[5]

In short, Darcy's patent was held void on the argument that it violated the right of others to carry on their trade.

If the common law recognized each man's right to work at a lawful trade, as the courts of this period became fond of asserting, that right was neither simple nor absolute. Its basis was the feeling that a man should not be denied the means to earn a living: he and his family ought not to starve, his neighbors ought not to be burdened by supporting him, and the Crown should not be deprived of his contribution to the nation's wealth and power. This right to work was defended by statute and proclamation against foreign competition. A typical statute of this sort, the "Act against Strangers Artificers," passed in 1484,[6] recited the complaint of certain English craftsmen that they were "greatly empoverished" and "likely in short time to be utterly undone for lack of occupation" because of foreign competition, and proceeded to limit importation of certain goods. This sort of protection of domestic workmen was enforced before this time and after—even toward the end of the seventeenth century, royal proclamations were issued to prevent the importation of rope, hats, knives, gloves, locks, and paper.[7] The common-law right to work was predicated on an eco-

[5] Gordon, *Monopolies by Patent,* 226.

[6] 1 Ric. III, c. 12 (1483).

[7] E.g., 18 Hen. VI, c. 4 (1439), and *Letter Book G,* 130 (Feb. 23, 1362). Charles II, Proclamations (Nov. 20, 1661); (Feb. 20, 1675); James II, Proclamations (Apr. 29, 1687); (Aug. 14, 1687); Steele, *Tudor and Stuart Proclamations* (1910).

nomic system that would protect the established trades from competition, whether from foreign workmen, improperly qualified English workmen, overly aggressive guilds, or domestic monopolists. The right to work was protected by giving each guild a monopoly, and Darcy's grant was condemned not because it was a monopoly and therefore necessarily bad, but because it was a bad monopoly.

While the law prior to the eighteenth century supported every man's right to follow his trade, it also strictly limited and regulated this right. The nature of such controls is well illustrated in the third leading case on monopolies decided before the Statute of 1624, the *Ipswich Tailors'* case of 1614.[8] The tailors' guild of Ipswich had a by-law forbidding anyone from practicing his trade in the town unless he had served his apprenticeship under the Company or had been given its approval. They brought suit against one Sheninge for breaking this rule, but the court held that the by-law was invalid, because "at the common law, no man could be prohibited from working in any lawful trade. . . ." In order to reach so broad a conclusion, the court must have closed its eyes to a series of customs and statutes of great age. The right to follow any lawful trade was qualified, for one thing, by the need to have served an apprenticeship—this condition was imposed not only by guild regulations, dating as far back as the thirteenth century in some cases,[9] but also by the statute of Artificers of 1562.[1] That statute had not lost its force by 1614, and despite the adverse decision in the *Ipswich Tailors'* and subsequent cases, it was still followed at the end of the seventeenth century.[2]

The right to follow a trade was limited also by the rule that no man might work at several trades simultaneously. The validity of this rule was argued in the *Ipswich Tailors'* case, for the guild main-

[8] 11 Co. Rep. 53, Godbolt 252 (1614).

[9] Cf., e.g., early charters printed in Consitt, *The London Weavers' Company* (1933).

[1] 5 Eliz., c. 4 (1562).

[2] Francis Kiderby was indicted under the statute in 1669, for setting up as a draper without having been apprenticed. He petitioned the Privy Council that the Crown might drop the prosecution, for, he said, "the Statute though not repealed yet, has been by most of the judges looked upon as inconvenient to Trade and to Encrease of Inventions." Nevertheless he felt sure that a common law court would find him guilty. His petition was granted. Privy Council Register (Oct. 29 and Dec. 17, 1669), quoted by Unwin, *Industrial Organization* 252. Cf. Wade v. Ripton, 2 Keble 125, Siderf. 303 (1666).

tained that it rightly refused to approve Sheninge since he was already doing another kind of work. The court apparently decided that the common law did not prohibit this; it seems to have accepted Coke's statement that the prohibition was first introduced by a statute of 1363, and that it was found so harmful that it was repealed in the following year.[3] But Coke was mistaken. The law of 1363 to which he referred ordained, among other things, that each merchant should deal in only one sort of merchandise and "that Artificers, Handicraft People, hold them every one to one Mystery."[4] It may be true, as Coke says, that before this time the common law did not require each artisan to keep to his own trade. It is quite certain, however, that the prohibition was not repealed in the following year. Only the section which directed merchants to restrict their trade to one commodity was repealed;[5] it would have been difficult to restrain a merchant who carried wool abroad from returning with wine, iron, or wax. The section which confined each workman to a single trade stayed in the books two hundred years more, and was indeed reinforced from time to time by specific acts such as that which forbade tanners to be shoemakers or shoemakers to be tanners.[6] The legal principle on which the Ipswich Tailors depended and which Coke denied was not just a momentary aberration from a long-standing common-law tradition. The fact is that the monopolistic powers of guilds, which Coke insisted repeatedly were always void at common law, had really been supported by law. That support first began to be withdrawn in the beginning of the seventeenth century,[7] under the pressure of, among other things, Coke's powerful but inaccurate polemics.

There is no doubt that the series of cases at the turn of the seventeenth century radically changed the attitude of the common law toward monopolies. But it must be borne in mind that this

[3] 11 Co. Rep. 53, 54 (1614).

[4] 37 Edw. III (1363), cc. 5, 6.

[5] 38 Edw. III, c. 2 (1364) repealed 37 Edw. III, c. 5 (1363).

[6] 37 Edw. III, c. 6 was repealed by 5 Eliz., c. 4 (1564). The Act on tanners and shoemakers was 13 Ric. II, s. 1. c. 12 (1389).

[7] They were still supported, for instance, in The Warden and Corporation of Weavers in London v. Brown, Cro. Eliz. 803 (1600), where the court held that Brown did not come under the weavers' control, for though he sold his goods in London, he wove them elsewhere; but the court added that this judgment did not question the guild's right to control weaving in London: "It were a good custom . . . being used time [immemorial]."

change was also a consequence of the decay of the monopolistic system from within. Pecche was not attacked by irate consumers for raising his prices, but by irate subjects objecting to an unpopular minister. Similarly, *Davenant v. Hurdis* was not a dispute between a freedom-loving tradesman and a tyrannical guild as much as a confict between two guilds for control of an industry. And *Darcy v. Allen* was not the action of a solitary champion bravely contesting the monopoly of a powerful courtier; it has been shown instead that Allen was supported in the case by the Mayor and Aldermen of London, who, regarding Darcy's patent as an attack on all the trades and privileges of the City, "comforted and animated [Allen] to continue his selling of cards" and promised to pay the costs of any legal action that might follow. When Allen submitted a bill for his costs in defending himself against Darcy, the Mayor refused to pay, but Allen sued him and recovered.[8]

Moreover, the mercantilist system of private and corporate monopolies, though very much weakened by 1600, was still too widespread to be destroyed by the application of common-law remedies in specific cases. It was seriously limited, and in the end destroyed, by legislation. The first important law contributing to that result was the Statute of Monopolies of 1624, which, however, has a deceptive ring. For though it was certainly directed against monopolies, it was based not on a preference for competition, but on constitutional objections to the power which the Crown presumed in granting monopolies and to the arbitrary reasons for which it had granted them. Parliament did not at this period oppose monopolies in themselves. As Bacon told the House of Commons in 1601, its attitude was inconsistent and suspect: "If her Majesty make a patent or a monopoly unto any of her servants, that we must go and cry out against: but if she grant it to a number of burgesses or a corporation, that must stand, and that forsooth is no monopoly."[9]

This inconsistency the House of Commons carried over into the Statute of Monopolies. The first section declared void "all monopolies and all commissions, grants, licenses, charters, and letter patents heretofore made or granted, or hereafter to be made or

[8] Davies, "Further Light on the Case of Monopolies," 48 *L.Q. Rev.* 394 (1932).

[9] Prothero, *Statutes and Constitutional Documents* 112 (1906).

granted to any person or persons, bodies politic or corporate whatsoever, of or for the sole buying, selling, making, working, or using of anything, or of any other monopolies." The ninth section nevertheless provides that the Act shall not apply to any cities or towns, or any of their privileges, "or unto any corporations, companies, or fellowships of any trade, occupation, or mystery, or to any companies or societies of merchants within this Realm, erected for the maintenance, enlargement, or ordering of any trade of merchandise. . . ." And this inconsistency, which symbolized Parliament's willingness to have monopolies, provided Parliament alone granted them, was not merely a matter of words in a statute. It justified the final irony in the case of *Darcy v. Allen:* only a few years after Darcy's monopoly of playing cards was judged void at common law, the same monopoly was given, under authority of the Statute of Monopolies, to the Company of Card Makers.[1]

The Statute of Monopolies soon put an end to the arbitrary granting of private monopolies, but it was not intended to abolish customary monopoly privileges of corporations. Cities and boroughs, guilds, and chartered trading companies continued to exercise their monopoly powers to exclude strangers from various trades.[2] The common law continued to protect them, though with lessening fervor as the influence of economic liberalism grew, and some of these monopolistic contróls were finally abolished only by legislation in the nineteenth century.[3]

English Common Law on Forestalling, Engrossing, and Regrating

Throughout the early monopoly cases the complaint was made that certain practices are objectionable because they tend to raise prices. But even this complaint did not arise from opposition to monopolies. It did not mean that the common law early in the seventeenth century favored competition or endorsed the deter-

[1] Fox, *Monopolies and Patents* 128 n. 21.

[2] Cases are voluminously noted in 32 *Halsbury's Laws of England* 345 n. 'o' (Hailsham's 2d ed., 1939).

[3] *Ibid.*, and see page 41 below.

mination of prices by the free play of the market. The common law favored "low" prices rather than free prices, and accepted as a matter of course that all important prices would be set by political or corporate authorities. The complaint meant only that Englishmen objected to private efforts to raise prices, and that they readily attributed a rise in prices to the evil machinations of profiteers. This superstition was written into the early common law in the form of provisions against forestalling, regrating, and engrossing.

The body of law concerning these crimes has been thought to be an integral part of the law on monopolies because "forestalling" and the associated offenses seem at first sight to be older names for the modern monopolistic tactic known as "cornering the market"; and because since the seventeenth century, "engrossing" has become synonymous with "monopolizing." Jeffreys coupled the terms in this way when he gave his opinion in *The East India Co. v. Sandys,* and so did the authors of the Sherman Act when they explained the meaning of the word "monopolize" in the second section of that Act.[4] But in fact the two bodies of law are quite distinct: they evolved from separate statutes; one did and the other did not raise questions of royal prerogative; and whereas the modern law on monopoly by patent was laid down early in the seventeenth century, that on forestalling did not take its present shape until almost two hundred years later. The basic legal difference is that the monopolist had a legal warrant for his activity, whereas the forestaller was justified by no custom, grant, or statute whatsoever.

Contrary to monopolies by patent, which always were and still are legal—the principal changes being in who gives and who may receive them—forestalling was always illegal, and ceased to be so only when the crime was altogether abolished. "Forestalling" in the common law before the thirteenth century is said to have been an inclusive term for all unlawful attempts to raise prices.[5] It came to be a more particular term: in the year 1266, the first statute prohibiting it defined forestallers as those "that buy any-

[4] 10 *Howell's State Trials* 372, 538 (1685): "though the word Monopoly, or Engrossing. . . ." 21 *Cong. Rec.* 3152 (1890): "monopoly . . . is the sole engrossing to a man's self. . . ."

[5] Illingworth, *Laws Respecting Forestalling* 14 (1800)

thing before the due hour, or that pass out of the town to meet such things as come to the market."[6] "Regrating" meant simply retailing, buying in bulk and selling in small lots, and "engrossing," in its original narrow meaning, was to buy crops in the field before they were harvested or at least before they were ready to come to market. These offenses were indictable at common law, and various statutes assigned punishments ranging, according to the temper of the time, from fines and forfeiture to banishment and even death.[7] Such statutes were passed periodically from the thirteenth until the late seventeenth centuries, in some cases against the forestalling of certain specified commodities, in others against forestalling generally. But the application of these general statutes, as of the common law itself, was relatively narrow, and usually only the forestalling of food—or more precisely, of "dead victuals"—constituted a crime. One statute forbade engrossing of hides and oak-bark, and another, of cloth;[8] but the fact that Parliament legislated for these commodities in particular argues that it did not consider them to be included under the general laws against forestalling. In a few scattered cases, also, courts found defendants guilty of forestalling land or houses,[9] but here "forestalling" could only be brought in by stretching an analogy, for the offense was generally understood quite literally as buying commodities before they had been carried into the actual market place or before the market had officially opened. Perhaps the strongest evidence on the point occurs in *Rex v. Waddington,* one of the last important English cases of this type, in which the defendant, having been charged with forestalling and engrossing hops, argued that it was no offense since hops were no victual, and the Court appeared to agree that if they had not been, there would have been no offense.[1]

[6] 51 Hen. III, §6 (1266).

[7] Banishment from the town where forestalling was committed was imposed by a statute of uncertain date, probably prior to 1327; 1 *Statutes of the Realm* 197, 202 et seq. But cf. Winfield, *Chief Sources of English Legal History* 93 (1925). Forfeiture was imposed by 25 Edw. III, c. 3, §4 (1350); death by 27 Edw. III, c. 11, §2 (1353), repealed 38 Edw. III, c. 6, §1 (1363).

[8] 1 Jac. I, c. 22, §§7, 19 (1604). 1 Phil. & M., c. 7 (1554). *Liber Albus* 172-73 is the case of a merchant fined by a London court for forestalling cloth; uncertain date prior to 1419.

[9] Fox, *Monopolies and Patents* 21 n. (1947).

[1] 1 East 143 (1800). Sanderson, *Restraint of Trade* 97 (1926).

The major objective of laws against forestalling was to keep food prices low. Such laws fit very neatly into the more general price-fixing program administered by medieval and, later, mercantilist governments. Local authorities of manors, cities, and guilds had customary rights to control food prices; kings issued proclamations and parliaments passed statutes for the same end; all these are implicitly confirmed in a statute of 1533 which gave certain members of the Privy Council as well the right to set "reasonable prices" of "cheese, butter, capons, hens, chickens, and other victuals necessary for man's sustenance." [2] The work of surveillance was much easier if all sales were made publicly in the market, and so forestalling and engrossing, means of evading the market, were seen as attempts to evade price controls.

But maintenance of low food prices was not the sole objective of the laws against forestalling. Just as monopolies by patent were attacked by those who feared to lose their own monopoly powers, so forestalling was abhorred not only by a public which hated high prices but also by those who saw in it an infringement of their privileges as owners of markets. Rights to hold markets were granted or confirmed by the Crown, and established local but powerful monopolies. What was given was not the mere right to hold a market, but an exclusive right. The extent of such privileges is illustrated in the case of the *Abbot of Westminster*.[3] The Abbot brought an action against one who sold cloth in London; William the Conqueror had given him a patent to hold a fair for thirty days, during which nobody should buy or sell merchandise at any other place within a radius of seven miles. The court presumably upheld the grant, and similar grants were upheld regularly. The owners of markets often had an intense interest in protecting their exclusive rights, for some of them had the right to charge a toll on certain goods sold in the market, and all of them were entitled to charge fees for market stalls put up on their land. To hinder sellers from coming to a market was therefore to deprive the owner of the market of stallage fees; thus the Prior of Coventry, in a suit

[2] 25 Hen. VIII, c. 2, §1 (1533).

[3] *Registrum Brevium,* f. 107. The case is cited in Darcy v. Allen, 11 Co. Rep. 84, Moore 671 (K.B., 1599), and East India Co. v. Sandys, 10 *Howell's State Trials* 372, 538 (1685).

against several who sold merchandise outside his market, declared that he thereby "lost stallage, terrage and cottage, etc., wrongfully and to his damage." [4]

The objectives of statesmen and the interest of owners of markets coincided with the prejudices of the public. They considered forestalling, engrossing, and regrating the typical tricks of middlemen and speculators, and were convinced that merchants who used such tactics were parasites profiting by the distress of others. They could see nothing but evil and selfishness in such practices. Thus a commission of inquiry into forestalling in Suffolk in 1411 reported that Geoffrey Russell bought sixty quarters of barley at forty pence a quarter and sold them for twice as much; "John Cok and John Joye . . . secretly bought, in private and secret places, sixty quarters of wheat . . . a quarter at eight shillings; whereas in open market, the same was sold for six shillings per quarter, &c, and so the aforesaid John and John are common forestallers of corn"; and "Simon Basket . . . bought at Beccles, Owtehole, and Brompton, and in divers other places, forty quarters of wheat, of the price of six shillings per quarter, and conveyed the same coastwise into divers other parts, whereby the price of a quarter of wheat was raised to ten shillings . . . and so the aforesaid Simon is a common forestaller." [5] The practices described show no sign of being, properly speaking, monopolistic; they appear on the contrary to have been acts of speculation, arbitrage, or wholesaling; but most men continued to identify the two phenomena until the new economic theory in the eighteenth century taught a few of them at least that speculation was no more profitable to the merchant than to the community at large, and that the community had as much to gain as the merchant from free trade.

The development of *laissez-faire* economic theory accounted for the abolition of the laws against forestalling. After 1552, when the great declaratory statute against forestalling was passed,[6] the general prohibitions were reasserted periodically when food prices

[4] *Year-Book 2 Edw. II,* pl. 141 (1308).

[5] Plea Roll 12 Hen. IV, 6 (1411), quoted in Illingworth, *Laws Respecting Forestalling* 240-42. Why Cok and Joye should have committed a crime at high prices rather than trade legally at low is either a mystery or the result of a black market.

[6] 5 & 6 Edw. VI, c. 14 (1552).

became unusually high. A Commonwealth Parliament passed a law in 1650 denying habeas corpus to defendants in any action concerning the buying or selling of foods, and William III issued a proclamation in 1698 insisting that the laws on forestalling be administered with full force.[7] Another such occasion arose in 1766 when corn prices were particularly high. Many complaints were voiced, tumults and riots took place, "in which, as usual in popular commotions, great irregularities took place," many lives were lost, order was restored only after the militia was called out and a number of rioters sentenced to death and hanged. George III tried to improve things by issuing a proclamation to put in force the statutes against forestallers. But, as *The Annual Register* noted, many doubted whether such action could be of any use: "It was apprehended that this measure would have an effect contrary to the intentions of the council, and by frightening dealers from the markets, would increase that scarcity it was designed to remedy."[8]

The doctrine hinted at in this comment, that public regulation of the market would produce worse results than the free action of merchants, was still novel in 1766 but was beginning to gain force. It dominated the committee of the House of Commons which reported in the following year "that the several laws relating to Badgers, Engrossers, Forestallers, and Regrators, by preventing the circulation of, and free trade in, corn, and other provisions, have been the means of raising the price thereof in many parts of this Kingdom."[9] The report suggested that those laws should be abolished, and action of this sort was finally taken in 1772, when a bill was prepared, reported by Edmund Burke (the main exponent in Parliament of this measure), and quickly passed by Commons.[1] The Act repealed the various statutes against forestalling because, as its preamble said, "it hath been found by experience that the restraints laid by several statutes upon the dealing in corn, meal, flour, cattle, and sundry other sorts of victuals, by preventing a free trade in the said commodities, have a tendency to discourage the

[7] Statute of Oct. 23, 1650, Firth and Rait, 2 *Acts and Ordinances of the Interregnum* 442 et seq. (1911). William III, Proclamation Oct. 13, 1698.

[8] *Annual Register* 39-40 (1767).

[9] *House of Commons Journal* (Apr. 8, 1767).

[1] *House of Commons Journal* (Mar. 13, May 6, May 20, 1772). For Burke's views on the subject, see his *Thoughts and Details on Scarcity*, *Works*, V, 133, 150 *et seq.* (Nimmo's ed., 1899).

growth, and to inhance the price of the same." [2] With the passage of this Act the cause of free trade seemed to be triumphant; the crime of forestalling had been abolished—so Blackstone, among others, thought[3]—and Adam Smith's remark, published three years later, that to fear forestalling was like fearing witchcraft seemed to be more useful as a contribution to public education than to practical policy.[4]

For a short while, however, the law against forestalling was revitalized by Lord Kenyon's decision in *Rex v. Rusby.*[5] Rusby was indicted in 1799 for regrating thirty quarters of oats, and presumably rested his defense on the Act of 1772. Kenyon held, however, that "though in an evil hour all the statutes which had been existing above a century were at one blow repealed, yet, thank God, the provisions of the common law were not destroyed" and found Rusby guilty at common law. The vigor of Kenyon's address against Rusby so inflamed the public that a mob of Londoners rioted, tried to lynch Rusby, and ended by pulling down his house;[6] the public was apparently not so convinced as Burke, Smith, and Parliament that forestalling was economically beneficial, or, at least, that laws prohibiting it were more harmful than the thing itself. After Kenyon's time, however, there were no further common-law prosecutions against forestalling,[7] and to make quite sure, Parliament in 1844 passed a law repealing all the remaining statutes against it, and utterly abolishing the common-law crimes of forestalling, engrossing, and regrating.[8]

Clearly, then, the laws against forestalling and engrossing, which some have tried to identify as a fount of modern antitrust law, did not have the required character. They were of narrow scope, applying almost exclusively to trade in foodstuffs; they were

[2] 12 Geo. III, c. 71 (1772).

[3] Blackstone, *Commentaries,* IV, 159 (5th ed., 1773).

[4] Smith, *Wealth of Nations,* II, 34-35 (Canaan ed., 1922).

[5] Peake Add. Cas. 189 (1800).

[6] Barnes, *History of the English Corn Laws* 81-82 (1930).

[7] Sanderson, *Restraint of Trade,* 98.

[8] 7 & 8 Vic., c. 24 (1844). Holdsworth, *History,* IV, 379 (1924), says that the forestalling laws were repealed by 6 Geo. IV, c. 129 (1825), under the influence of "the economists of the school of Ricardo." There is little evidence that Ricardo or his school particularly affected the passing of the act of 1844, and the act of 1825 which Holdsworth cites has no bearing on forestalling, being instead a combination act.

part of a program to regulate all economic activities; like the common law against monopolies by patent, they were supported by monopolists—in this case, the owners of markets—who found them useful protection; and they were finally repealed by the supporters of free trade and in the name of free trade.

English Common Law on Contracts in Restraint of Trade

Because the Statute of Monopolies settled that branch of law into its present narrow concern with patents, and the Acts of 1772 and 1844 did away altogether with the law against forestalling, modern antitrust law could only grow from the English bodies of law against contracts in restraint of trade and combinations in restraint of trade. The manner in which those laws were interpreted during the nineteenth century, however, very much weakened their capacity for controlling modern monopolies.

The common law relating to contracts in restraint of trade stems from the *Case of John Dyer,*[9] decided in 1414. The report of the case is meager. The defendant was sued for breaking his bond not to practice the trade of dyeing in his home town of Dale for a half year; he apparently maintained that he had not broken his bond, and seems to have won the case. One of the judges suggested that John could have used the stronger defense of demurring at law, as the condition of the bond was illegal, and he continued in words which have become all too famous in the literature on monopolies: "By God, if the plaintiff were here he should go to prison until he paid a fine to the King." The case was an extremely powerful precedent until the beginning of the eighteenth century.

But for all its legal power, the *Case of John Dyer* does not demonstrate—as so many have believed—that the common law always condemned restraints on trade. If one seventeenth-century lawyer could cite the case as authority for that view, his opponent could counter with a much older precedent, the *Case of the Archbishop of York,*[1] in which a court upheld the custom of the Archbishop's manor at Ripon that no one should operate a dyeing-

[9] *Year-Book 2 Hen. V,* 5f. (1414).

[1] *Reg. Brev.,* f. 105. The two cases were confronted in Darcy v. Allen.

house there without the Archbishop's license. If the common law is supposed to have been such an ardent protector of free trade, why was it prepared to uphold an Archbishop's power to keep a dyer from following his trade in Ripon forever, but not an ordinary man's power under a voluntary agreement to keep a dyer from following his trade in Dale for half a year?

The answer, of course, is that the common law prior to the fifteenth century did not favor free trade but reached its decision in *John Dyer*'s case on quite different grounds. The restraining agreement in the *Dyer*'s case was embodied in a bond, and it has been suggested that judges distrusted bonds because they were so often oppressive, and lost few opportunities to hold them void.[2] Lord Macclesfield, in his famous opinion in *Mitchel v. Reynolds,* held that the issue was not so much whether the restraining agreement was by bond or by contract but whether it was based on a good and adequate consideration. Yet, as he understood *John Dyer*'s case, the fact that it rested on a bond seemed material; "for suppose," he wrote,

> (As that case seems to be) a poor weaver [sic], having just met with a great loss, should, in a fit of passion and concern, be exclaiming against his trade, and declare, that he would not follow it any more, etc., at which instant, some designing fellow should work him up to such a pitch, as, for a trifling matter, to give a bond not to work at it again, and afterwards, when the necessities of his family, and the cries of his children, sent him to the loom, should take advantage of the forfeiture, and put the bond in suit; I must own, I think this such a piece of villainy, as is hard to find a name for. . . .[3]

Lord Macclesfield evidently thought that no court should uphold an agreement made in such circumstances, and perhaps earlier common-law judges did too.

But the more important basis for deciding against the restraint in the *Dyer*'s case was the principle, so important in the cases on monopolies by patent, of the individual's right to work. It may appear that to prevent a man from following one trade in one par-

[2] Sanderson, *Restraint of Trade* 14. Cf. Clerk v. Taylors of Exeter, 3 Lev. 241 (1685), in which the Exchequer held that in all the previous cases on restraint of trade the agreement had been disapproved if by bond, approved if by contract (assumpsit).

[3] 1 Peere Wms. 181, 193 (1711).

ticular town for six months did not very seriously limit his right to work: he might take up another trade or move to another town. But in the fifteenth century, those alternatives were not open to him. In order to take up another trade, he would have had to pass through an apprenticeship of seven years, or with great difficulty and expense satisfy a guild that he was a master of its craft; and this alternative was for all practical purposes ruled out. Nor could he more readily practice his old trade in a new town, for the guilds and municipal corporations of each place had by-laws to prevent strangers—that is, anyone not admitted to the privileges of the town or its guilds—from entering into competition with citizens.[4] The whole guild system, therefore, made it nearly impossible for a tradesman to earn his living if he did not practice his own trade in his own town, and this was the main reason why, as long as the guilds maintained their power, contracts in restraint of trade were held void. To have held otherwise would have been to concur in arrangements by which men deprived themselves of their means of support. The power of the guilds to regulate entrance into trade had begun to weaken by the sixteenth century, although cities and towns retained fragments of such powers until 1835, when the Municipal Corporations Act finally gave anyone the right to keep any shop or follow any trade in any borough.[5] It was with the decay of this power in the guilds that the law on contracts in restraint of trade came to change, and the time when the courts refused to uphold the restrictive powers of the Ipswich Tailor's guild was also the time when they first held valid a contract in restraint of trade.[6]

From then on, the law on the subject became more and more

[4] Cf. Sanderson, *Restraint of Trade* 15.

[5] 5 & 6 Wm. IV, c. 76 (1835). London was not considered a borough under the Act, and cases to exclude "foreigners" from certain employments in London continued until later in the nineteenth century; 32 Halsbury's *Laws* 345 (1939).

[6] Ipswich Tailors' case, 11 Co. Rep. 53 (1613); Rogers v. Parrey, 2 Bulst. 136 (1614). In the earlier cases, the restraints were held void, John Dyer's case being cited as authority for each: Anon., Moore 115 (K.B., 1578)—a mercer's apprentice bound himself not to exercise his craft for four years in Nottingham; Anon., Moore 242 (K.B., 1587), 2 Leonard 210—a blacksmith bound himself not to practice the trade in South-mims; Colgate v. Bacheler, Cro. Eliz. 872, Owen 143 (1601)—a haberdasher gave bond not to trade in Canterbury or Rochester for four years, of which Anderson, J. said that "he might as well bind himself, that he would not go to Church."

complex, since each case involved two contrary principles. On the one hand, the common law was inclined to uphold contracts in restraint of trade for the same reasons that moved it to sustain any good contract. To own property implied the right to dispose of property by contract, and if a reasonable man disposed of his property in a way he considered good, it was not for the court to tell him he was mistaken.[7] On the other hand, the common law was inclined to invalidate contracts in restraint of trade because they deprived a man of the means to earn a livelihood,[8] or because they deprived the public of the advantages of competition.[9] The first of these reasons prevailed until the eighteenth century; the second slowly replaced it. The conflict of these principles and their application to the particular circumstances of each case have resulted in the general rule, still true today, that some contracts in restraint of trade are good and others are bad. The basis on which the discrimination should be made was first formally stated in *Mitchel v. Reynolds,* decided in 1711; it was stated in broader terms—or, as some think, changed—by the decision in *Nordenfelt v. Nordenfelt* in 1894.

In *Mitchel v. Reynolds*[1] the defendant assigned to the plaintiff the lease of a bakery in a certain parish of London for five years, and undertook to pay the plaintiff £50 damages if he should work as a baker within that parish during those five years. The plaintiff brought suit for the damages, and though the defendant pleaded that since he had served his apprenticeship as a baker and had been admitted to the guild no private person could lawfully prevent him from working at that trade, Chief Justice Parker (later Lord Macclesfield) found for the plaintiff. The fame and great interest of this case lies not in the decision, but in the opinion, for

[7] Jollife v. Broad, 2 Roll. Rep. 201, Cro. Jac. 596, 1 Wm. Jones 13 (1620): Restraint ancillary to sale of a mercer's business in Newport held void in Common Pleas, reversed in King's Bench, affirmed in Exchequer. Dodderidge, J. in K.B.: "It is the usual course of men in their old age to turn over their trade to another. . . ."; 2 Roll. Rep. 201, 203. Similarly, Bragge v. Stanner, Palmer 172 (1621); Pragnell v. Goff, Style 111, Aleyn 67 (1648); Hunlocke v. Blacklowe, 2 Wms. Saunders 156, 2 Keble 674 (1670).

[8] See the cases listed at note 6, p. 41 above, and also Ferby v. Arrosmyth, 2 Keble 377 (1668).

[9] See the cases listed at note 5, p. 41 below.

[1] 1 Peere Wms. 181 (1711). See Blake, "Employee Agreements Not to Compete," 73 Harvard L. R. 625, 629-46 (1960).

there Lord Macclesfield very systematically classified all restraints of trade and arrived at his long-lasting rule for distinguishing good restraints from bad. He first divided all restraints of trade into involuntary or voluntary; the contract in issue was clearly a voluntary restraint. Among voluntary restraints he distinguished between those "where the restraint is general not to exercise a trade throughout the kingdom, and where it is limited to a particular place." General restraints, he held, had always been held void, and should be, "being of no benefit to either party, and only oppressive."[2] But particular restraints are of two sorts: without consideration, "all of which are void by what sort of contract soever created," and Macclesfield here cited the *Dyer*'s case as evidence for this point; and with consideration. Macclesfield's rule, therefore, was that a contract in restraint of trade can be good only if the restraint is particular and the contract "appears to be made upon a good and adequate consideration, so as to make it a proper and useful contract."[3] Lord Macclesfield had discovered this much from precedent, but being a lawyer of his time, he was interested to show not only what the law was, but also the reasonable explanation of why it should be so, and he added that one objection to voluntary general restraints is "the mischief which may arise from them, 1st, to the party, by the loss of his livelihood, and the subsistence of his family; 2dly, to the public, by depriving it of an useful member."[4]

These mischiefs might arise from general restraints but could not from particular restraints; the latter were good because the parties might gain and the public lose nothing from them. Once a man could reasonably be expected to enter a new trade if he sold his last one, or to move to a new place if he bound himself not to trade in his former one, the law became quite willing to uphold fair contracts in which he bound himself to desist from competition within a limited area. And so the test became whether the contract was fair and the area to which it applied limited.

For at least a century, Macclesfield's rule was followed religiously. But then new problems in the interpretation of the rule began to arise. How important a consideration was public policy; if a con-

[2] *Ibid.*, at 182.
[3] *Ibid.*, at 185-86.
[4] *Ibid.*, at 190.

tract did not injure either of the parties, might it still be bad because it interfered with competition? How large an area was "particular" rather than "general"; if the business of one party extended throughout the kingdom and real protection from competition could only be had by a "general" restraint, was a contract of this sort nevertheless to be held bad automatically? [5] How was the word "reasonable," recurring so often in Macclesfield's opinion, to be interpreted; was the real test of a restraint whether it was reasonable, and was Macclesfield only enunciating a special case of the rule, valid for his time but not for always, when he held that particularity and consideration made a restraint reasonable and therefore good? All these questions were decided one way or another by judges during the nineteenth century and finally settled by the decision of the House of Lords in *Nordenfelt v. Maxim Nordenfelt Guns and Ammunition Co.,*[6] and particularly by the rule laid down by Lord Macnaghten.

The case arose on a contract whereby Thorsten Nordenfelt agreed not to engage in the ammunition and armaments business except in behalf of the Company, the restraint to apply for twenty-five years and in all countries. The Company brought action to enforce the covenant by injunction, and Nordenfelt successfully defended himself in the lower courts by arguing that the restraint was general and therefore void. The Court of Appeals reversed the lower court[7] and Nordenfelt then appealed to the House of Lords. That body unanimously held that the restraint, though general, was valid because it was reasonable. Lord Macnaghten, in his concurring opinion, set down what has since been the governing rule in such cases; it very neatly coordinates considerations of public policy, generality of restraint, and reasonableness:

> The public have an interest in every person's carrying on his trade freely: so has the individual. All interference with individual liberty of action in trading, and all restraints of trade of themselves, if there is nothing more, are contrary to public policy, and therefore void. That is the general rule. But there are exceptions: restraints of trade and in-

[5] See, e.g., Wickens v. Evans, 3 Y. & J. 318 (1829); Wallis v. Day, 2 M. & W. 273 (1837); Mallan v. May, 11 M. & W. 652 (1843); Shrewsbury and Birmingham Railway Co. v. London and North-Western Railway Co., 21 L.J.Q.B. 89 (1851); and Tallis v. Tallis, 1 El. & Bl. 391 (1853).

[6] [1894] App. Cas. 535.

[7] [1893] 1 Ch. 630.

terference with individual liberty of action may be justified by the special circumstances of a particular case. It is a sufficient justification, and indeed it is the only justification, if the restriction is reasonable—reasonable, that is, in reference to the interests of the parties concerned and reasonable in reference to the interests of the public, so framed and so guarded as to afford adequate protection to the party in whose favour it is imposed, while at the same time it is in no way injurious to the public.[8]

Only the greatest optimism could have made it appear to Lord Macnaghten that contracts in restraint of trade are at all likely "to afford adequate protection" to a party and at the same time to be "in no way injurious to the public." What makes this entire area of law so difficult is precisely that the interests of the restraining party and of the public are so often opposed. This problem indeed seems to be at the core of *Nordenfelt v. Nordenfelt,* although the court very tactfully covered it over. Vague references were made to the public interest, which was said not to favor or require Thorsten Nordenfelt's competition with the Company. On the other hand, a great deal was said about the Company's need for adequate protection. The Lord Chancellor took notice of the improved means of communication that had become available since *Mitchel v. Reynolds,* and argued that under these new conditions "reasonable protection" may mean worldwide protection; he decided that because the Company sold its armaments mainly to governments, considering "the nature of the business and the limited number of customers," [9] it needed protection of such width. And Lord Watson, in his concurring opinion, made it quite clear why the public interest and the private interest of the covenantee could be so readily identified: "[But] it must not be forgotten that the community has a material interest in maintaining the rules of fair dealing between man and man. It suffers far greater injury from the infraction of these rules than from contracts in restraint of trade." [1]

This remark is the clearest possible indication that by 1894 English law on contracts in restraint of trade was not in any important respect an instrument for the maintenance of a competitive economic order. If ever, then only for a very short period after

[8] [1894] App. Cas. 535, 565.
[9] [1894] App. Cas. 548-50.
[1] [1894] App. Cas. 552.

Mitchel v. Reynolds did the courts give the public policy of promoting competition an important part in deciding cases on contracts in restraint of trade. The decision in *Nordenfelt v. Nordenfelt,* the words in which Lord Macnaghten expressed his rule of reasonableness, and the dictum of Lord Watson, all declared that competition was no longer public policy, or at least that freedom of contract had become a more important end than freedom of trade.[2]

English Common Law on Combinations in Restraint of Trade

The law on combinations in restraint of trade was by the end of the nineteenth century narrow and ineffective. Developments in both statute and common law joined to produce this result. The statute law governing combinations became increasingly lenient during the nineteenth century, in response to greater sympathy—abstract as well as sentimental—for the labor unions. The common law, influenced by a feeling that employers should not be denied rights granted to workers, matched the new legal power of the latter with a solicitous concern for employers' combinations; in the end it came to put a higher value on the freedom of entrepreneurs to use any means short of violence to outstrip competitors than on the right of the public to enjoy the advantages of competition.

Legislation governing wages and conditions of labor began with the Ordinance of Labourers passed in 1349,[3] which was confirmed and extended by numerous later statutes. In the sixteenth century, these occasional laws were consolidated in the great Elizabethan Statute of Artificers,[4] which governed apprenticeship and wages, and in the Act of 1548,[5] which provided criminal penalties against any workmen who conspired to raise wages or reduce hours of labor. But there was no thought in these statutes of making it possible for workmen to compete; on the contrary, the sixteenth-century legislators who passed these laws to fix the terms and wages of

[2] Cf. Morris v. Saxelby, [1916] 1 App. Cas. 688, 699.
[3] 23 Edw. III (1349).
[4] 5 Eliz., c. 4 (1562).
[5] 2 & 3 Edw. VI, c. 15 (1548), confirmed by 22 & 23 Car. II, c. 19 (1670).

labor hoped to recapture the economic stability that had been shaken by the movement of men from manors to towns, and the early industrial revolution.[6] They wanted competition no more than they understood it. Although these laws appear, in the light of later developments and interpretation, to express antagonism to monopolistic arrangements and approval of competition, they were really intended to reinforce the system of direct economic control.

The earliest instances of general labor legislation influenced by free-trade theories were the Combination Act of 1799, which prohibited combinations of workmen only, and the Combination Act of 1800, which superseded it and prohibited masters as well as workmen from combining.[7] It has been said that these Acts were prosecuted more severely against combinations of laborers than against those of masters; it appears that they were not very effective at all; it is certain that they did not settle the problem of changing from a legally regulated labor market to a free one.[8] Riots and violence continued as frequent incidents of labor relations after 1800, and Place, Joseph Hume, McCulloch, and other radical followers of Bentham argued that this disorder would not cease until workers were given a legal right to combine.[9] The Benthamites, in addition, advocated a statute permitting workers to combine because this law was implied by two of their basic political principles. These, as Dicey has expressed them, were "the belief that trade in labour ought to be as free as any other kind of trade," and "the well-grounded conviction that there ought to be one and the same law for men as for masters; Adam Smith had, about fifty years earlier, pointed out that trade combinations on the part of workmen were blamed and punished, whilst trade combinations on the part of masters were neither punished nor indeed noticed." [1] In the early decades of the nineteenth century, those who favored freedom of trade tried to achieve their other aim of equality before law by giving workers as well as masters freedom to associate. By rejecting the alternative that would have achieved both their ob-

[6] Nef, *Rise of the British Coal Industry,* I, 165-89 (1932).

[7] 38 Geo. III, c. 81 (1799); c. 106 (1800).

[8] George, "The Combination Laws," *Econ. Hist. Rev.*, VI, 172 (1935).

[9] Robbins, *The Theory of Economic Policy* 106 *et seq.* (1952).

[1] Dicey, *Law and Opinion* 196 (1905 ed.).

jectives, by not denying the right of combination to workers and masters alike, they wasted an opportunity to secure economic freedom against attack by monopolies of either.

In any case, so strong was the Benthamites' belief in freedom of association, so complete their inability to foresee the monopolistic position that labor unions and industrial combinations would in time achieve, so great their faith that if workers were allowed to combine in friendly associations they would desist from all violence and monopolistic activities, that in 1824 they successfully urged Parliament to pass the Act that gave combinations of workmen and masters alike immunity from all statutory and common-law prohibitions.[2] Workmen proceeded to make the most uninhibited use of that immunity. In the next session of Parliament, Huskisson brought in a bill that reversed the terms of the Act of 1824: where the old Act had given immunity for everything but intimidation and violence, the new bill—which very soon became law—restored the power of the common law over combinations, and excepted only a limited right to combine.[3] The pattern had, however, been established, and the increasing sympathy for the condition of workingmen excited by Tory reformers, early Socialists, and others, finally produced in 1871 the first Trades Union Act, and in 1875, a new Combination Act[4]—both of which had the effect of legalizing all combinations of workers and masters alike, provided those combinations were formed to settle labor disputes and to negotiate hours and conditions of labor.

The law on combinations which were labor unions or employers' associations was dominated by the statutes on the subject. On the other hand, combinations of merchants to fix prices of goods, share out a market, or otherwise limit competition, were governed by no general statutes, particularly after the laws against forestalling were repealed, and therefore remained under the jurisdiction of common law. In a few instances, such combinations were indicted as criminal conspiracies at common law.[5] But after the beginning

[2] 5 Geo. IV, c. 95 (1824).

[3] 6 Geo. IV, c. 129 (1825). Cf. Dicey, *Law and Opinion* 191 *et seq.*

[4] 34 & 35 Vic., c. 31 (1871); 38 & 39 Vic., c. 86 (1875).

[5] Rex v. Journeymen Tailors of Cambridge, 8 Mod. 10 (1721); Rex v. Eccles, 1 Leach 274 (1783); Rex v. Mawbey, 6 T.R. 619 (1796). See Winfield, *The History of Conspiracy and Abuse of Legal Procedure* 111-17 (1921).

of the nineteenth century, the common law came to regard an agreement between competitors to combine as analogous to a contract in restraint of trade, and judged such agreements by whether they left the parties reasonably free to act as they desired. All along, less attention was paid to whether the agreement seriously interfered with competition. In *Hearn v. Griffin*[6] the court upheld an agreement between two rival coach-owners to charge the same prices and provide no competing services; it was, wrote Lord Ellenborough, "merely a convenient mode of arranging two concerns which might otherwise ruin each other." In *Wickens v. Evans,*[7] three boxmakers had agreed to divide England into areas in which each was to be the exclusive seller. This arrangement was upheld on the grounds that it was only a partial restraint of trade, one of the judges maintaining that it was "not a monopoly, except as between themselves; because every other man may come into their districts and vend his goods: all they propose is, that they shall not carry on a rivalry. . . ." In *Hilton v. Eckersly,*[8] the court refused to enforce an agreement between eighteen mill owners to settle wages and hours by majority rule. The reason given was that the parties were not left free to trade on their own terms; but the case was decided before the Combination Act of 1875 authorized such agreements. In *Collins v. Locke,*[9] decided in 1879, an agreement between docking firms to distribute work and profits among themselves was upheld on the grounds that it did not unduly restrain the free action of the parties. But the modern common law on combinations in restraint of trade was established by the *Mogul Steamship* case,[1] which laid down the principle that although a trade combination might be destroyed by attack from within, it could not be successfully attacked by an outsider.

The *Mogul Steamship* case was decided two years before the *Nordenfelt* case; these two are among the chief reasons for the subsequent inability of English common law substantially to deter the growth of monopolies. The defendants in the *Mogul Steamship*

[6] 2 Chitty 407 (1815).

[7] 3 Y. & T. 318 (1829).

[8] 6 El. & Bl. 47 (1855).

[9] 4 L.R.A.C. 674 (1855). Cf. The Shrewsbury and Birmingham Railway Co. v. The London and North-Western Railway Co., 21 L.J.Q.B. 89 (1851).

[1] Mogul Steamship Co. v. McGregor [1892] App. Cas. 25.

case were a number of shipping lines who had formed an association; they had agreed to regulate by joint decision the number of ships each would send to Hankow or Shanghai during the brief tea-export season, the division of cargoes between those ships, and freight rates, to give a rebate to all shippers who dealt exclusively with members of the association, and to prohibit their agents in China from acting in the interest of competing shippers. Short of an outright merger or trust agreement, they could hardly have formed a more complete combination. The Mogul Steamship Company had been included in the association at first, was later excluded, but continued to send its ships to a Chinese port. The defendants retaliated by sending more of their ships to the port, underbidding Mogul rates, threatening to dismiss from their service agents who arranged to load Mogul ships, and circulating notices that they would not give their rebate to anyone who shipped by Mogul. The Mogul Company brought a suit for damages against the members of the association, alleging that they formed a conspiracy to injure Mogul interests. On the original action the Chief Justice, Lord Coleridge, judged for the defendants; this was affirmed by the Court of Appeals, three justices dissenting, and the plaintiff appealed to the House of Lords, which unanimously affirmed the decision.[2]

The principle on which all the justices agreed was that the agreement was unlawful in the sense that the courts would not enforce it, but that it was not *"contrary to law."* [3] It would become an illegal conspiracy at common law only if it sought an unlawful end or used unlawful means; and since, as the Lord Chancellor put it, the combination had neither acted with any "malicious intention to injure rival traders," nor used any unlawful means, such as violence, intimidation, molestation, or inducement to break contracts, it was innocent.[4] There were indeed some qualms among the justices as to whether all the means were lawful, whether the threatening notices distributed by the defendants did not amount to intimidation, but all these doubts they resolved in favor of the defendants. There were, on the other hand, no doubts at all about the propriety of defendants' ends. The defendants themselves had

[2] 21 Q.B.D. 544 (1888). 23 Q.B.D. 598 (1889). [1892] App. Cas. 25.
[3] [1892] App. Cas. 25, 39.
[4] [1892] App. Cas. 25, 36-37.

dismissed the public policy question, submitting that "[w]hether such combinations and agreements are on the whole beneficial or not to the public is a question not of law but of political economy as to which there will always be a difference of opinion";[5] but the court refused to accept this easy way out. Lord Bramwell maintained, on the contrary, that the public policy of free trade positively authorized such combinations: "It does seem strange," he wrote, "that to enforce freedom of trade, of action, the law should punish those who make a perfectly honest agreement with a belief that it is fairly required for their protection." And he went on to suggest that combinations of employers should be given equal treatment with combinations of workmen: "I have always said that a combination of workmen, an agreement among them to cease work except for higher wages, and a strike in consequence, was lawful at common law; perhaps not enforceable inter se, but not indictable. The Legislature has now so declared."[6] It followed that a combination of employers was lawful at common law. The law on combinations had by this time turned full circle: earlier in the century, unions had been legalized because combinations of masters were seldom if ever punished; by the end of the century, business combinations were held to be exempt from punishment because labor unions had been legalized.

By 1890, what little there had ever been of English common law against monopolies had become quite weak. The common law against monopoly proper had been superseded by the Statute of Monopolies. The common law against forestalling had been abolished by the statute of 1844. The common law against combinations of workmen and of masters had been overruled by the Trade Union Acts. The common law against contracts and combinations in restraint of trade alone remained in force, but it was governed by principles that condoned more than they prohibited. If monopolies were to be restrained, the common law would have to change its direction again, or legislation would have to remedy its weakness.

Legislation toward this end was provided in America, first by the antitrust laws of several states, and in 1890, by the Sherman

[5] [1892] App. Cas. 25, 34-35.
[6] [1892] App. Cas. 25, 47.

Act. Such legislation had a firmer foundation in the United States than in England, because American common law in 1890 still contained provisions that had been struck from the English common law by statutes which had no legal effect in the United States. Thus the common law against forestalling and engrossing was still in force in the United States; it could be made to serve purposes for which it had not been originally intended, and it was made the basis for section 2 of the Sherman Act, which prohibits "monopolizing."[7] Similarly, labor unions were not exempted from the American common law on combinations, and therefore the prohibition of combinations in section 1 of the Sherman Act could be used against certain activities of unions. But the Sherman Act went far beyond the common law when it authorized the Attorney General to indict violators of the Act, and gave injured persons the power to sue them, thus making it possible to enforce competition actively. The Act was therefore much more an innovation than its authors realized. It did not, as they thought, merely declare the common law. It can almost be said to have helped create the common law, insofar as its authors' convictions helped spread the belief that the common law always expressed as much antagonism to monopoly as they wrote into the Sherman Act.

[7] Adler, "Monopolizing at Common Law and under Sec. II of the Sherman Antitrust Act," 31 *Harv. L. Rev.* 246 (1917).

CHAPTER THREE

PASSING THE SHERMAN ACT

1888-1890

The deceptive simplicity of the Sherman Act has led many historians to believe that the intention of Congress was equally simple. Although they have not agreed on what the intention was, these historians have shared the view that the motives of Congress were elementary and unmixed and have differed chiefly over whether Congress was sincere. Some suppose that the congressmen of 1890 were committed to a policy of *laissez faire,* interpret that policy as a dogmatic faith in competition, and regard the Sherman Act as an effort to enforce that orthodoxy.[1] Others, less trustful, maintain that the Act was a fraud, contrived to soothe the public without injuring the trusts, and they insist that no other result was possible because the Republican Party, in control of the 51st Congress, was "itself dominated at the time by many of the very industrial magnates most vulnerable to real antitrust legislation." [2] Both these schools can draw support from distinguished men who lived while the Act was being passed.[3]

But the process by which laws are made in the American democ-

[1] See the authoritative text, Seager and Gulick, *Trust and Corporation Problems* 373 (1929) and Mund, *Government and Business* 145, 146, 150 (1950).

[2] Fainsod and Gordon, *Government and the American Economy* 450 (1941). Cochran and Miller, *The Age of Enterprise* 171-2 (1942). See also, Papandreou and Wheeler, *Competition and Its Regulation* 213 (1954), in which the Sherman Act is described as a measure of "appeasement."

[3] Senator Platt said that his colleagues were interested in only one thing, "to get some bill headed: 'A Bill to Punish Trusts' with which to go to the country." Coolidge, *An Old-Fashioned Senator: Orville H. Platt* 444 (1910). Justice Holmes thought that the Act was "a humbug based on economic ignorance and incompetence." *Holmes-Pollock Letters,* I, 163 (Howe ed., 1941).

racy is not so direct and obvious. Congress does not merely enact its private dogmas, nor does it simply supply whatever the people order. Public opinion is not so precise. Far from demanding a particular law, the public desires at most a certain kind of law, and more often only wants to be rid of a general evil. Sometimes, indeed, public opinion is practically silent and yet effective, for Congress often refuses to pass laws because it expects that the public would object, or adopts them in anticipation that the public will approve. Congress is not a factory that mechanically converts opinion into statutes. The congressman is a representative, who must recognize at least some tendencies of public opinion if he is to be re-elected. He is also a professional lawmaker, more likely than not a lawyer by training, who is not indifferent to his craft. He talks with lawyers, follows the decisions of judges, and reads law journals. He is willing to draw on the skill of other experts when the need arises, and will take advice from businessmen, reformers, or economists. He is a member of a political party and may feel loyal to its traditional policies and obliged to support at least part of its current platform. Finally, he is an individual with beliefs, interests, ambitions, and idiosyncrasies quite his own.

It should not be surprising then that although the Sherman Act was passed by a virtually unanimous vote, and although its language is disarmingly clear, the administrations and courts charged with enforcing it have experienced so much difficulty in settling its meaning. The Sherman Act reflects not only the uncertainty present in every general law because its authors cannot foresee the particular cases that will arise, but also the ambiguity that colors many democratic laws because the authors cannot completely resolve the divergent opinions and cross purposes that call it forth.

American Public Opinion on Monopolies

No one denies that Congress passed the Sherman Act in response to real public feeling against the trusts, but at this distance in time it is difficult to be sure how hostile the public was and why. The intensity of public opposition, difficult though it may be to assess, is of some importance in explaining what Congress did. If public hatred of trusts was violent, or if congressmen thought it was, then they might have felt so pressed to pass the law, whatever their own judgments, as to have done the work hastily and perhaps spitefully. If, on the other hand, the public opposition was firm but calm, then Congress may have felt free to pass the best law it could devise. In fact, though the public sentiment may not have been so intense as some believed, yet it was more deeply rooted than many have noticed, and sufficient in any event to persuade Congress that something had to be done. However, since the public, despite its hostility, did not and could not suggest any specific solution for the problem, Congress was left very much to its own devices in deciding what was to be done.

In the years immediately before the Sherman Act, between 1888 and 1890, there were few who doubted that the public hated the trusts fervently. Those who fanned the prejudice and those who hoped to smother it agreed that the fire was already blazing. Radical agitators and polite reformers spoke admiringly of the "people's wrath." Apologists for the trust did not deny its unpopularity. Dodd, the Standard Oil Company lawyer who invented the trust device, was properly mild when he told the merchants of Boston that there was "an earnest popular prejudice against trade combinations"; but George Gunton, a scholarly defender of Standard Oil, wrote that "the public mind has begun to assume a state of apprehension, almost amounting to alarm." [4] Those whose professional interests lay not so much in provoking or fearing the public reaction as in gauging it agreed that it was intense. Journalists gave every action of the trusts and of their critics ample publicity, which suggests that they did not find their readers indifferent. The din forced Charles Francis Adams, a calm and judicious man, to complain that an innocent plan for coordinating railroads was no sooner announced than it was "characterized in the papers as a vast 'trust'—in these days," he added, "everything is a 'trust'—and denounced as a conspiracy." [5] Another railroad president said that he knew of no trust that had injured the public, and thought that "the attitude of the press and the consequent temper of the

[4] Dodd, "Address Before the Merchants' Association of Boston," 5 *Ry. & Corp. L.J.* 97 (1889). Gunton, "The Economic and Social Aspect of Trusts," *Pol. Sci. Q.*, III, 385 (1888).

[5] Adams, Statement of Dec. 15, 1888, 4 *Ry. & Corp. L.J.* 579 (1888).

people are breeding a greater panic than the country has ever seen."[6] The editor of a law journal said that the ordinary man was "in a feverish state" about trusts even though he knew nothing about them; "He has been taught his terror by the newspapers and politicians."[7] It was true that politicians, whether or not they taught terror, assumed that it existed. Representative Rayner of Maryland urged a congressional committee in 1888 to waste no time on investigation; it need only "listen to the voice of a suffering people resounding through the homes and business centers of this country, and through the medium of an enlightened press appealing to their representatives to rescue them," to see the urgency of accepting his antitrust bill.[8] Many congressmen who participated in the debate on antitrust measures made declarations equally dramatic, if not always as dire as Senator Sherman's warning that the "popular mind is agitated with problems that may disturb social order."[9]

These impressions of the state of public opinion were supported by more nearly impartial contemporaries, including the judges who, with William Howard Taft, took it for granted that the Act "was a step taken by Congress to meet what the public had found to be a growing and intolerable evil."[1] Here and there a few doubts were expressed about the public's determination. Some extremists said that the populace could solve the trust problem—by establishing government ownership of all industry—if it would only awake and "prove itself worthy to be free."[2] Some free-traders said that trusts could be eradicated by abolishing protective tariffs, if the people would only "open their eyes."[3] A skeptic later argued that government would have destroyed the trusts if the people had really cared.[4] But these irregular views have not received much notice, and most later commentators have been satisfied to believe that there was a "great public outcry" against the trusts.

[6] Porter, writing in the Chi. *Trib.* (July 28, 1889), quoted in 6 *Ry. & Corp. L.J.* 103 (1889).
[7] 6 *Ry. & Corp. L.J.* 61 (1889).
[8] N.Y. *Times* p. 5, col. 1 (Feb. 11, 1888).
[9] 21 *Cong. Rec.* 2460 (1890).
[1] Taft, *The Anti-Trust Act and the Supreme Court* 2 (1914).
[2] Lewis, *A Talk About "Trusts"* [13] (1889).
[3] N.Y. *Times* p. 4, col. 3 (Dec. 28, 1887) (editorial).
[4] Wollman, "The Mortality of Trusts," 67 *Alb. L.J.* 227 (1905).

Those who have questioned this standard opinion have pointed out that few books or journal articles were published on the trust problem before 1890, fewer, at least, than were printed afterward. This fact led a leading historian of the Sherman Act, John Davidson Clark, to conclude that the public was not "hysterical" but rather indifferent to the trusts.[5] Unfortunately Clark exaggerated the evidence. Far more was printed than he realized,[6] especially in the newspapers. For instance, in February 1888, The New York *Times* published articles and editorials about trusts on every day but one.[7] If the *Times* was never again so persistent, neither did it become silent on the subject, and it certainly did not—as Clark asserted—ignore the hearings of the congressional committee investigating the trusts.[8] The most widely distributed newspaper in the Midwest, the Chicago *Tribune,* was at least as assiduously interested.[9] Moreover, there is evidence that other newspapers throughout the country were not much less attentive to the problem.[1]

Antitrust sentiment, in any case, cannot be measured merely

[5] Clark, *Federal Trust Policy* 27-37 (1931). Clark tried to bolster his case with other evidence, some of which, however, is erroneous and the rest capable of different interpretation. It is not true, for instance, that the political parties "wholly overlooked" the trust problem during the election campaign of 1888 (see discussion on p. 85 below); neither is it necessary to believe that the twelve states which passed antitrust laws before July 1890, were merely following a fashion—particularly since the statutes were quite different from each other.

[6] Sizable gaps in Clark's list of publications are indicated by Thorelli, *Federal Antitrust Policy* 137 (1954).

[7] The missing day was Feb. 8.

[8] The N.Y. *Times* reported on the hearings in its issues of Feb. 2, 11, 25, 29; March 9, 10, 11, 24, 26; April 7, 8, 14, 27, 28, 29; May 1, 2, 4, 5, 22; July 21, 28 of 1888. Compare Clark, *Federal Trust Policy* 33.

[9] During the first week of February, 1888, the Chicago *Tribune* published the following articles on trusts. Feb. 1: p. 3, col. 1, p. 4, col. 6, p. 9, col. 2; Feb. 2: p. 2, col. 3, p. 4, col. 1, p. 6, col. 5; Feb. 3: p. 1, col. 4, p. 1, col. 6, p. 3, col. 6, p. 6, col. 5, p. 8, col. 2, p. 8, col. 5; Feb. 4: p. 1, col. 4, p. 1, col. 5, p. 2, col. 6, p. 3, col. 6, p. 6, col. 1, p. 6, col. 6; Feb. 5: p. 10, col. 2, p. 14, col. 5, p. 17, col. 7; Feb. 6: p. 3, col. 4, p. 4, col. 1. The articles concerned the Standard Oil, Sugar, Whisky, Stove, Salt, Chicago Gas, Castor-Oil, Coal, and Starch trusts, and a New York antitrust bill.

[1] At least thirty-one newspapers outside New York published articles on trusts which were quoted by the journal *Public Opinion*. Thorelli, *Federal Antitrust Policy* 141, n. 138.

by counting the number of articles concerned exclusively with trusts that appeared exactly within the three years prior to the passage of the Sherman Act. The great political problems of a period are not so easily isolated. The true importance of the monopoly problem in public opinion is more nearly revealed by how much it pervaded discussion of the leading political questions of those years.

Between 1887 and 1890 the tariff question had priority in the newspapers, party platforms, and, as Senator Sherman himself said, in the work of the 51st Congress.[2] But the pre-eminence of the tariff question did not detract from the trust problem, and if the tariff constantly intruded in congressional debate on trusts, so did the trust problem regularly infiltrate discussion of tariffs. When Chicago meat packers petitioned Congress to repeal the tariff on salt, their congressman said that the strongest argument for their case was the Michigan salt monopoly.[3] When Representative Randall announced that the revenue bill he was introducing would, among other things, set a high duty on steel rails, those who saw in his proposal the hand of the Iron and Steel Association promptly labeled it "a bill for the perpetuation of trusts."[4] And in the Senate, debate on the Dependent Pension Bill—a scheme for disposing of surplus revenues—centered for a while on the accusation that Blair of New Hampshire, as an advocate of tariffs, was a defender of trusts, an accusation which he denied as one rejecting a heresy: "They are abhorrent to me."[5]

The trust problem was regarded as an integral part also of other leading political questions. Current discussions of how to improve Federal regulation of railroads were largely concerned with whether "pools" should be allowed, and it was repeatedly said that these would produce the same monopolistic combinations so objected to when they took the form of trusts. Labor unions, whose rights and limitations were a subject of angry debate, were on the one hand defended as necessary to enable workmen to deal with the trusts, and on the other hand condemned for being mo-

[2] Letter from Sen. Sherman to Gen. W. T. Sherman, Nov. 9, 1889, *The Sherman Letters* 379 (Thorndike ed., 1894).

[3] Chi. *Trib.* p. 1, col. 1 (Feb. 1, 1888).

[4] N.Y. *Times* p. 5, col. 1 (March 6, 1888).

[5] N.Y. *Times* p. 2, col. 6 (March 2, 1888).

nopolies as obnoxious as the trusts themselves. The low income of farmers, for which remedies were constantly being considered, was often said to be aggravated by various trusts, such as those that sold farmers bags and bought their linseed and cottonseed. The general problem of poverty, a great concern of the time, was regularly said to be accentuated by the trusts, which were accused of dividing the country into two classes, the very rich and the very poor.

The pervasive antitrust sentiment did not spring up overnight. Hatred of monopoly is one of the oldest American political habits and like most profound traditions, it consisted of an essentially permanent idea expressed differently at different times. "Monopoly," as the word was used in America, meant at first a special legal privilege granted by the state; later it came more often to mean exclusive control that a few persons achieved by their own efforts; but it always meant some sort of unjustified power, especially one that raised obstacles to equality of opportunity. The trust was popularly regarded as nothing but a new form of monopoly, and the whole force of the tradition was focused against it immediately.

The principle that government should create no monopolies was one of those deep political convictions that the colonists had brought with them from England. There the matter had been settled in 1624 by the Statute of Monopolies, which closely limited the King's power to grant exclusive privileges.[6] In America the same attitude was expressed when the colonial legislature of Massachusetts decreed that "there shall be no monopolies granted or allowed among us but of such new inventions as are profitable to the country, and that for a short time."[7] Soon after the Revolution several states included in their bills of rights rather more philosophic statements, similar to that adopted by Virginia: "No man, or set of men, are entitled to exclusive or separate emoluments or privileges from the community. . . ."[8] Jefferson thought that a prohibition to the same effect should appear in the Federal Bill of

[6] 21 James I, c. 3 (1623-24).

[7] c. 71 (1641); *Charters and General Laws of the Colony and Province of Massachusetts Bay* 170 (1814).

[8] Va. Bill of Rights §4 (1776); Mass. Const. Part I, Art. 6 (1780); Conn. Const. Art. 1, §1 (1818).

Rights,[9] and there are signs that his opinion was widely supported. Several of the states, having agreed to ratify the Constitution although they were not satisfied that it sufficiently guaranteed the people's rights, proposed amendments which they submitted with their acts of ratification. Among these were proposals offered by New York, "that the Congress do not grant monopolies," and by Massachusetts, New Hampshire, and Rhode Island, "that the Congress erect no company of merchants with exclusive advantages of commerce." [1] In the end, however, no specific prohibition of monopoly was included in the Federal Bill of Rights. Some afterwards maintained that since the power of creating monopolies had not been explicitly denied to Congress, it had been implicitly conceded,[2] others said that a legislature could not grant monopolies unless the Constitution expressly authorized it;[3] but no one argued that the prohibition was omitted because the public favored or was even indifferent to monopolies.

In spite of this hostility, the Federal Government after the Revolution did from time to time create private monopolies, but these did more to renew and deepen the public sentiment than to dilute it. The most numerous were patent monopolies granted to inventors, but the patent system was generally tolerated as a traditional exception to the traditional principle. Other monopolies, such as the two Banks of the United States,[4] were not toler-

[9] Letter from Jefferson to Madison, Dec. 20, 1787, in Jefferson, *Works*, V, 371 (Ford ed., 1904).

[1] Elliot, *Debates in the Several State Conventions*, I, 323, 326, 330, 337 (2d ed., 1854).

[2] Rep. Lawrence, in congressional debate on the first Bank of the United States, Feb. 4, 1791. *Debates and Proceedings in Congress of United States*, II, 1965 (Gales' comp., 1834).

[3] As Attorney General of the United States, Taney gave this opinion in 1833 concerning the monopoly granted the Camden and Amboy Railroad by the New Jersey legislature. Dodd, *American Business Corporations* 125 (1954).

[4] Their predecessor, The Bank of North America, incorporated in 1781 by the Continental Congress, was accepted because it would help finance the Revolution, and no great commotion was aroused by the recommendation of Congress that so long as the war lasted the states should neither incorporate nor endure any other banks. 20 *Journals of the Continental Congress* 547, 21 *ibid.* 1190 (Hunt ed., 1912). When the Bank, uncertain whether the congressional charter was valid, petitioned the states for reassurance, seven of them quickly passed acts confirming its legality and granting the requested

ated so quietly. The debates on the first Bank, both when it was created in 1791 and when it was discontinued twenty years later, were concerned mainly with the constitutional question whether Congress had authority to create corporations and especially banks. However, many objections besides the constitutional one were raised: that the plan for the Bank was ill-devised, that state banks would render better service, and not least, that the national bank would be a monopoly—since the plan committed the United States to establish no competing banks. In the Senate, an unsuccessful attempt was made to delete the monopoly clause; in the House, the Bank's opponents did not fail to seize on this objection. James Jackson of Georgia called the Bank "a monopoly, such an one as contravenes the spirit of the constitution—a monopoly of a very extraordinary nature—a monopoly of the public moneys for the benefit of the corporation to be created," while James Madison, its most active enemy, criticized it somewhat more guardedly as "a monopoly which affects the equal rights of every citizen." [5] The Bank's supporters did not deny the principle of this attack. Hamilton, in replying to the adverse opinion that Jefferson had submitted to Washington, did not maintain that monopoly was good but rather that the Bank's privilege did not constitute a monopoly. "Monopoly implies," he said, "a *legal impediment* to carrying on the trade by others than those to whom it was granted," [6] and since the Act to create a Bank of the United States did not prohibit the states from incorporating banks or citizens from operating unincorporated banks, it created no monopoly.

Opposition to monopoly, important but not critical in determining the affairs of the first Bank of the United States, became a chief weapon against the second Bank. President Jackson and his lieutenants, who led the movement, attacked the Bank on two scores: since its charter expressly guaranteed that the Federal

---

monopoly for the duration of the war. Davis, *Earlier History of American Corporations,* II, 38 (1917). But after 1784 the states withdrew the privilege: Massachusetts, New York and Maryland incorporated new banks, while Pennsylvania, the Bank's home state, was persuaded by attacks on the Bank's policies and privilege to repeal its charter and finally to grant a new and more restricted one (41-43).

[5] Clarke and Hall, *Bank of the United States* 33, 36, 37, 43 (1832).

[6] Clarke and Hall, *Bank of the United States* 101.

Government would create no other banks, it was a monopoly in the strict legal sense; since it was too big and rich, it was also a monopoly in the broader political sense. Thomas Hart Benton of Missouri, the Bank's chief opponent in the Senate, argued accordingly that it was objectionable not only "on account of the exclusive privileges, and anti-republican monopoly, which it gives to the stockholders," but also "because it tends to aggravate the inequality of fortunes" and is "an institution too great and powerful to be tolerated in a Government of free and equal laws." [7] Jackson, when he vetoed the bill renewing the Bank's charter, emphasized the "great evils to our country and institutions [that] might flow from such a concentration of power in the hands of a few men irresponsible to the people." [8] Amos Kendall, who as a member of Jackson's Kitchen Cabinet wrote the first draft of the veto message,[9] in his own public addresses also called the Bank a threat to democracy. All nations in the past, he said, had been controlled by "Nobility Systems," and now one was growing up in America: "Its head is the Bank of the United States; its right arm, a protecting Tariff and Manufacturing Monopolies; its left, growing State debts and State incorporations." [1] In the end this maneuver of repeatedly condemning the Bank as a "monster monopoly," a "moneyed power" that would establish an oligarchy and eventually a monarchy,[2] helped to defeat the Bank's supporters and led to its destruction.

There were other institutions, more numerous and permanent than the central banks, against which public opposition to monopoly was more regularly expressed. Chief among these was the corporation. The view that all corporations are monopolies was as old as the principle that all monopolies are evil, and like it, was founded on English experience. One of the most common forms of the early corporation in England was the guild—indeed there had been a time when "incorporated" was a synonym for "guildated" [3]—and the guild was a monopoly, since it could prevent

[7] 7 *Cong. Deb.* 50-54 (1831).

[8] 2 *Messages and Papers of the Presidents* 581 (Richardson ed., 1900).

[9] Schlesinger, *Age of Jackson* 89 (1945).

[1] Wash. *Globe,* Dec. 13, 1832, quoted in Schlesinger, *Age of Jackson* 97.

[2] Knox, *History of Banking in the United States* 69-70 (1903).

[3] Williston, "History of the Law of Business Corporations before 1860," 3 *Select Essays on Anglo-American Legal History* 195, 198 (1909).

everyone but its members from following its trade.[4] Another important group of corporations was composed of the great companies for foreign trade, most of which were monopolies, since their charters granted exclusive rights to commerce with certain parts of the world.[5] Since these prominent monopolies made up most of the private corporations, it was not hard to slip into thinking that all corporations were monopolies, and this belief became quite popular in the United States. This was not so much because American states continued the practice of English governments. They seldom gave corporations exclusive rights, and when they did it was to toll-bridge, turnpike, canal, and railroad companies. Though these grants did arouse some vigorous opposition, the fact that the recipients were "public service" corporations seems to have been regarded as a mitigating circumstance.[6]

In America every corporation, whether or not it had an express monopoly, was considered monopolistic simply because it was a corporation. This was partly because all corporations before the end of the eighteenth century, and most of them before the Civil War, were chartered by special legislation. Each was authorized by a separate act that prescribed its distinctive organization and defined the rights and duties peculiar to it. No group of men could form a corporation unless the state legislature passed a special act in their favor, and those who succeeded were regarded as privileged above their fellows. The mere existence of a corporation was therefore proof that it was a monopoly. So Theodore Sedgwick reasoned: "Corporations can only obtain existence . . . by a special grant from the Legislature. Charters of incorporation are therefore

[4] Davenant v. Hurdis, Moore 576 (K.B., 1599). See above, pp. 24-26.

[5] East India Co. v. Sandys, 10 Howell's St. Tr. 372, 90 Eng. Rep. 62 (1685) (The Great Case of Monopolies).

[6] The three earliest railroads in Massachusetts, incorporated in 1830, were given thirty year monopolies of their routes, Kirkland, "The 'Railroad Scheme' of Massachusetts," *J. Econ. Hist.*, V, 145, 164 (1945). Other instances of monopoly grants to such corporations are cited by Dodd, *American Business Corporations* 161, 127 n. 20, 162 (1954) and by Cadman, *The Corporation in New Jersey* 224-27 (1949). Instances of opposition to them are given by Davis, *Earlier History of American Corporations,* I, 193, 306, *et seq.,* and by Cadman, 74. The exception in favor of public service corporations was endorsed even by such antagonists of corporations as Taney, consult Swisher, *Roger B. Taney* 366-67 (1935), and Gov. Morton of Massachusetts, consult Dodd, 311-12.

grants of privilege, to be exclusively enjoyed by the corporators. . . . Every grant of exclusive privilege, strictly speaking, creates a monopoly. . . ."[7]

Also, every corporation had additional privileges, the real advantages that made men want to incorporate, such as long life, limited liability, and in some early cases, public subsidies. All of these aggravated the complaint that corporations were privileged, monopolistic bodies. The amplitude of privilege sometimes easily justified the charge. For instance, New Jersey's first business corporation, the Society for Establishing Useful Manufactures, was exempted from paying taxes on much of its property, was given authority to conduct lotteries and exercise the power of eminent domain, and enjoyed the additional subsidy that its workmen were exempt from all taxes and military service.[8] It was no wonder then that critics said it was a part of "a new system of monopolies," or that a writer who signed himself "Anti-Monopolist," in attacking it, bewailed "the present prevailing propensity for corporations and exclusive privileges, a system of politics well calculated to aggrandize and increase the influence of the few at the expense of the many."[9]

Even corporations that had no express monopolies and no extensive privileges were attacked in the same terms. It became an axiom that corporations were privileged bodies, monopolies incompatible with liberty, and this accusation was repeated through the years. It was one of the objections urged in 1785 against a bill to incorporate a society of tradesmen and mechanics in New York: "all incorporations imply a privilege given to one order of citizens which others do not enjoy, and are so far destructive of that principle of equal liberty which should subsist in every community."[1] It was one of the grounds on which Connecticut in 1787 refused to incorporate a medical society, which was denounced as "a combination of doctors . . . directly against liberty . . . a monopoly."[2] It was one of the arguments that Henry Clay in 1811 offered against the Bank of the United States, when he said that the Bank's

[7] [Sedgwick] *What Is a Monopoly?* 12 (1835).
[8] Davis, *American Corporations,* I, 384-85.
[9] Davis, *American Corporations,* I, 430, 431.
[1] Davis, *American Corporations,* II, 303.
[2] Davis, *American Corporations,* II, 304.

express monopoly was not as offensive as its corporate status, and that to incorporate competing banks would only compound the mischief, for "all corporations enjoy exclusive privileges. . . . And if you create fifty corporations instead of one, you have only fifty privileged bodies instead of one." [3] Finally, in the 1830's, it became the watchword of the great campaign that the Jacksonian Democrats led against all private corporations. One of their journalists wrote that "All Bank charters, all laws conferring special privileges, with all acts of incorporations [sic], for purposes of private gain, are monopolies, inasmuch as they are calculated to enhance the power of wealth, produce inequalities among the people, and to subvert liberty." [4] Another writer carried the argument one step further: "To have the land scattered over with incorporated companies, is to have a class of privileged, if not titled, nobility." [5] This doctrine, embellished with various expressions of fear and horror, was proclaimed on all sides.[6]

The natural solution, if all corporations were evil, would have been to destroy them all. There is a tone of martyred forbearance in the statements of those Jacksonians and Locofocos, who much as they would have liked to revoke the rights of all existing corporations, said that to do so would "stain the sacred faith of a whole people." [7] A more reasonable alternative was to extend the evil no further, and some therefore said that the legislature "ought cautiously to refrain from increasing the irresponsible power of any existing corporations, or of chartering new ones." [8] Others maintained that no new corporations likely to compete with individual enterprises should be created, and that in any case they ought not to enjoy the special advantage of limited liability.[9] The policy finally accepted was to reduce the privilege of incorporation, not by taking it from the few, but by opening it to the many: general incorporation

[3] Clarke and Hall, *Bank of the United States* 355.

[4] Cadman, *Corporation in New Jersey* 75.

[5] Cadman, *Corporation in New Jersey* 77.

[6] Cadman, *Corporation in New Jersey* 72 ff. Dodd, *American Business Corporations* 394 f., 414 f. Handlin, *Commonwealth Massachusetts* 229-35 (1947).

[7] Cadman, *Corporation in New Jersey* 76.

[8] Cadman, *Corporation in New Jersey* 76.

[9] Cadman, *Corporation in New Jersey* 78 ff. Dodd, *American Business Corporations,* chaps. 5 and 6, and esp. p. 385.

laws authorized state officials to issue charters to all qualified applicants. A few such laws had been passed before 1837 by legislatures that hoped to stimulate various branches of industry; they were recommended also as devices to save legislatures the time otherwise spent in considering special acts; but they became normal only after the great agitation against the monopolistic character of corporations created by special acts.[1] Connecticut, New Jersey, Pennsylvania, and Massachusetts passed general incorporation laws between 1837 and 1851, and during this period several of the younger states—California, Indiana, and Minnesota—adopted constitutions prohibiting legislatures from creating private corporations in any other way.[2] For a time special incorporation persisted: in New Jersey and in Maine, for instance, the number of incorporations under general law did not overtake those under special acts until 1875.[3] By the time of the Civil War incorporation under general laws had become so easy and frequent that the old complaint against "monopolistic corporations" could no longer be sustained.

Yet the distrust of corporations did not evaporate with the old complaint. After the middle of the nineteenth century new grounds were found for believing that corporations were monopolistic, and criticisms that had been subordinate now became prominent. They achieved their new importance partly because the fundamental American attitude toward government was changing at this time. The fear of oligarchy, which had been carried over from the colonial period and so carefully expressed in the Constitution, was subsiding. The fear of plutocracy, always present in some degree, grew sharper as Americans recognized the rapid growth of national wealth during and after the Civil War. Reasoning about monopolies accommodated itself to the new disposition: it was less often argued that monopolists would abolish representative government and more often they would use their wealth to make it serve their own interests. A great deal began to be said about the opulence of corporations. A Justice of the Supreme Court spoke in 1853 of "the vast amount of property, power, and exclusive benefits, prejudicial

[1] Dodd, *American Business Corporations* 316, 417 n. 28. Cadman, *Corporation in New Jersey* 21-27.

[2] Dodd, *American Business Corporations* 317, 449. Evans, *Business Incorporations in the United States,* II, 11 (1948).

[3] Cadman, *Corporation in New Jersey* 207 f. Evans, *Business Incorporations in the United States,* II, 12.

to other classes of society, that are vested in and held by these numerous bodies of associated wealth." [4] After the Civil War this idea became increasingly common, and frequent warnings were heard of "the rapid concentration of the whole political, commercial, and financial interests of the country in corporations and other monopolies." [5]

The chief attacks on monopolies after the Civil War became more specific. They were no longer directed at incorporation itself or corporations in the mass, but more particularly against certain practices—above all, economic abuses—that were attributed to some corporations. No one could by this time reasonably want or hope to solve the problem by abolishing corporations or by making it easier to establish more of them. The idea therefore began to spread that the power and injurious behavior of monopolistic corporations should be controlled by government regulation.

Agitation for antimonopoly laws was first led by the Grangers or Patrons of Husbandry. Founded two years after the Civil War and at first intended to serve the social and educational needs of farmers, it soon became involved in economic and political activities. By 1871, its founder reported that " 'Cooperation' and 'Down with monopolies' were proving popular watchwords"—indeed by 1875, when the Grange reached its peak, it had brought within its ranks at least one of every ten American farmers.[6] "Cooperation" meant organization of farmers' cooperatives, while "Down with monopolies" meant principally regulation of railroads. Granger opposition to railroads and monopolies was expressed in a host of manifestoes, declarations, petitions, and statements, of which the resolutions adopted by an Illinois Farmers' Convention in 1873 were fairly typical. The first two stated "that all chartered monopolies, not regulated and controlled by law, have proved detrimental to the public prosperity, corrupting in their management, and dangerous to republican institutions," and "that the railways of the world, except in those countries where they have been held under the strict regulation and supervision of the government, have proved themselves arbitrary, extortionate and as opposed to free institutions and free

[4] Catron, J., in Ohio Life Insurance Co. v. Debolt, 16 How. (U.S.) 416, 422 (1853).

[5] Cloud, *Monopolies and the People* 259 (1873).

[6] Buck, *The Granger Movement* 52-53, 58 (1913).

commerce between states as were the feudal barons of the middle ages."[7] The traditional theme, that monopolies are dangerous to liberty, was there as always, but with it a contemporary variation: the only cure is regulation by law. The resolutions went on to propose particular laws that would fix "reasonable maximum rates" and impose various other restrictions and duties on railroads. In a number of Midwestern and Western states, especially Illinois, Iowa, Minnesota, and Wisconsin, Grangers founded or supported independent parties—usually armed with the name "Anti-Monopoly"—that advocated railroad legislation of this sort. For a few years before 1875 they were surprisingly successful in having such laws enacted by the states,[8] but various difficulties prevented the laws from having any great effect, and indeed the railroad problem remained a leading aspect of the monopoly question until long after the Sherman Act was passed. Although the Grange had lost much of its power by 1880, it had served to stimulate a revival of antimonopoly sentiments which had been obscured by the more dramatic events of the Civil War.

Reformers with rather broader interests succeeded the Grange as leading antimonopolists during the early 1880's, and in their hands "monopoly" was a brush that could tar many rich or exclusive institutions. One crusader condemned as monopolistic not only railroads, banks, and public utility companies, but also speculative dealing in grains, restrictive licensing of businesses and professions, laws limiting the ballot to males, and "those nurseries of caste"—West Point and Annapolis.[9] John Jameson, a Chicago judge, speaking before the Illinois Bar Association in 1882, described as one of America's gravest problems the accumulation of capital into the "great moneyed institutions"—private corporations—that are "commonly stigmatized as monopolies." He gave three principal examples: the railroad corporation, typical form of the evil; the giant wheat farms of the northwest, which he described as novel, though his complaint echoed the cry of "land monopoly" that had been raised often before against speculators and absentee owners; and the "monster business establishments, owned by private indi-

[7] Periam, *The Groundswell* 286 (1874).

[8] Buck, *The Granger Movement*, c. 3.

[9] Bland, *The Reign of Monopoly* (1881).

viduals, of which the Standard Oil Company is the best known type."[1] General Ben Butler, presidential candidate of the Greenback and Anti-Monopoly parties in 1884, declared his hostility to monopolists in commerce, industries, and lands, and singled out the railroads that charged excessive rates, the sewing-machine monopoly, which derived its power from a patent, and the Standard Oil Company.[2]

Many other companies and institutions were attacked as monopolies during the years after 1880, but more and more attention was devoted to combinations of industrial firms, all of which, however organized, came by the end of the decade to be called trusts. Public prominence was achieved first by the Standard Oil Company, which by 1880 controlled much of the country's petroleum refining. Thereafter it became a favorite butt of the antimonopolists, none of whom castigated it more loudly than Henry Demarest Lloyd. His article, "The Story of a Great Monopoly," was so well received that the *Atlantic Monthly* had to reprint its issue for March 1881, six times.[3] In 1882, Standard Oil adopted the trust device, and the effectiveness of this method for making combinations permanently cohesive and easily manageable recommended it to others. The next two groups to use it were also oil businesses, whether by an association of ideas or because, as some thought, they were actively encouraged by Standard Oil.[4] The Cotton Oil Trust was organized in 1884 and the Linseed Oil Trust in the following year. The former is said to have angered Southern farmers and to have strengthened the demand for a Federal antitrust law; at the very least it provoked the Attorney General of Louisiana to proceed against it in the state courts.[5]

Trust-building did not begin in earnest until 1887, but then it took hold quickly. That year saw the formation of the Sugar and

[1] Jameson, *The Grounds and Limits of Rightful Interference by Law with the Accumulation and Use of Capital* 1-7 (1882).

[2] Butler, Speech of Aug. 30, 1884, appended to his pamphlet, *Address to His Constituents,* Aug. 12, 1884.

[3] Clark, *Federal Trust Policy* 17 (1931).

[4] Cook, *Trusts* 3 (1888).

[5] Clark, *Federal Trust Policy* 4 n. 5. The proceedings were begun in April 1887 and judgment given later in the year. Louisiana v. American Cotton-Oil Trust, 1 *Ry. & Corp. L.J.* 509 (1887).

Whisky Trusts, which until the end of the century contended for unpopularity only with Standard Oil. Others, affecting lesser industries or smaller markets, added to the list, which by the end of the year included the Envelope, Salt, Cordage, Oil-Cloth, Paving-Pitch, School-Slate, Chicago Gas, St. Louis Gas, and New York Meat trusts. When, in November, the president of the Paper-Bag Trust explained that trust-making was "the tendency of the times," his statement was not treated as startling news.[6] If we are to credit the judgment of most contemporary observers, the public seems to have had no difficulty in identifying the trusts as the latest version of monopoly and in transferring to them the antipathy which by long usage it had cultivated against all monopolies.

The great fervor against trusts in 1888, which bursts so unexpectedly on an historian like Clark, was for the people living at the time nothing so sudden or strange. It was simply a familiar feeling raised to a high pitch, intense because the speed with which new trusts were being hatched made it seem that they would overrun everything unless some remedy were found soon. The general disposition of the public was not in doubt. There were numerous objections to the trusts—complaints of a traditional sort as well as newer ones suited to the character of these particular monopolies. Trusts, it was said, threatened liberty, because they corrupted civil servants and bribed legislators; they enjoyed privileges such as protection by tariffs; they drove out competitors by lowering prices, victimized consumers by raising prices, defrauded investors by watering stocks, put laborers out of work by closing down plants, and somehow or other abused everyone. The kind of remedy that the public desired was also clear enough: it wanted a law to destroy the power of the trusts. The alternative suggestion that government should take over the trusts and operate them as public property had scant support. But the desire was not, and, in the nature of public opinion, could not be expressed in much greater detail. Any law might be acceptable if it really suppressed the worst abuses of the trusts, especially of those like the Standard Oil, Sugar, and Whisky Trusts, that were most noticeable and most important in the everyday life of many people. The public's mandate was clear, but so broad that Congress had to look elsewhere for advice on how to implement it.

[6] N.Y. *Times* p. 4, col. 5 (Nov. 7, 1887).

Expert Opinion on the Trust Problem

Expert judgment on how to solve the trust problem would naturally have been expected from the two professions most closely concerned with it, the economists and the lawyers.

OPINION OF ECONOMISTS

The general opinion of American economists during the years after 1885 was easier for legislators and the public to detect because the American Economic Association, which had just been formed, could be regarded as its official spokesman. A first attempt to organize a professional society had been made shortly after 1880 by Edmund James and Simon Nelson Patten, who had come to teach in the Wharton School of Finance after completing their studies in Germany. Following German models they had observed as students, they proposed a Society for the Study of National Economy. Since they believed that competition had very serious shortcomings as the basis of economic life,[7] they suggested that the aim of the Society should be

> To combat the widespread view that our economic problems will solve themselves, and that our laws and institutions which at present favor individual instead of collective action can promote the best utilization of our material resources and secure to each individual the highest development of all his faculties.[8]

In keeping with this aim, they suggested the Society should favor positive government intervention in economic life, particularly by means of Federal aid to education, forest conservation, mineral surveys, and agricultural experiment stations.[9] For one reason or another the proposal did not mature, and in 1885 Richard Ely made a fresh start. He circulated a statement setting forth the principles on which an American Economic Association should be based and outlining a platform that curiously blended the optimism, zeal, piety, and objectivity typical of younger economists of the time. It stated that economics was an immature science which

[7] E.g., Patten, *The Premises of Political Economy* (1885).

[8] Ely, *Ground Under Our Feet* 132, 296 (1938). See Coats, "First Two Decades of the A.E.A.," *Am. Econ. Rev.*, L, 555 (1960).

[9] *Ibid.*, 296-99.

could be improved greatly by statistical and historical research, intimated that the conflict between labor and capital could be resolved by the "united efforts of Church, state and science," and recommended that the Association avoid taking partisan positions on any matter of public policy and especially on the tariff question. But the essence of the program, virtually the same as that suggested by James and Patten, was stated in its first principle:

> We regard the state as an educational and ethical agency whose positive aid is an indispensable condition of human progress. While we recognize the necessity of individual initiative in industrial life, we hold that the doctrine of *laissez-faire* is unsafe in politics and unsound in morals; and that it suggests an inadequate explanation of the relations between the state and the citizens.[1]

This thesis was the main subject of discussion at the founding convention. Ely defended it. Others urged that it be modified; John Bates Clark, for instance, thought that "the point upon which individuals will be unable to unite is, especially, the strong condemnation of the *laissez-faire* doctrine."[2] Following a long debate the platform was finally revised, and the new version omitted the explicit denunciation, though it retained the fairly safe assertion that the state is indispensable to human progress.[3] This refusal to denounce *laissez faire* did not mean that the charter members of the Economic Association endorsed it. Most of them were evidently as skeptical as Ely, but they did not want to make a formal declaration that might suggest they favored socialism. In fact they preferred a middle, "balanced" position between liberalism and interventionism, between what they called the "English" and "German" views, in short, a distinctively "American" economic policy.[4] They concluded that as the "English" school believed competition was necessarily beneficial while the "German" school considered it inherently harmful, they themselves ought to regard it as a mixed bless-

[1] Ely, "Report on the Organization of the American Economic Association," *Pub. Am. Econ. Ass'n,* Vol. I, No. 1, 6-7 (1886).

[2] *Ibid.*, 29.

[3] *Ibid.*, 20, 35 and *passim.*

[4] *Ibid.*, 21, 23. Consult also, Adams, *Relation of the State to Industrial Action, Pub. Am. Econ. Ass'n,* I, No. 6, 29 (1887); Walker, *Recent Progress of Political Economy in the United States, Pub. Am. Econ. Ass'n,* IV, 245 (1889).

ing. Edwin Seligman said as much at the founding convention: "Competition is not in itself bad. It is a neutral force which has already produced immense benefits, but which may, under certain conditions, bring in its train sharply defined evils." [5] His colleagues agreed; their eagerness to construct a native economic policy increased their interest in what was anyway an important economic phenomenon, and many turned their energies to discovering when competition was useful and when it was inferior to combination or monopoly.

In order to judge the desirability of combination, they needed first to explain it. But this did not strike them as a particularly difficult task, for although they regarded the great wave of industrial combination as a new phenomenon, they were not surprised by it. Like many informed men of their time, they were convinced that Darwin's laws governed the evolution of human society, the social organism, no less rigorously than evolution of biological organisms.[6] Any social change in which they could detect "growth" or "centralization" struck them as "natural"; and as the combination—trust, pool, or syndicate—was an organization that many producers, who formerly had gone their own separate ways, formed in order to act jointly, these economists regarded it as an evolutionary advance. Combination was inevitable, an instance of the general law which ordained, as one writer put it, that "corporate action is ready to overshadow personal action." [7] The economists moreover could explain the inevitability of combination as the particular effect of technical progress. According to Davis Ames Wells, one of the most prominent economists of the older generation, the successful adoption of steam-driven machinery had made manufacturing so efficient that "industrial overproduction" resulted; a strenuous effort to sell unwanted goods had led to "excessive competition"; manu-

[5] Ely, *Ground Under Our Feet* 27.

[6] Wiener, *Evolution and the Founders of Pragmatism* (1949); Hofstadter, *Social Darwinism in American Thought* (1944). Ely later wrote: "The most fundamental things in our mind were the ideas of evolution and of relativity. I think that those two ideas were unanimously held by those who founded the American Economic Association." "The Founding and Early History of the American Economic Association," *Am. Econ. Rev.,* XXVI, Supp. 141, 144 (1936).

[7] Bascom, "Social Harmony," *Independent,* XL, 419, 420 (1888).

facturing firms were losing money, and could only correct the difficulty if they combined to reduce their output.[8] John Bates Clark, the best of the younger economists and not the most Darwinian of them, held much the same view:

> Combinations have their roots in the nature of social industry and are normal in their origin, their development, and their practical working. They are neither to be deprecated by scientists nor suppressed by legislators. They are the result of an evolution, and are the happy outcome of a competition so abnormal that the continuance of it would have meant widespread ruin. A successful attempt to suppress them by law would involve the reversion of industrial systems to a cast-off type, the renewal of abuses from which society has escaped by a step in development.[9]

Economists as different in spirit as Patten and Sumner agreed that improved transportation had been important in bringing about combinations.[1] Ely thought that "owing to discoveries and inventions, especially the application of steam to industry and transportation, it became necessary to prosecute enterprises of great magnitude."[2] And since the economists assumed that combination was the only way to correct excessive competition and the chaotic economic conditions that they thought it produced, as well as the most practicable way to get the positive advantages of large-scale production, they concluded that it was not only inevitable but in many instances beneficial.[3]

Nor did economists attribute such advantages only to combinations. They were adopting a theory which led them to conclude that even outright monopolies, or at least some of them, were also inevitable and potentially beneficial. This theory was by no means new, having been outlined by several great English economists

[8] Wells, *Recent Economic Changes*, c. 1-3, p. 74 (1889).

[9] Clark, "The Limits of Competition," reprinted in Clark and Giddings, *The Modern Distributive Process* 11 (1888).

[1] Patten, *The Principles of Rational Taxation* 5-7 (1890); Sumner, "Trusts and Trade Unions," *Independent*, XL, 482, 483 (1888).

[2] Ely, "The Nature and Significance of Corporations," *Harper's Magazine*, LXXV, 71, 75 (1887).

[3] This view had become more or less standard in the business community as well. See for an example the testimony of Francis Thurber, an important commodity broker, before the New York State Senate Committee on Trusts, reported in 5 *Ry. & Corp. L.J.* 20 (1889).

earlier in the century,[4] but American economists of this generation were especially struck by it on reading the monograph, *Relation of the State to Industrial Action,* which their colleague, Henry Carter Adams, published in 1887.[5] Adams distinguished three classes of industries according to the size that firms within them would naturally attain. In "industries of constant returns," every unit of capital and labor used in production yields equal quantities of output; a new firm in such an industry, say a new retail grocery, can sell its goods as cheaply as any older and larger store; and therefore competition can never fail to keep prices in such an industry from being exorbitant. In the second class, "industries of diminishing returns," small firms are more efficient than large ones because each additional unit of capital and labor produces a smaller quantity of goods; Adams cited agriculture as the typical industry of this sort, and concluded that individual interest will always maintain a large number of small producers in such industries. But in the third class, "industries of increasing returns," the opposite is true: since each successive unit of input produces more than the last, the largest firm is the most efficient and can eventually drive out all competitors. Industries of increasing returns, Adams concluded, must inevitably be controlled by monopolies.

Having decided that some combinations and all natural monopolies were inevitable, the economists did not hesitate to conclude that any attempt to prohibit them by law reflected the outworn belief "in the universal existence and beneficence of free competition."[6] Adams maintained that the only question of policy was whether an industry of increasing returns should become an "irresponsible, extra-legal monopoly, or a monopoly established by law and managed in the interest of the public." The public interest could be protected only by government intervention, but he was not sure which particular method would be most effective, whether the work should be done "through carefully guarded franchises, through official commissions, through competition of the state with

[4] *E.g.,* Senior, *Outline of the Science of Political Economy* 81 *et seq.* (reprint, 1938) (1834); Mill, *Principles of Political Economy,* Bk. III, c. 2, §2, 444 (Ashley's ed., 1909) (1848).

[5] Adams, *Relation of the State to Industrial Action, Pub. Am. Econ. Ass'n,* Vol. I, No. 6, 55-60 (1887).

[6] Seligman, "Railway Tariffs and the Interstate Commerce Law," *Pol. Sci. Q,* II, 374 (1887).

private industries, or through direct government management."[7] Ely, who with many of his prominent colleagues immediately adopted Adams' theory of natural monopolies,[8] was of two minds, because though in the abstract he preferred public ownership, especially municipal ownership of public utilities, he conceded that a system of control by limited charters and taxation might be more readily established.[9] Others, like Hadley, thought it would be best to subject all monopolies to some scheme of regulation like that imposed by state railroad laws, "under which the necessity for combination was at least tacitly admitted, but where the combinations were held to a larger degree of publicity and responsibility than before";[1] they did not, however, specify the rules of such a scheme.

Although they differed as to the exact action government should take, nearly all the economists were convinced that any attempt to prohibit combinations would be either unnecessary or futile. Since many of the trusts were "natural," the law could not destroy them. "If," as Adams summarized this view, "it is for the interest of men to combine no law can make them compete."[2] Those trusts, on the other hand, that were "artificial" could be destroyed by withdrawing the tariffs and other legal privileges that protected them or by regulating the natural monopolies that created them. Ely, when discussing the latter method, had in mind, for instance, the rebates and extraordinarily low rates that railroads were supposed to have granted the Standard Oil Company.[3] Moreover, some economists argued, any combination that was not justified by the underlying conditions of its industry would decay of its own accord or be controlled by what came to be called "the active influence of the poten-

[7] Adams, *Relation of the State to Industrial Action* 53, 64.

[8] Ely, "Nature and Significance of Corporations," *Harper's Magazine*, LXXV, 259, 261 (1887); Hadley, "Private Monopolies and Public Rights," *Q. J. Econ.*, I, 40 (1887); James, *Relation of the Modern Municipality to the Gas Supply*, *Pub. Am. Econ. Ass'n*, I, 29 *et seq.* (1886).

[9] Ely, *Problems of Today* 129-30, 189-94 (1890).

[1] Hadley, "Private Monopolies and Public Rights," *Q. J. Econ.* I, 44; and see his speech reported in N.Y. *Times* p. 1, col. 2 (Feb. 6, 1888). Cf. Seligman, "Railway Tariffs," *Pol. Sci. Q.*, II, 374 (1887).

[2] Adams, *Relation of the State to Industrial Action* 64.

[3] Ely, *Problems of Today*, c. 3, esp. 201.

tial competitor."[4] Even when they were most vehement in denying English *laissez faire* or the "orthodox" theories of the older American school, the economists granted that competition was inevitable and beneficial in some industries. But they insisted that in other industries combination was equally inevitable and beneficial. Younger and older economists alike agreed with Wells's judgment that "Society has practically abandoned—and from the very necessity of the case has got to abandon, unless it proposes to war against progress and civilization—the prohibition of industrial concentrations and combinations." Wells went on to say:

> The problem, therefore, which society under this condition of affairs has presented to it for solution is a difficult one, and twofold in its nature. To the producer the question of importance is, How can competition be restricted to an extent sufficient to prevent its injurious excesses? To the consumer, How can combination be restricted so as to secure its advantages and at the same time curb its abuses?[5]

He offered no solution to the problem, nor indeed did the economists as a group. They insisted that the government must somehow allow both competition and combination to play their proper parts in economic life, that it must regulate both, that it could not reasonably prohibit either. Beyond this, they offered no unified or precise suggestion about the law Congress should pass.

OPINION OF LAWYERS

The legal profession was more likely to suggest means that Congress might use in solving the trust problem, since most lawyers believed that laws could prohibit monopolies. Indeed, they thought that the common law already did so, although their conviction rested on a somewhat tenuous basis. There was no question that the common law had at various times condemned monopolies—or, more often, behavior that was supposed to be monopolistic. There were many precedents to this effect in the bodies of law concerning chartered monopolies, forestalling and engrossing, contracts in restraint

[4] Gunton, "Economic and Social Aspects of Trusts," *Pol. Sci. Q.*, III, 385, 403 (1888); Clark, "The 'Trust'," *New Englander*, LII, 223 (1890).

[5] Wells, *Recent Economic Changes* 74-5 (1889).

of trade, and combinations in restraint of trade. Nevertheless, it was doubtful whether the common law was powerful enough in 1888 to destroy the monopolies of that time. Yet many lawyers felt sure that it embodied a spirit unalterably opposed to monopoly and that this spirit—the "public policy" of the law—would somehow prevail against any trust it encountered. The only problem they admitted was how to enforce and strengthen the common law.

Of the four branches of common law particularly concerned with monopoly, two had hardly any direct bearing on the trust problem. The common law concerning chartered monopolies, which had been used in England during the seventeenth century to destroy or weaken monopolies created by the Crown, had little force as precedent in nineteenth-century American courts. Moreover, it had no relevance to the trusts. The editor of one contemporary law journal wrote that "the word, 'monopoly,' in its only legal sense means an exclusive right to deal in and sell certain articles, . . . guaranteed . . . by positive law." [6] Though it was an exaggeration to insist that "monopoly" still had an unequivocal legal sense,[7] it was undoubtedly true that trusts could not be condemned under this branch of the common law since their monopolistic power had not been conferred on them by government.

The body of common law that prohibited engrossing had no more direct bearing on the modern monopoly problem. It had grown out of English cases and statutes against practices whereby merchants evaded the regulations of medieval markets. Yet although in England, under the influence of free-trade ideas, this body of law had been repealed, in the United States it persisted. The ancient definitions of the crimes were forgotten, but "engrossing" came to mean cornering the supply of a commodity, "monopolizing" came to serve as a synonym for it, and in a few scattered cases American courts judged it illegal.[8] There was accordingly some point in declaring, as one lawyer did in 1889, that the trusts "literally *engross,* to borrow a word from the common law, the market in respect of the particular commodity," [9] though using the common-law word did not prove that trusts were prohibited by

[6] 27 *Cen. L.J.* 205 (1888).

[7] See below, p. 81.

[8] Adler, "Monopolizing at Common Law," 31 *Harv. L. Rev.* 246 (1917).

[9] "The Theory of a Trust," 23 *Am. L. Rev.* 103 (1889).

American common law as it stood in 1888. There was much sounder historical evidence for maintaining, as did Theodore Dwight, Dean of the Columbia Law School, that the common law against engrossing was practically extinct; but he weakened his case by adding the disingenuous argument that the trusts could not be accused of engrossing, because a necessary part of that crime was the intent to raise prices, and the trusts had no purpose except the laudable one "to regulate prices and keep them steady." [1] Moreover, Dwight emphasized, even supposing that the law against engrossing retained any vigor, it could hardly be used against trusts in general. Engrossing was traditionally a crime only if it affected food, or later, "necessaries of life," and although the definition of "necessity" had been broadened by American courts, it did not include many commodities in which trusts might deal.[2]

Although the common law against contracts in restraint of trade was distinctly more alive and more pertinent to the activities of trusts, it too was incapable of destroying them. Although such contracts were at first altogether condemned by common law, in time more and more of them were permitted, until, after the early eighteenth century, lawyers assumed they were valid if the restraint were "partial"—if the person undertaking the obligation not to engage in a certain business were excluded only from a small area and only for a short time.[3] Some American lawyers during the 1880's thought this rule—that all "general" restraints were void—still governed the decisions of American courts.[4] Others were beginning to believe that the true test was whether the restraint was "reasonable," and that the courts would consider unreasonable any restraint broader than the party imposing it needed or than the interest of the public could tolerate.[5] There are good grounds for believ-

[1] Dwight, "The Legality of 'Trusts'," *Pol. Sci. Q.*, III, 592, 594, 609-10 (1888).

[2] A catalogue of commodities that American courts classified as necessities was given by Boisot, "The Legality of Trust Combinations," 39 (N.S. 30) *Am. L. Reg.* 751, 762 (1891). See also Allen, "Criminal Conspiracies in Restraint of Trade at Common Law," 23 *Harv. L. Rev.* 531, 543, 547 (1910).

[3] See pp. 42-43 above.

[4] Kerr, "Contracts in Restraint of Trade," 22 *Am. L. Rev.* 873 (1888).

[5] McQuillan, "Validity of Contracts in Restraint of Trade," 33 (N.S. 24) *Am. L. Reg.* 217, 218 (1885). Eaton, "On Contracts in Restraint of Trade," 4 *Harv. L. Rev.* 128 (1890).

ing, as Dwight evidently did,[6] that the test of reasonableness was rather more lenient than the older one and that by 1888 even the older one might permit almost any restraint. Dwight cited as chief evidence the case of *Diamond Match Co. v. Roeber,* which decided that a contract to restrain Roeber from engaging in the match business anywhere in the United States, except Nevada and Montana, was still "partial" and therefore valid.[7] The courts' willingness to uphold rather broad restraints was only one reason for doubting that this body of common law could damage the trusts. A more important reason was that such contracts could be brought before the courts only by parties to them. If trusts were to be attacked by this means either they themselves or those who did business with them would have to initiate the action, and there were few instances of this kind. No outsider could attack such a contract, no public official could bring a suit to have it declared void, and a court could at most invalidate the contested agreement. There was little hope of destroying trusts in this way.

Nor were the trusts likely to be destroyed by the common law on combinations in restraint of trade. This body of law prohibited some, but only some, of the agreements by which a number of producers combined to reduce competition, either by setting uniform prices, fixing production quotas, dividing the market into exclusive dealing areas, or pooling their profits. The principle by which American courts distinguished between legal and illegal combinations was rather obscure, though they seemed to consider void any agreement that was "part of a conspiracy to create a monopoly."[8] There was enough doubt so that a lawyer well-disposed toward the trusts could argue that the courts were beginning to be more lenient toward industrial combinations,[9] while one of the leading opponents of the trusts could maintain that even the decisions which appeared

[6] Dwight, "The Legality of 'Trusts'," *Pol. Sci. Q.,* III, 610-11; and see pp. 43-45 above.

[7] 106 N.Y. 473 (1887). Dwight, 607.

[8] Marsh v. Russell, 66 N.Y. 288, 291 (1876). This doctrine seems to have been followed equally in cases where the combination was held valid and in those where it was not: Central Shade Roller Co. v. Cushman, 143 Mass. 353 (1887); Skrainka v. Scharringhausen, 8 Mo. App. 522 (1880); Craft v. McConoughy, 79 Ill. 346 (1875). Consult Allen, "Criminal Conspiracies," 23 *Harv. L. Rev.* 531.

[9] Dwight, "The Legality of 'Trusts'," *Pol. Sci. Q.,* III, 608-9. As evidence that the courts were becoming lenient he cited two English cases, Wickens v.

lenient really sustained the severity of the principle.[1] However, the main defect of this branch of the law, considered as an antitrust device, was that the courts could decide cases involving combinations only when brought by persons who belonged to, or did business with, a combination. No public official could start proceedings to dissolve a combination or to punish its members.[2]

Although none of these branches of the common law was sufficiently powerful to be used in an active campaign to destroy the trusts, all of them together convinced lawyers that the law opposed monopolies. It had once prohibited chartered monopolies, it still prohibited "engrossing" or "monopolizing," "general" or "total" restraints of trade, and combinations "tending toward monopoly." On the basis of such precedents judges had constructed the theory that the "public policy" embodied in the common law opposed monopoly.[3] This doctrine had become firmly established among lawyers,[4] and it was not denied even by those who disapproved of it. The very lawyers who insisted that the trust was not an illegal form of organization usually argued that nothing about the nature of the trust made it necessarily monopolistic, and in doing so they conceded that any trust which was a monopoly would probably be illegal.[5]

Evans, 3 Y. & J. 318 (1829) and Collins v. Locke, 4 L.R.A.C. 674 (1879). The American cases would not have supported this argument so clearly.

[1] Cook, *Trusts* 27 (1888). Cook was the author of a frequently quoted treatise on the Law of Stock and Stockholders, and was on a committee of well-known lawyers who drafted an antitrust bill for the N.Y. state legislature. 3 *Ry. & Corp. L.J.* 121 (1888).

[2] Allen, "Criminal Conspiracies," 23 *Harv. L. Rev.* 531.

[3] A few of the opinions in which judges held that public policy favored competition are: Central Ohio Salt Co. v. Guthrie, 35 Ohio St. 666 (1880); India Bagging Ass'n v. Kock & Co. 14 La. An. 164 (1859); Stanton v. Allen, 5 Denio (N.Y.) 434 (1848). Consult also, Greenhood, *The Doctrine of Public Policy,* 674-75, 685-89 (1886). An example of the tendency to identify a "general restraint of trade" with "monopoly" appears in Skrainka v. Scharringhausen, 8 Mo. App. 522 (1880).

[4] Cook, *Trusts* 28; Kerr, "Contracts in Restraint of Trade," 22 *Am. L. Rev.* 879; McQuillan, "Validity of Contracts in Restraint of Trade," 33 (N.S. 24) *Am. L. Reg.* 227; Mickey, "Trusts," 22 *Am. L. Rev.* 538, 544, 547 (1888).

[5] Dwight, "The Legality of 'Trusts'," *Pol. Sci. Q.*, III, 592; Beach, editorial, 3 *Ry. & Corp. L.J.* 217, 219 (1888); Abbott, 34 *Daily Register* 484, 572 (1888), cited and criticized in 22 *Am. L. Rev.* 926 (1888); Dodd, 5 *Ry. &*

To say that monopolies were illegal at common law was one thing; to destroy them by using the common law was another. It was true that in at least three prominent instances between 1887 and 1890 courts judging private suits refused to uphold agreements in restraint of trade.[6] Such results were comforting indications of "the tendency of the judicial mind," as one contemporary law journal put it,[7] but they were clearly not enough to put an end to the trust problem. Active prosecution of trusts was needed, and indeed a few public officials managed to do it. If they could not sue monopolies in any other way, they could and did use the legal weapons provided by their power over corporations. Between 1887 and 1890 the attorneys general of five states more or less enthusiastically initiated suits to dissolve corporations that exceeded their chartered powers or to destroy associations that exercised corporate powers without having charters.[8] Most of the lawyers who insisted on the

---

Corp. L.J. 98 (1889); Heinsheimer, "The Legal Status of Trusts," 2 *Columbia L. Times* 51 (1888).

[6] In Chicago Gas Co. v. People's Gas Co., 121 Ill. 530 (1887), the court refused to enforce an agreement by which two gas companies partitioned Chicago into two exclusive markets; it considered the contract a partial restraint, but invalid because the parties were engaged in public service. In Mallory v. Hanaur Oil Works, 86 Tenn. 598 (1888), the court would not enforce a combination of five cottonseed oil manufacturers, because whether or not it was a monopoly, its members were corporations and had no proper authority for participating in a partnership. In Richardson v. Buhl, 77 Mich. 632 (1889), the court would not enforce a contract between organizers of the Diamond Match Co. on the ground that any contract for the formation of a monopoly was illegal.

[7] 25 *Cen. L.J.* 482 (1887), referring to Chicago Gas Co. v. People's Gas Co., 121 Ill. 530 (1887).

[8] In Louisiana v. American Cotton-Oil Trust, 1 *Ry. & Corp. L.J.* 509 (1887), the court declared the trust unlawful, because it was not a corporation and the state's statutes forbade joint-stock companies. In People v. Chicago Gas Trust Co., 130 Ill. 268 (1889), the court held that the Company must sell the stocks it owned of four other gas companies, because its corporate charter did not give authority to operate other corporations or to form a monopoly. In California v. American Sugar Refining Co., 7 *Ry. & Corp. L.J.* 83 (1890), the court dissolved the corporation on the ground that it had forfeited its franchise by surrendering its business to the Sugar Trust. In People v. North River Sugar Refining Co., 121 N.Y. 582 (1890) aff'g 22 Abb. N.C. (N.Y.) 164 (1889), the court dissolved the corporation because it exceeded its chartered powers by entering a combination, the Sugar Trust, which moreover was a monopoly. In State v. Nebraska Distilling Co., 29 Neb. 700 (1890), the court annulled the franchise of the corporation because

legality of trusts argued that they were either unincorporated joint-stock companies or partnerships of shareholders, both perfectly lawful forms of organization.[9] The public prosecutors set out to prove the opposite, and in every case they won. The reactions to these cases were mixed. Some lawyers felt that this sort of attack might solve the problem: they hailed one decision as a "crushing" blow, another as a "setback" for the trusts, a third as a "victory" for the people, and concluded that at least in New York the trust had received its "judicial quietus."[1] Others were less certain that the solution was general: they pointed out that the Louisiana decision would not be followed elsewhere, since other states did not prohibit joint-stock companies, and that the Illinois decision was not a blow against trusts because the defendant, the Chicago Gas Trust Company, was not properly speaking a trust but a corporation.[2] In any case, few monopolies had been destroyed in this way by 1890.

Still, these few attacks on monopolies, together with the current view that the common law expressed a public policy hostile to monopolies, made lawyers confident that the common law went in the right direction. Some of them thought it went far enough. The members of the New York Senate committee on trusts were so impressed by the *North River Sugar* decision that they proposed to defer legislation for the time being—or rather, the Republican majority of the committee thought that no new law might be needed, whereas the Democrats believed that none likely to be passed would be as favorable as the common law declared in that decision.[3]

---

in selling out to the Whisky Trust it had made an unlawful contract. The New York sugar case was called a "Tammany Hall suit," 4 *Ry. & Corp. L.J.* 241 (1888), and was part of a Democratic campaign to make capital of the trust question, 5 *Ry. & Corp. L.J.* 53 (1889). The Chicago Gas case was prosecuted by Attorney General Hunt, at the instance of the Chicago Citizens' Association. His first reaction to their suggestion was that he could not bring the case without "backing" and that he had no money to pay for collecting evidence. Chi. *Trib.* p. 6, col. 5 (Feb. 3, 1888).

[9] Consult authors cited note 5, p. 81 above.

[1] Comments on the La. decision, 29 *Cen. L.J.* 41 (1889); Cal., 30 *Cen. L.J.* 69 (1890); Ill., 24 *Am. L. Rev.* 143 (1890); N.Y., *Albany L.J.*, quoted in 5 *Ry. & Corp. L.J.* 144 (1889).

[2] Mickey, "Trusts," 22 *Am. L. Rev.* 542; 30 *Cen. L.J.* 2 (1890); 6 *Ry. & Corp. L.J.* 441 (1889).

[3] 5 *Ry. & Corp. L.J.* 478 (1889).

The editor of the *American Law Review,* in commenting on Sherman's antitrust bill, said that as the trusts were making war on society, society was bound to make war upon them, but concluded that society could carry on its war without enacting criminal statutes: "The common law is good enough, if it were only administered."[4] Other lawyers, however, said that more force was necessary. One, after arguing that the trusts, as monopolies, were prohibited by the common law, suddenly ended with a warning that they could be checked only by "wisely and fearlessly executed legislation."[5] The editor of the *Central Law Journal,* commenting on the Tennessee case in which the operation of the common law dissolved a combination of cotton-oil manufacturers, nevertheless differed with the suggestions that the common law was a sufficient weapon. The trusts, he said, were "vast masses of aggregated capital, completely organized; and fully supported by numerous corporations, many of them improvidently endowed by their charters with extraordinary powers"—they were too powerful to be destroyed without legislation.[6]

Few of the lawyers who believed that statutes were needed—at least, few who wrote in legal periodicals—suggested how the statutes should be framed. One of the rare proposals was that laws be passed to subject the trust to corporation law, and to prohibit any corporation from holding stock in any other.[7] This second hint was rather far-sighted, for the author understood, as few yet did,[8] that the corporate holding company or merged corporation might be a much safer method of organizing monopolies than the trust. But there was a serious flaw in this scheme, as in all antitrust laws proposed or passed by the states (the Missouri antitrust law, for instance, had already encountered it by March of 1890)[9]: the states lacked authority to regulate corporations engaged in interstate commerce. It seemed therefore that if antitrust legislation were

[4] 22 *Am. L. Rev.* 926 (1888).

[5] Mickey, "Trusts," 22 *Am. L. Rev.* 549.

[6] 27 *Cen. L.J.* 277 (1888), commenting on Mallory v. Hanaur Oil Works, 86 Tenn. 598 (1888).

[7] Stimson, "Trusts," 1 *Harv. L. Rev.* 132 (1887).

[8] 30 *Cen. L.J.* 257 (1890); see also the remarks of Senators Teller and Sherman in 21 *Cong. Rec.* 2560, 2462 (1890). All of these, however, recognized the fact three years later than Stimson.

[9] 30 *Cen. L.J.* 1 (1890); 7 *Ry. & Corp. L.J.* 241 (1890).

needed, and if it were to be effective against the largest and most powerful trusts, it must be passed by Congress.[1]

The lawyers and the economists offered Congress little specific help and much conflicting advice. Yet, although the economists advocated some sort of public regulation while the lawyers suggested nothing but prohibitory laws, their underlying views were well adapted to each other. The economists thought that both competition and combination should play their parts in the economy. The lawyers saw that the common law permitted combination in some instances and prohibited it in others. Congressmen seized on this hidden agreement, and set out to construct a statute which by the use of common-law principles would eliminate excesses but allow "healthy" competition and combination to flourish side by side.

Legislative History of the Sherman Act

The political parties officially recognized the trust problem soon after it arose. The "third parties" needed no urging; they were eager to extend the campaign that the Greenback and Anti-Monopoly parties had carried on since 1880 against "land, railroad, money and other gigantic monopolies." [2] It was a matter of course that the Union Labor Party, formed by a coalition of Greenbackers, Knights of Labor, and farmer organizations, should make much of this new opportunity, and indeed they made it one of their great causes. The platform they adopted in the spring of 1888 concluded with the declaration: "The paramount issues to be solved in the interests of humanity are the abolition of usury, monopoly, and trusts, and we denounce the Democratic and Republican parties for creating and perpetuating these monstrous evils." [3]

The major parties were anything but anxious to appear as champions of the trusts. The Democrats had made the appropriate

[1] 30 *Cen. L.J.* 1,365 (1890); 22 *Am. L. Rev.* 269 (1888).

[2] Greenback platform of 1884; a virtually identical expression appeared in their platform of 1880, and a more expanded version in the Anti-Monopoly platform of 1884. McKee, *National Conventions and Platforms* 215, 192, 224 *et seq.* (1901).

[3] *Ibid.*, 251. Anti-monopoly planks appeared also in the 1888 platforms of the Prohibition Party and of the United Labor Party. *Ibid.*, 247, 252 *et seq.*

general statements against monopoly in 1880 and 1884,[4] but they had especially good reasons for carrying these further in 1888. For one thing, they could cite the new offense as additional evidence against their old enemy, protection. President Cleveland, in his annual message to Congress at the end of 1887, said it was "notorious" that the "combinations quite prevalent at this time, and frequently called trusts," strangled competition; he urged that action be taken against them, and suggested that Congress reduce the customs duties protecting them against foreign competitors.[5] Moreover, the trust issue was especially useful for appealing to farmers and laborers who might otherwise shift their vote to the third party. Cleveland, during his term of office, opposed the easy-money and silver-coinage schemes, supposedly popular in the South and West, that were advocated by the Union Labor Party[6] and supported by a wing of his own party. As a candidate for re-election he was no more pliable, and the Democratic national convention of 1888 was the only one between 1880 and 1896 that did not advocate silver coinage; it did not even mention the word "silver" in its platform. The party apparently felt obliged to make up for this somehow, and amidst sympathetic references to "the industrious freemen of our land," "every tiller of the soil," and "the cry of American labor for a better share in the rewards of industry," it asserted that, "Judged by Democratic principles, the interests of the people are betrayed when, by unnecessary taxation, trusts and combinations are permitted to exist, which, while unduly enriching the few that combine, rob the body of our citizens. . . ."[7]

The Republican Party had even more compelling need to condemn the trusts. They had since 1880 achieved the reputation of being the party of the rich, and in 1884 Ben Butler began calling them the "Party of Monopolists."[8] This label became especially current after their presidential candidate was given a banquet by a group of businessmen, among them Gould, Vanderbilt, and Astor, which the New York *World* titled "The Royal Feast of Belshazzar

[4] *Ibid.*, 184, 206.

[5] Richardson, *Messages and Papers of the Presidents,* VIII, 588 (1900) (Message of Dec. 6, 1887).

[6] McKee, *National Conventions and Platforms* 250.

[7] *Ibid.*, 235.

[8] Butler, *Address to His Constituents* 8 (Pamphlet of Aug. 12, 1884).

Blaine and the Money Kings," and during which, it said, the "Millionaires and Monopolists" sealed their allegiance to the party.[9] A party whose policies were subject to so crudely cynical an interpretation and was undoubtedly supported—as were the others—by some millionaires, must have condemned the trusts in self-defense even if it had not objected to them in principle. In their convention of 1888 the Republicans accordingly condemned "all combinations of capital, organized in trusts or otherwise, to control arbitrarily the conditions of trade among our citizens," and recommended "such legislation as will prevent the execution of all schemes to oppress the people by undue charges on their supplies, or by unjust rates for the transportation of their products to market."[1] Because they elected President Harrison and won decisive control of Congress in the following election, responsibility for carrying out the recommendation became theirs.

Congress began to concern itself with the trust problem in January of 1888. An antitrust bill was brought to the floor of Congress by Senator John Sherman, by now an aging man at times impatient and confused, but still the most prominent and esteemed Republican in Congress. He had served as representative for eight years, senator for over twenty-five, and had been Secretary of the Treasury under Hayes. He had been a candidate for the presidential nomination since 1880, and seemed finally to be winning it at the convention of 1888 until Harrison took the lead during the seventh ballot. Soon after this defeat he began to take serious interest in the trust question. His seniority and experience gave him great authority on financial questions and his recent disappointment gave him the urge to do something memorable. He began by establishing personal jurisdiction over the antitrust problem. The antitrust bills introduced earlier in the year[2] had been referred to committees, but none had yet been debated when, on July 10, Sherman successfully introduced a resolution directing the Senate Committee on Finance, of which he was a ranking member, to investigate all antitrust

[9] N.Y. *World* p. 1 (Oct. 30, 1884).

[1] McKee, *National Conventions and Platforms* 241.

[2] 50th Cong. 1st Sess. Sen. 2906; H.R. 6113, 6117, 8036, 8054, 9449, 10049 (1888). The bills, as well as debates directly concerned with them, are conveniently gathered in 57th Cong. 2d Sess., Sen. Doc. No. 147, *Bills and Debates in Congress Relating to Trusts* (1903), from which, however, some relevant matter is omitted, e.g., H.R. 4406.

bills.[3] He maintained that the Committee would investigate antitrust bills "in connection with" tariff bills, which were undoubtedly its proper province; but this argument had its danger as well, for by stressing the connection between trusts and tariffs he was playing into the hands of the Democrats. He had already made this blunder when, in replying to Cleveland's annual message, he agreed that the trusts might be fought by reducing duties that protected them—though he then added that he knew of no trusts which had such protection.[4] Now he was a little more on guard, and argued that the trusts not only prevented "freedom of trade and production" but also subverted the tariff system; they undermined "the policy of the Government to protect and encourage American industries by levying duties on imported goods."[5]

The effect of Sherman's maneuver became evident a month later, when Senator John Reagan, a Democrat from Texas, introduced an antitrust bill which was read and about to be referred to committee.[6] At this point Sherman rose to insist that according to the resolution the bill should be sent to the Finance Committee. He maintained that this was appropriate because the only constitutional provision enabling Congress to legislate against trusts was the power to levy taxes: though the Federal Government might not be able to attack trusts like Standard Oil, it could certainly use the taxing power to control monopolies like the Sugar Trust, which were aided by tariffs. But this doctrine was far from congenial to him, and when Senator Ransom replied that Congress derived its jurisdiction over trusts from its constitutional power to regulate commerce, Sherman was ready to shift ground. He answered: "I always take the revenue laws as commercial laws. They always go together, interchangeably."[7] Though this may have been an accurate interpretation of the Constitution,[8] it was less than an adequate reason for referring trust bills to the Finance Committee rather than the Commerce Committee, but the Senate was impressed by Sherman's determination and agreed to send Reagan's

[3] 19 *Cong. Rec.* 6041 (1888).
[4] 19 *Cong. Rec.* 190.
[5] 19 *Cong. Rec.* 6041.
[6] 19 *Cong. Rec.* 7512.
[7] 19 *Cong. Rec.* 7512.
[8] Crosskey, *Politics and the Constitution* parts 1-2 (1953).

bill to his committee. Sherman immediately capped the day's work by introducing an antitrust bill of his own.[9]

His bill, unlike Reagan's, was returned in short order to the Senate floor, where it was briefly debated and considerably amended in January 1889.[1] By now it had begun to look like a serious effort, and was honored with a long attack by Senator James George of Mississippi, formerly a Confederate general and Chief Justice of the state supreme court, a Democrat and fevent upholder of states' rights.[2] George questioned both its effectiveness and its constitutionality. He declared that although he firmly opposed the trusts and was eager to destroy them, he saw no hope that the bill could do so. It declared illegal "all arrangements, contracts, agreements, trusts, or combinations between persons or corporations made with a view, or which tend, to prevent full and free competition" in certain goods, or "to advance the cost to the consumer"; yet these words, George said, would condemn not only the trusts and combinations but also arrangements made "for moral and defensive purposes." It would penalize not only the Southern farmers who had organized a boycott against the Jute-Bag Trust, but also combinations of farmers to raise the prices of their products and of laborers to raise their wages, and even temperance societies whose members compacted not to use spirits. However serious this defect—and Sherman immediately assured the Senate that it was unintentional—the great objection to the bill was its utter futility. The bill, as it now stood, supposed that Congress derived its power over trusts from the commerce clause of the Constitution; it therefore outlawed combinations dealing in goods that had been imported from abroad or that might "in the due course of trade" be transported from one state to another. But according to the established interpretation of the Constitution, George insisted, Congress could control commerce only while goods were in the actual process of being transported into the country or from one state to another. It was apparent that a law punishing combinations because they dealt in goods that might once have been imported or that might some day be sent from one state to another was either unconstitutional, or if constitutional, then so limited in application as to be worthless. Having

[9] 19 *Cong. Rec.* 7512.

[1] 20 *Cong. Rec.* 1167-69 (1889).

[2] 20 *Cong. Rec.* 1459-61.

ended his critique, he took a little time to point out, with some relish, that Sherman had admitted that an antitrust law could not be based on the commerce power and had recognized, as he himself would, that trusts could be controlled in a constitutional manner only by reducing protective tariffs. Sherman did not answer, and before there was another opportunity for debate, the 50th Congress disbanded.

These preliminary skirmishes were continued during the early months of the 51st Congress. The moment the session began Sherman introduced a bill that, except for changes in detail, contained the words and principles of his previous drafts. It declared unlawful and void all combinations preventing competition in foreign and interstate commerce; it authorized any person injured by such combinations to recover damages; and it subjected all members and agents of such combinations to fine and imprisonment.[3] The bill, introduced on December 4, 1889, and very slightly amended by the Finance Committee, was brought to the floor of the Senate in February 1890, whereupon Senator George once again made a full-scale attack on it. He repeated his previous objections, and as before concluded that the bill was "utterly unconstitutional, and even if constitutional, utterly worthless."[4] The matter was left there, and it began to look as though antitrust legislation was a dim prospect. More than two years had passed since the first bills had been put before Congress, and as yet only one had been briefly considered. The machinery seemed to have come to a standstill. Two other bills in the Senate, introduced by George and Reagan, were still being held up by committees, as were seventeen bills that had been introduced by Representatives.[5] It was rumored that the reason for the delay since December was that McKinley, chairman of the House Ways and Means Committee, was thinking of attaching

[3] 51st Cong. 1st Sess., Sen. 1 (1889).

[4] 21 *Cong. Rec.* 1765-72 (1890).

[5] Sherman's Resolution (see p. 87 above) having expired with the end of the 50th Congress, Reagan's bill (51st Cong. 1st Sess., Sen. 62, [1889]) was referred to the Judiciary Committee, but George's bill (51st Cong. 1st Sess., Sen. 6, [1889]) was sent to the Finance Committee. Of the bills in the House (H.R. 91, 179, 202, 270, 286, 313, 402, 509, 811, 826, 839, 846, 3294, 3353, 3819, 3844, 3925 [1889]) nine were referred to the Way and Means Committee, six to the Judiciary, and two to Manufactures. 51st Cong. 1st Sess., H.R. 30 (1889), a proposal for a constitutional amendment prohibiting trusts, was also before the Judiciary Committee.

an antitrust section to his tariff bill,[6] which had already been passed by the House and was quite certain to become law. For the moment, however, nothing seemed to be happening.

Suddenly the situation changed, and in the last weeks of March 1890 the serious work of preparing an antitrust law was begun. The burst of energy may have come because the Republican congressmen gave up the idea, assuming they had ever had it, of treating the trust problem in the McKinley Tariff Bill. To have done so would have given the impression that they agreed with the Democrats about the causes of trusts and the constitutional powers available to destroy them. They may have felt that the public was becoming impatient, for congressmen were receiving an increasing number of petitions advocating antitrust legislation.[7] Or the new activity may have come at Sherman's insistence. He announced a few days before it began that he had revised his bill to meet George's objections, having deleted the provisions George had criticized because they would make the law a criminal one and thus oblige the courts to interpret it narrowly.[8] In any case, by the time Sherman submitted his new bill on March 21, the Senate was prepared to concentrate on it and spent the next five days doing little else.

The great debate opened with a long, formal address in which Sherman praised his bill.[9] He began by explaining its political and legal theory. It was intended, he said, to destroy combinations—not all combinations, but all those which the common law had always condemned as unlawful. It was not intended to outlaw all partnerships and corporations, though they were by nature combinations. The corporations had demonstrated their usefulness by the vast development of railroads and industry, and Sherman added—bearing in mind the lingering prejudice against them—that as long as every man had the right under general laws to form corporations, they were "not in any sense a monopoly." But any combination

[6] 7 *Ry. & Corp. L.J.* 201 (1890).

[7] A few public petitions and resolutions from state legislatures were read into the record during the second session of the 50th Congress (Dec. 3, 1888 to March 3, 1889), 20 *Cong. Rec.* 514, 1234, 1253, 1273, 1500, 1589, 2135 (1888-89). But between Dec. 2, 1889 and March 21, 1890, forty-nine were entered. 21 *Cong. Rec.* (listed in Index, sub. "Trusts, Petitions").

[8] N.Y. *Times* p. 6, col. 1 (March 19, 1890).

[9] 21 *Cong. Rec.* 2456 (1890).

which sought to restrain trade, any combination of the leading corporations in an industry, organized in a trust to stifle competition, dictate terms to railroads, command the price of labor, and raise prices to consumers, was a "substantial monopoly." It smacked of tyranny, "of kingly prerogative," and a nation that "would not submit to an emperor . . . should not submit to an autocrat of trade." Sherman went on to say that all such combinations in restraint of trade were prohibited by the common law, wherever it was in force; it had always applied in the states, and the "courts in different States have declared this thing, when it exists in a State, to be unlawful and void." Senator Cullom interrupted to ask, "Everywhere?" "In every case, everywhere," Sherman replied, and went on to list the recent decisions supporting his view. He first read the full opinion of the Michigan Supreme Court in the case of *Richardson v. Buhl,*[1] which had a double attraction for him. It struck at the Diamond Match Company's monopoly, and it branded as a monopolist General Russel Alger, one of his chief rivals in 1888 for the Republican presidential nomination, whom Sherman blamed for his unexpected defeat and publicly accused of having bribed delegates.[2] Sherman then cited other cases, which if they did not hold the same personal interest for him, all supported the view that monopolies and combinations in restraint of trade were unlawful and void in courts of common law.[3] But, he contin-

[1] 77 Mich. 632 (1889).

[2] The rumor that Alger, or his managers, bought votes of Southern delegates, reputedly at $50.00 each, was reported at the time and has been repeated since by disinterested witnesses: N.Y. *Trib.* (June 10, 1888); Stephenson, *Nelson W. Aldrich* 71, 434 n. 7 (1930); Gresham, *Life of Walter Quintin Gresham,* II, 574, 632 (1919). Sherman was convinced of its truth and was openly antagonistic to Alger. When President Harrison signed the Antitrust Bill, he is said to have remarked, "John Sherman has fixed General Alger," though this story may well be apocryphal. Gresham, II, 632. Though revenge cannot have been Sherman's chief motive in pressing for the Act, there is no doubt that he was bitter about the incident; he still referred to it angrily in his autobiography. Sherman, *Recollections of Forty Years,* II, 1029 (1895). And he did not forego the opportunity to indulge the passion; contemporary observers remarked the relish with which he read the opinion in Richardson v. Buhl. N.Y. *Times* p. 4, col. 3 (March 25, 1890).

[3] Craft v. McConoughy, 79 Ill. 346 (1875); Chicago Gas Co. v. People's Gas Co., 121 Ill. 530 (1887); People v. Chicago Gas Trust Co., 130 Ill. 268 (1889); People v. North River Sugar Refining Co., 22 Abb. N.C. (N.Y.) 164 (1889), aff'd, 121 N.Y. 582 (1890).

ued, the trusts were threatened by no similar law in the Federal courts and a statute was needed to enforce the common law that already applied in state courts. Once again, he insisted that Congress was authorized alike by the commerce and revenue clauses of the Constitution to regulate combinations affecting interstate and foreign commerce; and he concluded that his bill, based on this constitutional power and declaring the common-law rule, would effectively destroy the power of the trusts.[4]

The debate which occupied much of the following week was untidy but not without pattern. Many senators delivered great orations, but few were heard to say that the trusts were desirable or an antitrust law unnecessary. George repeatedly questioned the bill's constitutionality; certain of his Democratic colleagues took occasion to avow their opposition to tariffs. A number of senators tried to substitute their own bills for Sherman's; failing this, they attached them to his bill as amendments. By the end of the third day, the bill before the Senate consisted of sixteen sections.[5] Sherman's bill now had tailing after it: Reagan's bill, which, instead of relying on common-law formulas, gave a long explicit definition of the term "trust";[6] Ingall's bill, which was a more or less independent effort to prohibit speculation in farm products; and George's clause, which exempted labor unions and farmers' organizations from the general prohibitions. Moreover, the constitutional issue was still confused, and George suggested that the bill be referred to the Judiciary Committee, whose members, chosen for their legal wisdom, might be able to restore order to the law. Sherman, piqued and impatient, objected that it was most unusual to transfer a bill from one committee to another; Reagan, whose original bill had never been reported to the floor by the Judiciary Committee, was equally adamant; and Vance called the Judiciary Committee a "grand mausoleum of Senatorial literature" in which this bill would be buried. But after two more days in which further amendments were added

[4] 21 *Cong. Rec.* 2458 *et seq.* (1890).

[5] *Bills and Debates* 217-22 (1890).

[6] Reagan defined a trust as a "combination of capital, skill, or acts" by two or more persons or associations for any of the following purposes: to restrict trade, to limit production, to increase or reduce price, to prevent competition, to fix prices, to "create a monopoly," to make any agreement to set minimum prices, to agree to "pool, combine, or unite" so as to affect prices. 51st Cong. 1st Sess., Sen. 62 (1889).

and further profound doubts expressed, the matter had become so tangled that little alternative remained, and the bill was referred to the Judiciary Committee with instructions to report within twenty days.[7]

The Judiciary Committee took the matter out of Sherman's hands, much to his regret and anger. But within a week, surprising everyone, the Committee produced a bill of its own. The work was done largely by its chairman, George Edmunds of Vermont. He disposed of the constitutional question very quickly: when the Committee first met to consider the bill, he proposed to his colleagues "that it is competent for Congress to pass laws preventing and punishing contracts etc. in restraint of commerce between the states." And they, including George, who had raised objections to this theory all along, unanimously agreed.[8] Edmunds then presented drafts of the critical sections of the Act, that made it a misdemeanor to engage in any combination in restraint of trade or to "monopolize" trade, and these were agreed to by all the committeemen present. Two of the remaining sections were written by others: George prepared the section authorizing the Attorney General to sue for injunctions against violators, and Hoar wrote the section authorizing private persons to sue violators for triple damages.[9] The Committee's draft was in broad outline the same as Sherman's original bill, yet Sherman was not pleased. He immediately denounced it as "totally ineffective in dealing with combinations and trusts. All corporations can ride through it or over it without fear of punishment or detection."[1] His reaction was particularly ungenerous, since aside from the fact that the new bill was simpler than his, it differed mainly in providing a greater number of more severe penalties. But when the time came, he voted for it, and as a matter of courtesy it bears his name. The Senate as a whole seemed well sat-

[7] 21 *Cong. Rec.* 2600 *et seq.*, 2604, 2610, 2731 (1890).

[8] Senate, Committee on the Judiciary, Minute Book 226 (March 31, 1890) (Ms. in U. S. Archives).

[9] The Committee Minute Book 227-33, shows that sections 1, 2, 5, and 6 were drafted by Edmunds, section 4 by George, section 7 by Hoar, and the phrase "in the form of a trust or otherwise" by Evarts. It does not indicate who drafted sections 3 and 8. There is a strong presumption, but no proof, to support Walker's assertion that Edmunds did; Walker, "Who Wrote the Sherman Law?," 73 *Cen. L.J.* 257, 258 (1911).

[1] N.Y. *Times* p. 4, col. 4 (April 8, 1890).

isfied, and after hearing Edmunds' plea that they "pass a bill that is clear in its terms, is definite in its definitions, and is broad in its comprehension, without winding it up into infinite details," [2] they passed it by fifty-two votes to one.

The action of the House was less systematic. Representative Culberson, who was in charge of the debate, tried to limit it to one hour. His colleagues, who had not until now considered any anti-trust bill, complained that they could not get printed copies of the one before them. A strong group insisted that a section should be added to the bill specifically aimed at outlawing railroad and meat-packing pools. After a rather desultory debate, the House passed the bill with one amendment, on May 1. During the next two months, conferences were held between the two chambers, and the House was eventually prevailed on to withdraw its amendment.[3] President Harrison signed the bill, and it became law on July 2, 1890.

Law and Policy in the Sherman Act

The Sherman Act was as good an antitrust law as the Congress of 1890 could have devised. Congressmen had been called on to give the Federal Government novel powers to control, directly and generally, the organization of economic life. They had little experience to teach them how such a law should be written or to inform them how the courts might interpret it. They realized from the beginning that whatever law they composed would be imperfect. Its strongest advocates frankly admitted that it would be "experimental," [4] and in the end the whole of Congress was reconciled to the limitation Sherman recognized when he said, "All that we, as lawmakers, can do is to declare general principles." [5] Yet if the Sherman Act was an experiment, it was the safest one Congress could make, and if it only declared general principles, they were at least the familiar ones of the common law. Sherman had repeatedly said that his bill

[2] 21 *Cong. Rec.* 3148 (April 8, 1890).

[3] *Bills and Debates* 327-402 (1890).

[4] E.g., Senators Sherman, Edmunds, Turpie, and Representatives Culberson and Heard; 21 *Cong. Rec.* 2460, 2557-58, 3148, 4089, 4101 (1890).

[5] 21 *Cong. Rec.* 2460 (1890).

was based on a tried formula: "It does not announce a new principle of law, but applies old and well-recognized principles of the common law to the complicated jurisdiction of our State and Federal Government."[6] Edmunds, principal author of the Judiciary Committee bill, and Hoar, who guided it through debate on the floor, said the same.[7] Of the eighty-two senators, sixty-eight were lawyers, and as one of them said, "I suppose no lawyer needs to have argument made to him that these combinations and trusts are illegal without statute."[8] They could not tell how the courts would construe a statute that gave the government power to indict and sue the offenders, but they believed that the courts would experience little difficulty in recognizing the offense.

Congress had reason to think, further, that the Act aimed at the proper goals. On the one hand, it satisfied the public demand for an antitrust law. It prohibited trusts in so many words: it declared illegal "every contract, combination in the form of a trust or otherwise, or conspiracy, in restraint of trade or commerce among the several States or with foreign nations." This specific mention of "trusts" had almost been omitted, for Edmunds so strongly desired to define the offense in "terms that were well known to the law already"[9] that his draft of the section used only the common-law words, "contract," "combination," and "conspiracy." But a majority of his colleagues on the Judiciary Committee had seen the political value of adding a term that was well known to the public and had agreed to insert Evart's phrase, "in the form of a trust or otherwise."[1]

On the other hand, the Act did not go farther than Congress thought it should. Congressmen were no more in favor of unlimited competition than the economists were. Sherman, in his great address, had emphasized that many combinations were desirable. He was sure that they had been an important cause of America's wealth, and he had no intention of prohibiting them. It was only "the unlawful combination, tested by the rules of common law and human experience, that is aimed at by this bill, and not the lawful

[6] 21 *Cong. Rec.* 2456.
[7] 21 *Cong. Rec.* 3146, 3148, 3152.
[8] Sen. Teller, 21 *Cong. Rec.* 2458.
[9] 21 *Cong. Rec.* 3148.
[1] See note 9, p. 94 above.

and useful combination." [2] Edmunds and Hoar later said they had the same intention.[3] A majority of the representatives who conferred with senators about the House amendment opposed it for similar reasons. They said that the bill's "only object was the control of trusts, so called," but that the scope of the amendment was broader, and indeed too broad: "It declares illegal any agreement for relief from the effects of competition in the two industries of transportation and merchandising, however excessive or destructive such competition may be." [4] Senator Teller meant the same, although he used impolitic language, when he said that "a trust may not always be an evil. A trust for certain purposes, which may mean simply a combination of capital, may be a favorable thing to the community and the country." [5] Perhaps the clearest statement of this view, held by many congressmen as well as by many economists of the period, was that of Representative Stewart of Vermont:

> [T]here are two great forces working in human society in this country to-day, and they have been contending for the mastery on one side or the other for the last two generations. Those two great forces are competition and combination. They are correctives of each other, and both ought to exist. Both ought to be under restraint. Either of them, if allowed to be unrestrained, is destructive of the material interests of this country.[6]

The common law was a perfect instrument for realizing the policy supported by Congress. It prohibited some monopolies but not all combinations, and congressmen felt that a statute based on it would have equally qualified effects.

Though the pattern of the law was sound, there were nevertheless defects in detail. Various ambiguities had crept in because so many men had taken part in drafting it, because they wanted it to be simple and general, and because they wanted to use common-law terms to define the offenses. In order to keep the law broad,

[2] 21 *Cong. Rec.* 2457, and also 2460.

[3] Washburn, *The History of a Statute* 9 (1927); United States v. Joint Traffic Ass'n, 171 U.S. 505, 544 *et seq.* (1898); *Hearings before Senate Committee on Interstate Commerce, pursuant to Sen. Res. 98,* 62d Cong. 1st Sess., Vol. II, pp. 1550, 2430 (1912).

[4] 21 *Cong. Rec.* 5950.

[5] 21 *Cong. Rec.* 2471.

[6] 21 *Cong. Rec.* 5956.

Congress did not specifically exclude labor unions from its scope or include railroad pools. So far as their sentiments were expressed in debates and bills, they had favored unions or wanted to leave them immune from this law. Sherman said they should be specifically exempted and many agreed with him.[7] Edmunds almost alone spoke against a specific exemption, because he thought that labor unions should be treated like any other combination.[8] But when he came to write the bill he was mainly concerned with keeping it unqualified. His colleagues seem to have been convinced by his arguments in favor of simplicity. Although during the debates four of the eight members of the Judiciary Committee spoke for exempting labor unions,[9] they all voted for Edmunds' draft, probably because they agreed that the law should not be cluttered with details and felt that, in any case, it would not be construed against unions. Reasoning of the same sort explains why railroad pools were not specifically named as offenders, for Senator Vest, a member of the Judiciary Committee, in commenting on the House amendment said that he too had wanted to add an explicit prohibition, until the other committeemen convinced him it would be redundant.[1] In order to make the Act more inclusive, Congress introduced another note that added to its ambiguity. "Restraints of trade," as the common law understood them, could only come about through agreement between persons; but the Judiciary Committee felt that the Act should also condemn any individual who restrained trade by himself, and they therefore drafted a section making it illegal for any individual to "monopolize." Hoar and Edmunds assured the Senate that the word had a well-known meaning at common law,[2] and their advice was followed, although the word meant little more at common law than the engrossing of a local food supply. These were only a few of the blemishes that marred the Act; the courts in

[7] Sherman, 21 *Cong. Rec.* 2562, 2611-12; Hiscock, at 2468; Teller, at 2561-62; Reagan, at 2562; Gray, at 2657. Consult also note 9 below. The exemptions were included in 51st Cong. 1st Sess., Sen. 1, 6, and H.R. 91, 402, 509, 826, 3819, 3844 (1890).

[8] 21 *Cong. Rec.* 2726-29.

[9] Hoar, 21 *Cong. Rec.* 2728; Wilson, at 2658; Coke, at 2613-15. George was the author of the proviso in the first place. It appeared in his 51st Cong. 1st Sess., Sen. 6 (1890), from which Sherman borrowed it, 21 *Cong. Rec.* 2611.

[1] 21 *Cong. Rec.* 6116. See also the remark by Hoar, at 4560.

[2] 21 *Cong. Rec.* 3151-52.

time found many more. But to have drawn up a more satisfactory solution for a new and difficult problem, congressmen would have had to be much more adept, much more remote from public opinion, and much more unanimous in their own views than the lawmakers of a democracy ever can be.

CHAPTER FOUR

ADMINISTERING THE SHERMAN ACT

1890-1901

When the Sherman Act was passed in 1890, it was taken by some to mean the end of trusts. Once it became apparent, however, that the mere enrollment of the Act in the statute books would not do away with every activity that might be called a trust or be condemned as monopolistic behavior, critics began to search for a scapegoat. Common complaints were that Congress had deliberately passed a mock law, too weak and badly worded to accomplish anything; and that the courts' antiquated ideas prevented them from countenancing or even understanding the purpose of the Act. Other critics rejected these explanations, however, and maintained that the fault lay in the administration of the Act. Thus, as early as 1892, Senator Edmunds, a principal author of the statute, remarked: "the law is all right, the courts are all right, and the people are all right. Let the officers charged with the enforcement of the law do their full duty and Trusts and combinations will go to pieces as quickly as they sprang into existence."[1] The critics who have adopted Senator Edmunds' view speak as though all statutes work automatically, halted only by the sabotage of indifferent or hostile prosecutors; in fact, the implementation of any law, far from being a matter of "full duty" or even plain duty, often requires delicate discrimination.

Even ancient and familiar laws, like those proscribing murder, do not enforce themselves. A conspicuous dead body will command the attention of public officials; but the public prosecutor must decide how much effort should be spent on ferreting out hidden corpses. Once a crime is known, he must decide what re-

[1] N.Y. *Times* p. 4, col. 2 (Nov. 25, 1892).

sources should be allocated to discovering the criminal and evidence against him. Finally, he must determine whether the particular sort of killing is prohibited by the murder laws as they are then interpreted, or, if not, whether he can persuade a judge to read the laws to cover the case. Although the prosecutor must protect the public from crime, he must also respect the right of citizens to be free from wanton prosecution when there is no likelihood of their being convicted. Nor can he escape the responsibility of his role in deciding whether a law should be extended to a new class of case, for the courts can only act upon cases laid before them. Thus, no prosecutor can avoid acting as a policy maker. He affects the law no matter how he chooses to execute it.

The breadth of his discretion allows a public prosecutor, and particularly the Attorney General of the United States, to adopt a theory of his office anywhere between two extremes. At the least, he must attack some abuses presumed to be violations, and he may select those that the public considers outrageous, those that he estimates would best serve to warn other violators, or those where evidence is readily available and victory most certain. The opposite limit is harder to define. It seems clear, however, that a prosecutor who sought to stretch statutes beyond their ordinary meaning in order to prohibit the widest range of conduct, or to prosecute every person against whom a shred of evidence could be found, would be weakening the presumption of innocence and overly extending the power of government. Equipped with enough resources, such an officer might turn any modern society into a police state without invoking any authority beyond the already existing statutes.

Exactly where between these extremes of enforcement policy a particular Attorney General will choose to stand depends on his estimate of the capacities of various statutes and the policies they tend to serve. He may feel that some laws are dead, feeble, or harmful, and may therefore plan to leave them unused, unless or until the public cries out for their enforcement. He may believe that other statutes are not yet exerting the force they should, and may begin a campaign to invigorate them. Guiding the prosecutor's actions, in part, will be his convictions about what laws should do. Clearly, his private opinion that a law is undesirable would not justify a categorical refusal to enforce, any more than the opposite view would warrant his concentrating all efforts on catching anything that might be termed a violation of the statute.

Since no one will believe that all existing statutes are equally necessary, useful, or wise, and since the Attorney General must exercise discretion in deciding which laws he will enforce and to what extent, his views on the quality of the laws do, and should, affect the exercise of his office. Moreover, since he serves not only as the Government's chief attorney but also as a cabinet member, and as such is the representative of a particular administration, the policy of his office may properly be influenced by his party's standards of what is wise legislation and enforcement policy. To be sure, our framework of government contains no provision for rewriting the statutes as each new administration takes office. But if it were not intended that law enforcement should be subject to some political control, it would have been more reasonable to provide that the Attorney General should be a civil servant with life tenure, rather than a political appointee.

There are consequently two distinct grounds on which the execution of a law can be criticized. The prosecutor may be attacked for having willfully misused his office, either to protect criminals or to oppress the innocent. Or he may be criticized for being more (or less) energetic than the public interest requires. The first line of censure questions the prosecutor's good faith; the second, his political wisdom; and, though both attacks may at times be justified, they should be recognized as distinct. Reviews of the early administration of the Sherman Act have generally failed in this regard. The critics notice only that the Attorneys General between 1890 and 1901 were less vigorous in executing the Sherman Act than its most fervent advocates might have wished, and they forget the wide range of honest choice that was open to the Federal prosecutors of this period in determining the best way to implement the new antitrust law. These critics also do not take into account the more material circumstances under which the Attorneys General had to work.

Administrative Difficulties Facing the Attorney General

Anyone accustomed to the spending habits of mid-twentieth-century government must be astonished by the poverty of the Department of Justice in the 1890's. However eager an Attorney General might have been to prosecute antitrust cases, he would have been seriously hampered by the resources at his command. Congress had supplied no special funds for enforcing the Sherman Act, and even before antitrust work was added to his duties, the chief prosecutor was complaining that his forces were too small and cramped for want of money. In 1890 the Department of Justice occupied the upper stories of a bank building, employed eighty persons, of whom eighteen were lawyers, and had an increasingly heavy load of routine work. Cases before the Supreme Court—the responsibility of the Solicitor General and one of the assistant attorneys general—had risen from an average of 60 during each of the previous ten years to 180 in 1890. Suits in the Court of Claims had increased almost twentyfold since 1880, but the Assistant Attorney General in charge had no more help than before.[2] Aiding him in his principal work were six attorneys, each of whom had to prepare about ten cases every month; he directed, in addition, one attorney and two law clerks who dealt exclusively with French spoilation claims. In 1890 this group of ten lawyers was responsible for the 13,000 claims then pending against the Government. The remaining Assistant Attorney General worked chiefly on Indian depredation cases—claims for damages done in the period between the Creek War of 1836 and the Sioux uprising of 1890. Over 5000 such petitions had been submitted during the first six months following their congressional authorization, and many more were expected. The officer in charge complained that "there are only two regular employés in the office . . . and it is impossible with this force to keep up the dockets, records, and history of the cases, as they are daily being filed, as they should be kept for the proper administration of my office, to say nothing of the very important work of examining witnesses and preparation

[2] *Att'y Gen. Ann. Rep.* 3, 11 (1891).

of cases for trial."[3] Another official reported that *"it is physically impossible that the force assigned by the present law will be able to adequately transact the business. . . ."*[4]

The Attorney General's annual accounting indicates the care with which every penny was doled out. When Solicitor General William Howard Taft traveled on government business, his omnibus fares, twenty-five cents, were carefully entered. Another twenty-five cent amount—for stationery purchased by an employee—was recorded as reimbursed, the employee having certified that the item was necessary because the stationery "furnished by the Department was not properly ruled, and could not be used for the purpose." Eight cents spent for mailing a deposition to a witness was not reimbursed, perhaps because the acting commissioner who claimed it had not submitted a voucher. The costs of "1 Yale Key," $0.36, of one and one half dozen pins, $0.83, of "1 fitch, round," $0.10, found their appointed places, as did the less plausible item "500 clock dials, $2.50." Nothing was spent at mere discretion, and in order to repair a Federal jail, defective among other things in that "the lever that locks one tier of cell doors [was] out of order and useless," the Attorney General had to petition Congress for a special appropriation of $300.[5]

The restricted personnel and finances of his Washington office were not the worst of the Attorney General's problems. If his Washington staff was overworked, at least it worked under his control. His subordinates in the field, including the district attorneys, were much more difficult to supervise. Troubles with them arose in part from the manner in which they were paid. Although the district attorneys earned a fixed salary of $200 a year, most of their income came from fees paid by the Government according to the number of cases they conducted. These fees amounted on the average to about $4000 a year, and in some instances even exceeded the compensation of Federal judges.[6] As might be expected, some of the district attorneys responded more enthusiastically to

[3] *Att'y Gen. Ann. Rep.* 15 (1891).

[4] *Att'y Gen. Ann. Rep.* 10 (1891).

[5] *Att'y Gen. Ann. Rep.* 97, 117, 128, 148, 168, 169, xv (1891).

[6] *Att'y Gen. Ann. Rep.* 37, 46-51 (1891). There were seventy-two district attorneys and the appropriation for their regular fees was $280,000; there were in addition special appropriations and special compensations.

piecework pay than to the Attorney General's policies, and in 1890 the Attorney General urged, neither for the first nor last time, that the fee system be abolished. It led to "prosecutions with a view solely to make fees against persons who ought not to be prosecuted at all," and frequently encouraged fraudulent claims.[7] It disposed some district attorneys to avoid difficult cases and to spend little effort searching out and investigating possible crimes. Quite apart from the fee system, the Attorney General could not feel confident that his instructions would be followed. He might admonish, cajole, and scold the district attorneys; he could refuse to furnish temporary assistants and special funds; his six examiners occasionally inspected their accounts and records. But he did not appoint and could not easily dismiss these attorneys, whose positions were secured by the assumption that, as qualified professionals who had special knowledge of local conditions, they were most competent to resolve problems arising within their own districts.

Neither could the Attorney General, even if he wished to, offer much help in the preparation of their cases. Funds available to pay for assistant attorneys were never ample enough to satisfy the many requests, and he had virtually no resources for investigation. Only occasionally would United States marshals investigate local crimes, usually crimes of violence, which were still common and flagrant in the frontier territories. The six examiners of the Washington office were kept busy with routine work and were not, in any case, skilled detectives. Even had there been enough money with which to hire private investigators, the prejudice against Pinkerton agents was so well established that to use their services was out of the question. Investigation was, therefore, always difficult and often impossible. As late as 1903, when a father appealed for help in finding his kidnapped child, the acting Attorney General was forced to reply with the comforting words: "You should furnish me with the names of the parties holding your daughter in bondage, the particular place, and the names of the witnesses by whom the facts can be proved."[8] Such difficulties would have impeded even the most determined enemy of trusts; they could have been overcome only by an Attorney Gen-

[7] *Att'y Gen. Ann. Rep.* xxvii (1891). See also Cummings and McFarland, *Federal Justice* 493-94 (1937). The fee system was finally abolished in 1896.
[8] *Att'y Gen. Ann. Rep.* 374 (1903).

eral who determined to slight his other work and lead his grouped forces into an unknown field.

Enforcement During President Harrison's Administration: 1890-1892

William H. H. Miller, the Attorney General in 1890, moved slowly in administering the new act. Leaving enforcement mainly to the efforts of his district attorneys, he gently prompted them from time to time, encouraging them when it did not cost money, more closely supervising a few important cases. Consistent with this policy, the first case under the Sherman Act was instigated by a minor official and directed against obscure offenders. John Ruhm, the United States Attorney in Nashville, Tennessee, wrote to Miller a month after the Act was passed that he would like to use it against a combination of mine owners and coal dealers who had raised the price of coal in Nashville several cents a bushel higher than it was in Memphis. He added that the ice dealers of Nashville were also "an unlawful combination" and offered to investigate them as well.[9] Though the ice dealers passed out of the picture, the coal suppliers became the defendants in the first Federal antitrust suit.[1]

In answering Ruhm, Miller adopted his characteristic attitude. "If, in your judgment, after careful examination, a case can be made against any of the parties named, then, I take it, it is your duty to cause the necessary affidavit to be made, and have an examination before the commissioner, if that is deemed the proper course." After some further correspondence, Ruhm was authorized to file suit against the combination,[2] but not before he sent the

[9] Letter from Ruhm to Miller, Aug. 7, 1890, Dep't Justice File 8247-J.1-1890.

[1] United States v. Jellico Mountain Coal & Coke Co., 43 Fed. 898 (1890), 46 Fed. 432 (C.C.M.D. Tenn. 1891).

[2] Letter from Miller to Ruhm, Aug. 13, 1890, D.J. Instr. Bk. No. 4, at 224; Letter from Ruhm to Miller, Aug. 15, 1890, D.J. File 8247-c-1890; Letter from Taft to Ruhm, Aug. 25, 1890, D.J. Instr. Bk. No. 5, at 22; Letter from Ruhm to Miller, Aug. 30, 1890, D.J. File 8247-c-1890; Letter from Miller to Ruhm, Sept. 2, 1890, D.J. Instr. Bk. No. 5, at 124.

bill in equity to Washington for approval.[3] It was handed to the Solicitor General, William Howard Taft, who suggested certain changes, especially the addition of a paragraph alleging "that the coal mines owned by the defendant corporations include all those from which it is practicable or profitable to send coal for consumption in the Nashville market. . . ."[4] Taft apparently hoped to strengthen the case by arguing that the Nashville Coal Exchange was not only a combination in restraint of trade but also a monopoly. Ruhm filed the bill with the circuit court, which in due course granted an injunction, observing "that the purposes and intentions of the association could hardly have been more successfully framed to fall within the provisions of the act. . . ."[5]

The *Jellico Coal* victory, unqualified and undisputed, since the defendants failed to appeal, was a hopeful beginning. By itself, however, it did not make a very impressive record for the administration, and the Act was by now almost a year old. A few weeks later, G. A. Copeland, an editor of the Boston *Daily Advertiser,* wrote to Miller asking about his policy. Had he urged the district attorneys to act against the trusts? Had he tried to get evidence against "the well known Standard Oil Trust, the reorganized sugar trust of New Jersey, the cotton oil trust, or any of the better known combinations to restrict interstate trade?" If not, how did he propose to enforce a law that had been shown to be constitutional? These questions, Copeland said, were not intended as criticism; they arose from his "anxiety as a loyal Republican that the mark of the present administration shall be above honest and fair criticism."[6] Miller, who of course recognized the implicit reproach, replied:

No special instructions have been issued to all the District Attorneys, with reference to the anti-trust law. We have, however, made a test case in Tennessee, and have obtained a decision in the United States Circuit Court in that state, sustaining the anti-trust law. Much doubt was expressed as to the validity of the law, and it was thought best, be-

[3] Letter from Ruhm to Miller, Sept. 5, 1890, D.J. File 8247-c-1890; Letter from Miller to Ruhm, Sept. 5, 1890, D.J. Instr. Bk. No. 5, at 186.

[4] Letter from Taft to Ruhm, Sept. 12, 1890, D.J. Instr. Bk. No. 5, at 290.

[5] United States v. Jellico Mountain Coal & Coke Co., 46 Fed. 432, 436 (C.C.M.D. Tenn. 1891).

[6] Letter from Copeland to Miller, June 24, 1891, D.J. File 8247-J.1-1890.

fore taking any general action, to test this question. The District Attorneys of the Districts involving the operations of some of these larger trusts will soon be instructed to investigate and prosecute, if they can find any violations of the law.[7]

The instructions mentioned went out in July and August of 1891,[8] but beyond this the district attorneys were left to their own devices. When the district attorney in St. Louis asked for more detailed information, Miller wrote: "You can act upon your own judgment as to the best way of acquainting yourself with violations of the anti-trust law. Doubtless you will find the Tennessee case reported in Federal Reporter now or very soon."[9] To another district attorney who asked about the meaning of the circular letter of instruction, Miller answered that "it was my intention to authorize and direct District Attorneys, in case there were indications of the existence of any trust or combination in violation of the law, to investigate thoroughly, and if any infraction of the law was found, to prosecute vigorously." The Department had not assigned any agent to make such investigations; "the case is like any other case of an alleged violation of Federal law, no special provision being made for compensation for its investigation or prosecution."[1] And in general this was his policy. Once, when asked whether he would order the Sherman Act to be used against an alleged offender, he replied that he was not in the habit of directing district attorneys to bring particular cases, and had already gone further than was customary in issuing general instructions to enforce the act.[2]

During the first eighteen months, therefore, attempts at enforcement depended on local conditions. Success encouraged the victor to seek fresh glory and inspired others to imitation. Ruhm, for one, was so elated by his first case that even before it was won,

[7] Letter from Miller to Copeland, July 1, 1891, D.J. Misc. Letter Bk. No. 5, at 340.

[8] *E.g.*, Letters from Miller to Dist. Attorneys S.D.N.Y., N.J., E.D. Pa., July 2, 1891, D.J. Instr. Bk., No. 13, at 414; Circular from Att'y Gen. to D.A.'s, July 20, 1891, Circular F-8247-1890.

[9] Letter from Miller to Reynolds, July 15, 1891, D.J. Instr. Bk. No. 14, at 61.

[1] Letter from Miller to Remick, D.A., N.H., July 31, 1891, D.J. Instr. Bk. No. 14, at 314.

[2] Chicago *Tribune* p. 9, col. 1 (Aug. 5, 1891).

he eagerly offered to begin two or three more.[3] Later he tried to enlist himself in the struggle against the whisky trust, and to engage in sole combat against the Southern Wholesale Grocers' Association.[4] These additional ventures were not authorized by his chief, and his glowing promise was never fulfilled. On the strength of his single victory, however, newspapers celebrated him as "one of the keenest and most aggressive officers in the Department of Justice."[5] Some colleagues rushed to follow his example, and for a few weeks it seemed as if the Sherman Act might become a weapon specially adapted to chastising coal merchants. On August 3, 1891, the district attorney in Chicago announced that he was beginning to look into the combination of coal dealers there.[6] On August 4, it was reported that Federal officials in New York State had investigated the Lockport Coal Exchange and the Buffalo coal syndicate.[7] On the same day, the Attorney General was urged to invoke the act against a Tennessee coal mine that was said to have combined with several railroads.[8] In all of these instances, however, the first spurt of energy was the last. A few other district attorneys, on their own initiative, tried their hands against assorted offenders. James Remick, in New Hampshire, unsuccessfully urged a grand jury to indict the bobbin trust, and John Reed made an abortive attempt against the oleomargarine trust.[9]

Meanwhile, the Attorney General passed along information and complaints. He recommended that district attorneys pay "careful attention" to "Drug Trusts."[1] He forwarded to the district attorney

[3] Letter from Ruhm to Miller, Sept. 22, 1890, D.J. File 8247-1890.

[4] Letter from Ruhm to Miller, March 29, 1892, D.J. File 8247-J-1890. Letters from Ruhm to Miller, April 13, May 20, July 18, 1892, in Thorelli, *Federal Antitrust Policy* 375 n. 34.

[5] Chicago *Tribune* p. 9, col. 1 (Aug. 5, 1891).

[6] Chicago *Tribune* p. 1, col. 5 (Aug. 3, 1891).

[7] N.Y. *Times* p. 1, col. 1 (Aug. 4, 1891).

[8] Chicago *Tribune* p. 9, col. 1 (Aug. 5, 1891).

[9] N.Y. *Times* p. 1, col. 4 (Dec. 16, 1891); p. 4, col. 3 (March 10, 1892); Letter from Remick to Miller, Dec. 21, 1891, in Thorelli, *Federal Antitrust Policy* 376 n. 35. Letter from Reed to Miller, Jan. 11, 1892, in Thorelli, *Federal Antitrust Policy* 376 n. 35; Chicago *Tribune* p. 4, col. 3 (Jan. 9, 1892).

[1] Circular from A.G. to D.A.'s, Aug. 13, 1891, D.J. File 8247-1890; Letter from Miller to Marshall, D.A., N.D. Tex., Aug. 13, 1891, D.J. Instr. Bk. No. 14, at 514.

in Iowa a letter complaining about the formation of a "wheat trust," a scheme supposedly sponsored by the Farmer's Alliance whereby farmers would raise the prices of grain by withholding their crops from the market.[2] Having read in the newspapers that a window-glass combine had been formed in Pittsburgh, he asked the attorney there whether he was taking action. The attorney answered that he would promptly investigate if only he were told which newspaper contained the report, to which Miller responded: "I beg to say that I do not now remember in what paper I saw the reference to the alleged violation. . . . However, you will be able, I suppose, to find out the state of matters by inquiry in your city." [3] Judicious and necessary as this reliance on the initiative of district attorneys may have been, it had nevertheless produced only one prosecution. Hostile newspapers were not long in alleging that "department agents" were "trying to make the statute an object of contempt." [4]

This criticism was all the more damaging because none of the major trusts had yet been so much as threatened. Not that Miller had entirely overlooked them. During the summer of 1891, he had ordered the district attorney in Ohio to investigate the Standard Oil Company, referring to "a popular belief that its operations are in gross violation of the purposes of the [antitrust] law"; [5] but nothing further came of it. Moreover, Miller apparently desired that action be brought against the whisky trust, which reached a peak of unpopularity after George Gibson, one of its officers, was indicted for plotting to dynamite a competitor's factory.[6] Here, Miller was frustrated for half a year by Milchrist, the

[2] Letter from Miller to O'Connell, D.A., Iowa, Aug. 14, 1891, D.J. Instr. Bk. No. 14, at 527. Rumors of the plan to form a "trust" were current in the newspapers. See Chicago *Daily News* p. 2, col. 7 (July 29, 1891).

[3] Letter from Miller to Lyon, Sept. 24, 1891, D.J. Instr. Bk. No. 15, at 339; Letter from Lyon to Miller, Sept. 25, 1891, D.J. File 8247-1890; Letter from Miller to Lyon, Oct. 1, 1891, D.J. Instr. Bk. No. 16, at 93.

[4] N.Y. *Times* p. 4, col. 3 (March 10, 1892).

[5] Letter from Miller to Brinsmade, Aug. 14, 1891, D.J. Instr. Bk. No. 14, at 517.

[6] Gibson was arrested on Feb. 11, 1891, and the story was prominent in the newspapers during the following week. See N.Y. *Times* p. 1, col. 3 (Feb. 12, 1891); p. 8, col. 3 (Feb. 13, 1891). See also Gresham, *Life of W. Q. Gresham*, II, 640-47 (1919). Milchrist was responsible for the prosecution, which was unsuccessful, and a final *nolle prosequi* was entered on June 24, 1892, just as the Sherman Act indictment was being quashed. N. Y. *Times* p. 5, col. 6 (June 25, 1892).

district attorney in Chicago, within whose jurisdiction the whisky trust had its headquarters. Although Milchrist kept promising to investigate, he ultimately reported his belief that the trust was immune from the Sherman Act.[7] One day he announced to the newspapers that though the trusts had held "almost absolute sway," "the hour of retribution is at hand."[8] A few days later he told interviewers:

> Now a great many people believe I ought to begin proceedings at once against the so-called whisky trust, but an examination I have made has cleared away an impression I had that the Cattle Feeding and Distilling company is a combination we can reach under the anti-trust law. The company cannot be reached under the Federal statutes as it owns all its distilleries and is simply a large concern. . . .[9]

That this was a plausible view of the matter was demonstrated later, when the courts held that the whisky trust, being a single corporation, could not by its mere existence violate section one of the Sherman Act.[1] At this time, however, Miller apparently did not share Milchrist's conviction. He may have believed, as many did, that a corporation formed by merging the members of a combination would be construed as a combination under the Sherman Act; or he may have thought, as the Government's eventual pleadings against the whisky trust suggest, that a successful attack could be launched, if not against its mere existence, then against its activities. Yet Milchrist would not be persuaded to act. In August he again promised Miller to investigate,[2] and in January of 1892, he signified that he had enough evidence to go before a grand jury. But this report was premature, and for all his earnest investigating, he did not bring the "hour of retribution" closer.[3]

With the beginning of 1892, however, Miller's own efforts began to produce some action. District Attorney Frank Allen in Boston,

[7] Letter from Milchrist to Miller, June 24, 1891, D.J. File 8247-J-1890.

[8] Chicago *Tribune* p. 1, col. 5 (Aug. 3, 1891).

[9] Chicago *Inter Ocean* p. 7, col. 2 (Aug. 5, 1891).

[1] *In re* Greene, 52 Fed. 104 (C.C.S.D. Ohio 1892). See below, pp. 147-49.

[2] Letter from Miller to Milchrist, Aug. 14, 1891, D.J. Instr. Bk. No. 14, at 518; Letter from Milchrist to Miller, Aug. 21, 1891, D.J. File 8247-J-1890.

[3] Chicago *Tribune* p. 5, col. 7 (Jan. 8, 1892). But in his letter to Olney on Oct. 2, 1893, D.J. File 8247-1890, Milchrist said that there had never been enough evidence to support an indictment.

to whom Miller, despairing of Milchrist's willingness, had assigned the duty of destroying the whisky trust, reported that he was ready to proceed. His preparation had been facilitated by unusual assistance: he had been allowed to borrow one of the Department's investigators;[4] and, with this aid, had gathered enough evidence to request an indictment, which a grand jury issued in February.[5] But hope quickly faded. By May, Judge Nelson of the district court in Boston had quashed the indictment, maintaining that it was "clearly insufficient according to the elementary rules of criminal pleading," because, although it alleged that the trust had been engaged in monopolistic activities, it neglected to mention their interstate character, a necessary averment under the statute.[6]

Miller, who had seen Judge Nelson's decision reported in the newspapers, sought an explanation. The defect, Allen wrote, was the fault of a typist who omitted the vital line. "The amount of work which we have had to do in this office, with the really insufficient clerical force renders us at times liable to some slip of this kind, which I am very glad to say, was only a slip and not the result of carelessness in the preparation of the indictment." [7] He could, however, begin again, for, having recognized the weakness in the original accusation as soon as the defense moved to quash, he had prepared an improved and more detailed indictment, which the grand jury returned several days before Nelson's opinion was published.[8] On the strength of this new indictment, the officers of the trust were arrested again. This time they refused to give bond for appearance in Boston, preferring to contest the indictment in

[4] *Att'y Gen. Ann. Rep.* xix, 84-85 (1892); Letter from Allen to Miller, Jan. 11, 1892, D.J. File 8247-1890. Somewhat later, the investigator, D. M. Horton, was seeking evidence against the cordage trust in Chicago; Boston *Herald* p. 3, col. 2 (Mar. 6, 1892).

[5] N.Y. *Times* p. 2, col. 3 (March 1, 1892).

[6] United States v. Greenhut, 50 Fed. 469, 471 (D.C. Mass. 1892).

[7] Letter from Allen to Miller, May 14, 1892, D.J. File 8247-1890. It is difficult to see from the text of the indictment, as quoted in the N.Y. *Times* p. 6, col. 2 (March 3, 1892) how any omission occurring, as Allen put it, "in the last line," could possibly have created the difficulty.

[8] N.Y. *Times* p. 3, col. 2 (March 20, 1892). Letter from Allen to Miller, May 24, 1892, D.J. File 8247-1890. The indictment was returned on May 10 and filed in the circuit court on May 14.

courts in their various districts.[9] The case against the trust thus became three preliminary proceedings in different parts of the country, and now, for the first time, long letters traveled between Washington and the outposts, the Attorney General giving minute advice, the district attorneys carefully revising their plans.[1] All the hard work did not help. Although the new indictment corrected the faults of the original, the judges were evidently captivated by Nelson's opinion, and each of them found more subtle defects rendering it insufficient.[2] The case having collapsed completely by June, Miller and Allen agreed that attempts at resuscitation were pointless.[3]

Miller's second great effort fared little better. Since the beginning of 1892, rumors had been circulating that the sugar trust was about to buy out its last substantial competitors, four refineries in Philadelphia that reputedly produced one third of the country's output.[4] For some time the story was denied by the principals. John Searles, treasurer of the trust, told the stockholders that "so far as the American Sugar-Refining Company is concerned, we have nothing to do with the store on the other corner." Claus Spreckels, one of the independents, said that he would never sell. Even after the contract had been signed, E. C. Knight would only concede that it was "not improbable an understanding [might] . . . be reached" between the trust and him.[5] But, by the end of

[9] N.Y. *Times* p. 6, col. 6 (June 10, 1892); p. 9, col. 5 (June 12, 1892); Letter from Herron, D.A., S.D. Ohio, to Miller, May 24, 1892, D.J. File 8247-1890.

[1] D.J. File 8247-1890, and, *e.g.,* Letter from Miller to Brinsmade, D.A., N.D. Ohio, June 6, 1892; Letter from Miller to Herron, May 27, 1892, June 6, 1892; D.J. Instr. Bk. No. 22, at 318, 206.

[2] *In re* Corning, 51 Fed. 205 (N.D. Ohio 1892); *In re* Terrell, 51 Fed. 213 (C.C.S.D.N.Y. 1892); *In re* Greene, 52 Fed. 104 (C.C.S.D. Ohio 1892). See below, pp. 145-49.

[3] Letter from Wyman, Acting DA., Mass., to Miller, Sept. 6, 1892, D.J. File 8247-1890.

[4] The Government asserted that at this time 65% of the nation's refined sugar was produced by the trust, 33% by the four Philadelphia firms—Knight, Spreckels, Franklin, and Delaware—and the remaining 2% by the Revere Refinery of Boston. Record, United States v. E. C. Knight Co., 156 U.S. 1 (1895), filed March 29, 1894.

[5] N.Y. *Times* p. 3, col. 4 (Jan. 14, 1892); p. 8, col. 2 (March 20, 1892). The contract between the trust and Knight was dated March 4, 1892. Record, p. 83, United States v. E. C. Knight Co., 156 U.S. 1 (1895).

March, it was known that the merger had been arranged—a transaction by which the trust would perfect its control and become, for the time being at least, virtually absolute. No circumstance could more clearly test the willingness of the Government to use the Sherman Act and the power of the Act to control the big trusts. It was not long, therefore, before Owen Scott, a Democrat from Illinois, introduced a resolution in the House of Representatives asking the Attorney General what he proposed to do.[6] Miller's answer was ready; he had anticipated prompting of this sort, and had already begun a suit to invalidate the sale.[7] Yet he had no reply for critics who wondered why a civil suit should be brought against these offenders when the officers of the whisky trust had been indicted as criminals.[8] The sugar trust proceedings moved so slowly, however, that it was almost two years before the case reached the courts, and by then Miller had left office.[9]

There were other defeats on the record. In a criminal action brought against the Mississippi River Valley Lumbermen's Association for concerted action to raise lumber prices, the indictment was found insufficient.[1] And a suit to dissolve the Trans-Missouri Freight Association, one of the most important railroad pools in the west, begun in January of 1892, was lost by autumn.[2] Joseph

[6] 23 *Cong. Rec.* 3366, 3926-29 (1892). The resolution was introduced on April 16, 1892, and adopted on May 4, 1892.

[7] 52d Cong. 1 Sess., H.R. Exec. Doc. No. 225 (1892). Miller reported that suit had been filed on May 2, 1892. Apparently, the resolution came after the action began, for Miller instructed Ingham on April 11 to institute proceedings; and on April 14 the acting Attorney General wrote Ingham asking what aid he would like. Record, p. 2, United States v. E. C. Knight Co., 156 U.S. 1 (1895); D.J. Instr. Bk. No. 21, at 77.

[8] E.g., editorial, N.Y. *Times* p. 4, col. 4 (June 8, 1892).

[9] The defendant's answers were filed between July 1892 and January 1893; the examiner held hearings in October 1892 and January and February 1893; and he filed his report in October 1893. The case was not argued in court until January 19, 1894. Record, pp. 14-75, 208, United States v. E. C. Knight Co., 156 U.S. 1 (1895).

[1] United States v. Nelson, 52 Fed. 646 (D. Minn. 1892). The indictment was returned on Jan. 20, 1892, CCH, *Federal Antitrust Laws* 68 (1952); the warrants issued on Feb. 10, 1892, N.Y. *Times* p. 9, col. 3 (Feb. 11, 1892); p. 1, col. 6 (Feb. 13, 1892); and the opinion was filed on Oct. 10, 1892.

[2] Although the opinion was not delivered until Nov. 28, 1892, United States v. Trans-Missouri Freight Ass'n, 53 Fed. 440 (C.C.D. Kan. 1892), it was

Ady, district attorney in Topeka, who was so devoted to this cause that he paid for an assistant counsel from his own pocket, urged Miller to authorize an appeal, arguing that, if the opinion stood unchallenged, it would provide a complete defense for almost all "of those great aggregations of capital which the public has been used to look upon as a menace to our institutions, and therefore a popular subject of prohibitory legislation."[3] Miller consented; but the appeal was decided against the Government a year later.[4]

Few compensating victories stood out against this string of defeats. In its first effort to apply the Sherman Act to a labor dispute, the Government succeeded in having a general strike in New Orleans enjoined, though the injunction was not granted until months after the strike ended.[5] An indictment against the cash-register trust was upheld, at least in part.[6] Although the decision may have soothed District Attorney Frank Allen, who, following his abortive whisky-trust prosecution, had been suffering from a bad rash of insufficient indictments,[7] the case was eventually

---

generally believed soon after the argument was concluded in August that the decision would favor the defendants. N.Y. *Times* p. 2, col. 5 (Aug. 4, 1892).

[3] Letter from Ady to Miller, Dec. 2, 1892, in Thorelli, *Federal Antitrust Policy* 377-78 (1954). Ady hoped that Miller would ask Congress for a special appropriation to reimburse him. Letter from Ady to Miller, Dec. 1, 1892, D.J. File 8247-1890.

[4] Letter from Miller to Ady, Dec. 6, 1892, D.J. Instr. Bk. No. 26, at 351. United States v. Trans-Missouri Freight Ass'n, 58 Fed. 58 (8th Cir. 1893), *rev'd,* 166 U.S. 290 (1897).

[5] United States v. Workingmen's Amalgamated Council, 54 Fed. 994 (C.C.E.D. La.), *aff'd,* 57 Fed. 85 (5th Cir. 1893). The bill for injunction was authorized on Nov. 8, 1892, and filed on Nov. 10, when the strike was at its height. Letter from Miller to Earhart, D.A. La., Nov. 8, 1892, D.J. Instr. Bk. No. 25, at 457, in Cummings and McFarland, *Federal Justice* 437-38 (1937).

[6] United States v. Patterson, 55 Fed. 605 (C.C.D. Mass. 1893) (demurrer to indictment sustained as to fourteen counts, overruled as to four). Subsequently, a petition for rehearing was granted. 59 Fed. 280 (C.C.D. Mass. 1893). For details of the indictment, see N.Y. *Times* p. 17, col. 2 (July 10, 1892).

[7] Not only were Allen's indictments against the whisky trust held to be insufficient, see pp. 112-13 above, but in United States v. Potter, 56 Fed. 83 (C.C.D. Mass. 1892), a case involving the banking laws, the court sustained demurrers to two of the three indictments for the same reason. The New

dropped.[8] The cash-register proceeding is nevertheless of special interest because it was one of the several cases in which the Government cooperated with private persons injured by trusts. In this instance, the indictment was drawn by the attorney for the Lamson Store Service Company, one of the firms alleging that its business was being destroyed by the trust's coercive acts.[9] On another occasion, when the Mather Electric Company complained that coercive practices of the General Electric Company jeopardized its business, Allen supported the private suit by filing a similar one on behalf of the Government.[1]

When all was said and done, the Government during President Harrison's administration had brought seven antitrust cases to court and won only two. This record caused some anxiety among Republican leaders during the presidential campaign of 1892, and some of them sought to attribute the poor showing to a weakness in the Act itself.[2] But the party platform generally reaffirmed its faith in the statute and endorsed the record of its administration.[3]

York *Times* did not hesitate to suggest that the defects were deliberate: p. 4, col. 2 (June 13, 1892); p. 4, col. 5 (June 16, 1892); p. 4, col. 5; p. 4, col. 3 (June 20, 1892).

[8] The Government entered a *nolle prosequi* on Nov. 10, 1894. *Decrees and Judgments in Federal Anti-trust Cases* 1890-1918, 680.

[9] See Letter from Hoar (Allen's successor as D.A., Mass.) to Att'y Gen., Oct. 11, 1893, in Thorelli, *Federal Antitrust Policy* 378 (1954). Thorelli describes the participation of the Lamson Company as "rather sensational," apparently unaware that the practice was neither novel, irregular, or in this instance, unknown to Miller. See Letter from Miller to Allen, June 3, 1892, D.J. Instr. Bk. No. 22, at 283½.

[1] On July 16, 1892, two bills in equity were presented to Judge Colt of the circuit court in Boston; in one, the Mather Electric Company was the complainant; in the other, the Government. Both bills alleged that the Mather Company stood in danger of losing a contract because the General Electric Company, a combination, fraudulently represented that the Mather Company was infringing its patents and unable to fulfill the contract. Colt refused to grant a temporary injunction, and set a hearing for July 25. N.Y. *Times* p. 16, col. 5 (July 17, 1892). There seems to be no further record of the case.

[2] See N.Y. *Times* p. 4, col. 4 (June 8, 1892) (quoting statement at the Republican national convention by ex-Gov. Brackett of Massachusetts).

[3] McKee, *National Conventions and Platforms* 272 (1901).

The Program of Richard Olney, Attorney General under President Cleveland

OLNEY'S ATTITUDE TOWARD THE SHERMAN ACT

The election of 1892 was fought mainly on the tariff issue. The Democrats emphasized as before their conviction that the tariff was the mother of trusts, though they were willing to agree with their opponents that prohibitive antitrust legislation could be of some value in controlling the combines. Their platform asserted: "[W]e believe [the trusts'] . . . worst evils can be abated by law, and we demand the rigid enforcement of the laws made to prevent and control them, together with such further legislation in restraint of their abuses as experience may show to be necessary."[4] This demand for "rigid enforcement," however sincere, was partly conventional, since no campaign manager could present to the public a proposal for lax enforcement; more important, it was an obvious attack on the record of the previous administration. The Democratic announcement nevertheless failed to recognize that by now any enforcement policy would face the difficult problem of persuading the judiciary that the act was not toothless. Cleveland recognized this difficulty, and in his inaugural address made a more guarded promise to assault the trusts: "To the extent that they can be reached and restrained by the Federal power the General Government should relieve our citizens from their interference and exactions."[5]

Richard Olney, Cleveland's Attorney General, did not believe that the Sherman Act could reach or restrain monopolies to any great extent. Since Olney did not hide his skepticism, he has often been held culpable for the Act's weakness—on the theory that a man who questions the sharpness of his knife really does not want to cut anything. But this argument is inapplicable to an Attorney General, who, like a surgeon, may refuse to work with instruments that might injure rather than cure. The precise question is whether

[4] McKee, *National Conventions and Platforms* 264.

[5] Inaugural Address, March 4, 1893, in Richardson, *Messages & Papers of the Presidents,* IX, 391.

Olney refrained from employing the Act because he believed it to be ineffective or only because he was hostile to its purposes.

The evidence that is supposed to impugn his sincerity is sparse. Much has been made of the fact that among Olney's clients were a number of large corporations, as though a lawyer must always be prejudiced in favor of his clients. Still more sinister conclusions have been drawn from a letter Olney wrote, soon after being offered the cabinet office, to the president of the Chicago, Burlington & Quincy Railroad, which he served as counsel: "Among other things that I want to find out is where I am going to stand with my present clients. . . . I am not a millionaire and cannot take any office of the sort without a good deal of pecuniary sacrifice—just how much I should like to ascertain." The railroad's president answered, "It shall make no difference in our relations except such as you may think it expedient to make." Olney's law partners also approved of his accepting the post.[6] It was perhaps timorous of Olney to worry about the consequences of injuries he might cause his clients while Attorney General—the office is supposed to demand fearless performance of duty. The letter nevertheless testifies to his good faith, since it would have been superfluous had he already decided to suit his future actions to the desires of his clients.

Possibly, however, Olney believed that the Sherman Act was harmful and ought to be repealed. Such a belief is suggested by a letter that he wrote to Secretary of the Treasury Carlisle in 1893 informing him that certain people Olney knew wished to organize an attempt to repeal the Act, and asking for a list of senators "who ought to be persuaded to see the thing in the right light."[7] Certainly, by about 1906, when he wrote a series of articles on the subject, he had come to believe that the policy of the Act was misconceived.[8] His arguments were familiar ones at the time, much like

[6] See Letter from Olney to Perkins, Feb. 16, 1893, in Olney Papers (Lib. Cong.); Letters from Perkins to Olney, Feb. 17, 1893, Feb. 18, 1893, in Olney Papers; Letter from Forbes to Perkins, Feb. 20, 1893, in Olney Papers and Cummings and McFarland, *Federal Justice* 321 (1937).

[7] Letter from Olney to Carlisle, July 5, 1893, in Olney Papers (Lib. Cong.) and Cummings and McFarland, *Federal Justice* 322 (1937).

[8] His views may, of course, have changed in the meantime, perhaps even as a result of his experience as Attorney General. A hint that the later articles represented an earlier view, however, is contained in *Att'y Gen. Ann.*

those advanced by the great trust-buster, Theodore Roosevelt. Olney maintained that while very large firms were beneficial because they could produce so efficiently, they were also dangerous. By concentrating wealth in a few hands, the trusts tended to separate the country into distinct classes of rich and poor, and those who controlled these great accumulations of wealth were powerful enough to represent a menace to free institutions.[9] But it was ridiculous, Olney believed, to try to overcome these defects by outlawing trusts: if they could be successfully prohibited, the community would be deprived of their positive advantages; as a matter of fact, they could not be abolished. In an article published in 1906, Olney argued that their benefits were proved by their persistence:

> . . . the "trust" has earned the right to be regarded as an economic evolution. That it is such there could be no stronger proof than that the "trust" not only continues to exist but to actually grow and flourish. It has encountered such a degree of popular prejudice, has been so bitterly condemned by the press and from the platform, has been such a favorite theme for denunciation by political demagogues, and has been so unrelentingly harried by legislatures and by courts, that its unimpaired and even increased vitality must be deemed to be another signal instance of the ineffectiveness of artificial restraints when opposed to the operation of natural laws.[1]

The problem was how to ensure that the community would enjoy the benefits of trusts without suffering from their "sinister and injurious operation." Olney's answer, an early hint at the "countervailing power" theory, was that the trusts would be sufficiently restrained by labor unions and potential competitors; the government need only deny tariff protection to those who abused it, prevent discrimination by public utilities and railroads, and perhaps eliminate patent monopolies.[2]

The theory of the Sherman Act, Olney had concluded by 1907,

Rep. xxvi-xxvii (1893), where Olney wrote, "all ownership of property is of itself a monopoly. . . ." This remark, so reminiscent of William Graham Sumner, has its counterparts in the later articles, in such phrases as "economic evolution," "artificial restraints and natural law."

[9] Olney, "Labor Unions and Politics," *The Inter-Nation* 23-24 (Dec. 1906); Olney, "Modern Industrialism," *The Inter-Nation* 29, 32 (Feb. 1907).

[1] Olney, "Labor Unions and Politics" 24.

[2] Olney, "Modern Industrialism" 39-42.

was altogether mistaken. In the first place, it sought to prohibit the progressive tendency of capital and of labor to form themselves into large units of operation. If a statute was necessary at all, it ought to be an intelligent and impartial one which would be "in the interests of both classes—, of both labor and capital; [and would] concede the right to combine and organize to each class. . . ."[3] Second, the Sherman Act failed to provide for what might be useful—regulation, rather than a futile and misdirected effort at prohibition. On this point, Olney said:

> The hoary axiom—"Competition is the life of Trade"—in the sense in which it has been heretofore understood and acted upon is, I believe, thoroughly discredited. The competition of the future promises to be a regulated competition—a competition regulated by law, so regulated as to be fair. . . . [I]f business enterprises and the mutual relations of business men ought to be regulated in the interest of fair play, justice, and equality of opportunity and treatment—such assuredly meritorious objects are not to be refused recognition because not within the conception of men of past generations.[4]

In short, Olney believed at this time that the Sherman Act was based on a false economic theory and was therefore incapable of achieving even its misguided goals.

Still, there is no reason to think that this view, assuming Olney already held it in 1893, affected his administration of the Act. He could, and did, amply justify his policy by the antitrust decisions the courts had thus far handed down. In a review of these cases, published in his first annual report, he showed that the Act as it had been interpreted could not really affect many of the supposed offenders. As a matter of constitutional principle, it could govern only businesses engaged in interstate commerce. Nor did it actually affect every one of these, since the courts had held in the *Trans-Missouri* case that the Sherman Act was inapplicable to railroads, and, in one of the whisky trust prosecutions, that it did not reach monopolies unless they were exclusive. "[T]he cases popularly supposed to be covered by the statute," he wrote, "are almost without exception obviously not within its provisions,

[3] Olney, "Modern Industrialism" 42.

[4] Address by Olney before the Merchants Club of Boston, 1913, in James, *Richard Olney and his Public Service* 190-91 (1923).

since to make them applicable not merely must capital be brought together and applied in large masses, but the accumulation must be made by means which impose a legal disability upon others from engaging in the same trade or industry." Since this was for the moment the unvarying opinion of the courts, the Attorney General quite properly announced that he would not prosecute where statutory authority seemed so feeble.[5]

THE SUGAR TRUST TEST

Although he had stated a position on which he could quite easily have rested, Olney saw fit to test his conclusions. Despite his estimate of how the courts would interpret the Act and regardless of any views he might have had about the wisdom of Congress's antitrust policy, he decided to obtain a more authoritative judgment by bringing a test case before the Supreme Court as soon as possible.[6] For this test, he chose the suit against the sugar trust. It was ideal for his purpose. It could be brought to trial quickly, since the preliminary preparations were finished. Briefs and answers had been filed, the examiner had completed his hearings, and Ellery Ingham, the district attorney at Philadelphia, who had been in charge of the proceedings since they began, was ready to proceed.[7] Moreover, the sugar trust was extremely unpopular and as clearly monopolistic as any. Until such an offender had been tried, a doubt would always remain about the Act's meaning.

The subsequent history of the Sugar Trust case bore out Olney's judgment of the law's ineffectiveness. During 1894 the Govern-

[5] *Att'y Gen. Ann. Rep.* xxvii (1893). The decisions to which Olney referred as limiting the scope of the act were: United States v. Trans-Missouri Freight Ass'n, 53 Fed. 440 (C.C.D. Kan. 1892), *aff'd,* 58 Fed. 58 (8th Cir. 1893), *rev'd,* 166 U.S. 290 (1897); *In re* Greene, 52 Fed. 104 (C.C.S.D. Ohio 1892) (opinion by Jackson, J.).

[6] *Att'y Gen. Ann. Rep.* xxvii (1893).

[7] Olney entered office on March 6, 1893. The bill of complaint in United States v. E. C. Knight Co., 156 U.S. 1 (1895), had been filed May 2, 1892; answers had been entered Jan. 17, 1893; and the examiner had completed his hearings on Feb. 8, 1893. The examiner was apparently responsible for much of the delay from that time forward, for his report was not filed until Oct. 27, 1893. See Record, pp. 1, 72, 75, United States v. E. C. Knight Co., *supra.*

ment was defeated in the circuit court and then in the court of appeals.[8] And, early the following year, the Supreme Court upheld the lower court decisions. The court ruled that even if the trust monopolized the manufacture of sugar, it had not been shown to have a monopoly of interstate commerce and therefore was not subject to the Federal statute.[9] This outcome was exactly what Olney's analysis of previous decisions had suggested to him. As he wrote to his secretary after the final decision was published: "You will have observed that the government has been defeated in the Supreme Court on the trust question. I always supposed it would be and have taken the responsibility of not prosecuting under a law I believed to be no good." [1] That he was justified in not enforcing the Act if he believed it was ineffective, seems beyond doubt, and the defeat in the sugar trust test seemed to vindicate his policy.[2]

[8] United States v. E. C. Knight Co., 60 Fed. 306 (C.C.E.D. Pa.), *aff'd,* 60 Fed. 934 (3d Cir. 1894).

[9] United States v. E. C. Knight Co., 156 U.S. 1 (1895).

[1] Letter from Olney to Straw, Jan. 22, 1895 in Olney Papers (Lib. Cong.) and Cummings & McFarland, *Federal Justice* 323 (1937). He made a similar statement to the press. See N.Y. *Times* p. 16, col. 2 (Jan. 22, 1895).

[2] The seriousness of the defeat, and the Supreme Court's insistence that the case presented before it did not involve interstate commerce, has led many critics to maintain that the Government was not well prepared. Senator Edmunds held that the bill of complaint did not sufficiently stress the sugar trust's activities in interstate commerce, Letter from Edmunds to Sleicher, Jan. 2, 1903, in 36 *Cong. Rec.* 1901 (1903), and William Howard Taft later agreed; Taft, *The Anti-Trust Act and the Supreme Court* 59 (1914). Even if this be true—and by no means is it certain that greater emphasis on the jurisdictional point in the bill of complaint would have impelled the Supreme Court to decide for the Government—it is no reflection on Olney, for the bill was filed on May 2, 1892, almost a year before Olney became Attorney General. See note 7, p. 121 above. Nevertheless, later attempts to explain the defeat assumed an increasingly personal flavor, as in Nevins' remark that "Olney allowed the suit against the Sugar Trust to go to trial in deplorably weak form. . . ." Nevins, *Grover Cleveland* 722 (1932). But there is no evidence to show that the case was carelessly prepared, or that Olney, as Nevins implies, allowed it to proceed knowing that it had remediable flaws.

Still less warranted is the conclusion drawn by Mrs. Gresham and endorsed by Thorelli that District Attorney Ingham deliberately sabotaged the Government's case, omitting evidence on interstate commerce because he had been bribed by the trust. Gresham, *Life of W. Q. Gresham,* II, 653 (1919); Thorelli, *Federal Antitrust Policy* 387 (1954). No doubt the sugar trust was capable of such maneuvering; in fact, at the very time the case was before

THE PULLMAN STRIKE

After the sugar trust suit, Olney allowed the Sherman Act to be used only once—during the Pullman strike of 1894. The dispute began in May, when workers at the Pullman factory struck against a cut in wages. The American Railway Union, led by Eugene Debs, decided to support their fellows by refusing to handle after June 26 any train carrying Pullman cars; the boycott quickly became a general railroad strike throughout the Central and Western states. The Federal Government was drawn in when the acting Postmaster General notified Olney that strikers were obstructing the passage of the United States mails. Olney immediately instructed United States attorneys to apply to Federal courts for orders restraining this interference, and several courts issued in-

---

the Supreme Court, a congressional committee was investigating charges that the trust had bribed senators to pass more favorable tariff rates. Moreover, according to an unsupported statement by Mrs. Gresham, Ingham was later convicted for complicity in counterfeiting. Gresham, II, 653.

These two indications of criminality, however, form the basis of a conclusion which, apart from its logical defects, is falsified by other facts. First, Ingham never had a free hand in preparing the case. The original bill seems to have been drawn up by Solicitor General Charles H. Aldrich. Thorelli, 386. A special counsel, former Solicitor General Samuel F. Phillips, appeared at Ingham's side during most of the proceedings. (He was appointed Sept. 13, 1892, by Miller, *Att'y Gen. Ann. Rep.* xx, 249 (1892), and was present at the pretrial hearings between October 1892 and February 1893, as well as before the court of appeals, Record, p. 75, United States v. E. C. Knight Co., 156 U.S. 1 [1895].) And when the case came before the Supreme Court, Ingham took no part at all. Second, and even more significant, the judges who heard the case were not unanimous in holding the evidence of interstate commerce insufficient. Justice Harlan thought it was ample. See United States v. E. C. Knight Co., 156 U.S. at 43-44 (dissent). And the trial court was convinced by the evidence that the trust sold sugar throughout the country and that its object in buying the refineries was "to obtain a greater influence or more perfect control over the business of refining *and selling sugar in this country.*" United States v. E. C. Knight Co., 60 Fed. 306, 308 (C.C.E.D. Pa. 1894). (Emphasis added.) This fact, often forgotten, tends to vitiate allegations that the Government failed altogether to introduce evidence on commerce. The opinions suggest that the fatal flaw was elsewhere: since the complaint was directed against the acquisition of refineries, the case was about refining and not about the trust's commercial activities as such; on this view, no amount of evidence on commerce would have been enough to change a decision directed to the essence of the complaint. See below, pp. 161-67.

junctions against the strikers. During the first week of July, the situation deteriorated. Mobs gathered at railroad yards, blocked the rails, overturned cars, and jammed switches; they refused to disperse and, in some instances, went on to burn cars, bridges, and depots, to derail locomotives, and to attack police and deputy marshals. Vigorous action of some sort had to be taken and, after the strikers had refused to obey Federal court injunctions, the Government decided to command obedience by sending in Federal troops.[3]

That Olney should have authorized action under the Sherman Act in such circumstances may seem especially incongruous, for he had written only a few months earlier:

> It should, perhaps, be added, in this connection—as strikingly illustrating the perversion of a law from the real purpose of its authors—that in one case the combination of laborers known as a "strike" was held to be within the prohibition of the statute, and that in another, rule 12 of the Brotherhood of Locomotive Engineers was declared to be in violation thereof.[4]

Moreover, when, in May 1893, he had been asked to authorize proceedings against the Tonawanda Lumber Shovers' Union—which had been accused of interfering with the business of certain importers—he had refused. Maintaining that the Sherman Act was not intended as a sanction against labor organizations, he had said that to employ the Act in this particular instance would unfairly place "the whole power of the federal government on one side of a civil controversy, of doubtful merits, between the employers of labor on one hand and the employed on the other."[5] But, in fact, the plan of introducing the Sherman Act into the Pullman strike was not of his making.

Olney's first reaction to the Postmaster General's complaint

[3] The official correspondence on the Pullman strike is gathered in *Att'y Gen. Ann. Rep.* App. (1896) [cited as 1896 Appendix]. For a systematic account, see Lindsey, *The Pullman Strike* (1942).

[4] *Att'y Gen. Ann. Rep.* xxvii-xxviii (1893). The cases Olney referred to are United States v. Workingmen's Amalgamated Council, 54 Fed. 994 (C.C.E.D. La.), *aff'd,* 57 Fed. 85 (5th Cir. 1893), and Waterhouse v. Comer, 55 Fed. 149 (C.C.W.D. Ga. 1893).

[5] Letter from Olney to Alexander, D.A., N.D.N.Y., May 12, 1893, D.J. Instr. Bk. No. 30, at 71, in Cummings & McFarland, *Federal Justice* 438 (1937).

was not to give precise instructions to the district attorneys, but rather to send them an order in quite general terms:

See that the passage of regular trains carrying United States mails in the usual and ordinary way, as contemplated by the act of Congress and directed by the Postmaster-General, is not obstructed. Procure warrants or any other available process from United States courts against any and all persons engaged in such obstruction and direct marshal to execute the same by such number of deputies or such posse as may be necessary.[6]

Two days later, however, he particularly reminded Milchrist, the district attorney in Chicago, which was the center of the tumult, of a series of precedents that he should consider in applying for a restraining order. The cases Olney listed clearly indicate that he did not have the Sherman Act in mind. All of the precedents tended to demonstrate that Federal courts could restrain the strikers without invoking the authority of any statute; two of them involved the Sherman Act, but in both cases it was extraneous to the court's theory; and, most significantly, the *Workingmen's Council* case was conspicuous by its absence.[7] Milchrist clearly saw the point

[6] Telegram from Olney to Milchrist, June 28, 1894, in 1896 Appendix 55. The text of the order is similar to that of the directive Olney issued when western counterparts of Coxey's Army seized trains in April 1894; this suggests that Olney contemplated using the same remedies, which in the former case had not included any action under the Sherman Act. See Cummings & McFarland, *Federal Justice* 439 (1937); McMurray, *Coxey's Army*, c. 10 (1929).

[7] See Telegram from Olney to Milchrist, June 30, 1894, in 1896 Appendix 57. Olney cited: United States v. Clark, 25 Fed. Cas. 443 (No. 14805) (E.D. Pa. 1877); United States v. Claypool, 14 Fed. 127 (W.D. Mo. 1882); United States v. Kirby, 74 U.S. (7 Wall.) 482 (1868); Toledo, A.A. & N.M. Ry. v. Pennsylvania Co., 54 Fed. 730 (C.C.N.D. Ohio 1893); Blindell v. Hagan, 54 Fed. 40 (C.C.E.D. La.), *aff'd,* 56 Fed. 696 [miscited in Olney's telegram as 596] (5th Cir. 1893); Waterhouse v. Comer, 55 Fed. 149 (C.C. W.D. Ga. 1893); Farmers' Loan & Trust Co. v. Northern Pac. R.R., 60 Fed. 803 (C.C.E.D. Wis. 1894) [miscited as 16 Fed. 803].

In the first three of these cases, courts ruled on indictments for obstructing the mail in contravention of Rev. Stat. §3995 (1875) (now 18 U.S.C. §1701 [1952]). In the *Toledo Ry.* case, the court enjoined a strike on the authority of the Interstate Commerce Act, 24 Stat. 379 (1887), 49 U.S.C. §§1-22 (1952). The *Blindell* case held that a court of equity could enjoin a strike if the threatened damages were irremediable at law. And *Waterhouse* and *Farmers' Loan* were precedents for the proposition that a court of equity could enjoin a strike directed against property being administered by a re-

and answered that he would apply for an injunction on the authority of the Interstate Commerce Act.[8] During the next few days, however, he became persuaded that the Interstate Commerce Act did not apply to laborers. He therefore asked permission to proceed on the authority of the Sherman Act and the *Workingmen's Council* case, and added an alarming comment on the situation: "The general paralysis of interstate and general business warrants this course. Very little mail and no freight moving. Marshal is using all his force now owing to mob and obstruction of tracks. . . . His force is clearly inadequate." [9]

Milchrist's view of the strike as a critical emergency was widespread; the news of disorder, frightening enough in itself, awakened memories of the succession of violent incidents over the past few years—the Haymarket riot, the Coeur d'Alene troubles, the Homestead strike, and the march of Coxey's Army—incidents which, like the present strike, seemed to verge on armed insurrec-

---

ceiver under its superintendence. The Sherman Act was mentioned in the *Blindell* case, but the court there held the act inapplicable since it did not authorize private parties to sue for injunctions. In the *Waterhouse* case, the Sherman Act and the Interstate Commerce Act were said to make strikes against interstate railroads illegal, but this view was *obiter;* the court was able to base its objection to rule 12 of the Brotherhood of Locomotive Engineers, which authorized secondary boycotts, on a broader principle: "[I]f there were no statutory enactments upon the subject, no court of equity could justifiably direct its receiver to enter into a contract with a body of men who hold themselves bound to repudiate their contract, and disregard a grave public duty, because of real or alleged grievances, which some other person or corporation, not a party to the contract, inflicts or is alleged to inflict, not upon a party to the contract, but upon somebody else." (55 Fed. 149, 158).

[8] Telegram from Milchrist to Olney, June 30, 1894, in 1896 Appendix 57.

[9] Letter from Milchrist to Olney, July 1, 1894, in 1896 Appendix 60-61. Milchrist prepared the bill after consulting with the railroads' attorneys, and Thorelli, who exaggerates the influence on the proceedings of Walker, the government's special counsel, makes the very doubtful suggestion that the conference was "presumably instigated by Walker himself." Thorelli, *Federal Antitrust Policy* 390. As evidence to the contrary, Walker was not in Chicago during the early days of the strike and did not return until after the conference; moreover, Milchrist had been conferring with the railroad attorneys several days before Walker was appointed special counsel. See Letter from Milchrist to Olney, June 30, 1894; Telegram from Milchrist to Olney, July 2, 1894; Telegram from Walker to Olney, July 2, 1894; all in 1896 Appendix 57-58, 63.

tion and aroused the anger of responsible men. William Howard Taft's views were not at all extreme when he wrote to his wife:

The situation in Chicago is very alarming and distressing and until they have had much bloodletting, it will not be better. The situation is complicated by the demagogues and populists . . . who are continually encouraging resistance to federal authority. Word comes tonight that thirty men have been killed by the federal troops. Though it is a bloody business, everybody hopes that it is true.[1]

In circumstances like these, an Attorney General could not insist too firmly on his own view of the Act's proper functions. Besides, the district attorneys were primarily responsible for getting the indictments, and Olney could not tie their hands by denying them the use of a statute which, by judicial construction, was applicable. Hence, a few days before Milchrist's request, when Charles Garter, district attorney in San Francisco, expressed his belief that the strike violated the Sherman Act, Olney had answered: "Act upon your view of the law, which is certainly sustained by adjudications so far as they have gone." [2] Although the tone of the message suggests that Olney did not share that view of the law or consider the decisions authoritative, he evidently felt that the time was not one for cavil. Presumably for the same reason, when Milchrist requested similar authority, Olney approved, and soon was recommending that other district attorneys follow Milchrist's successful example.[3]

Olney's reluctance to base the injunction on the Sherman Act is indicated also by his suggestion to Walker in September, when the strike was over and Debs and other union officers were being tried for violating the injunction, that he need not rest the Government's case solely on the Act. Courts of equity, he argued, had always exercised the power to enjoin the obstruction of public highways at the instance of the Government, and railroads were in

[1] Letter from W. H. Taft to Helen H. Taft, July 7, 1894, in Pringle, *William Howard Taft,* I, 128 (1939).

[2] Telegram from Garter to Olney, June 28, 1894; Telegram from Olney to Garter, June 29, 1894; both in 1896 Appendix 17-18.

[3] See, *e.g.*, Telegram from Olney to Garter, D.A., N.D. Cal., July 2, 1894; Telegram from Olney to Cleveland, D.A., S.D. Ohio, July 3, 1894; both in 1896 Appendix 20, 171 and *passim*.

effect public highways.[4] Walker used this argument in addition to the one founded on the Sherman Act, and Judge Woods of the circuit court in Chicago sustained the injunction on both grounds.[5] The following spring, when the case came before the Supreme Court, Olney gave Assistant Attorney General Edward B. Whitney the responsibility for preparing the brief and presenting the discussion insofar as it bore on the Sherman Act.[6] He himself maintained in his oral argument that, though the Act did apply, "under all the circumstances of this case, it seems to me quite inadvisable that the jurisdiction of the court below should be thought to turn upon the Government's technical relation to the mails and the mail bags, or should appear to depend upon the novel provisions of an experimental piece of legislation like the Act of 1890."[7] Reverting to the theory he had implied in his first instructions to Milchrist and had more recently suggested to Walker, he maintained that Federal courts had broad powers to restrain interference with interstate commerce and thus needed no special statute to support them. The Supreme Court may have accepted this argument; in any event, it apparently decided the case without relying on the Sherman Act.[8]

OLNEY'S POLICY AFTER THE PULLMAN STRIKE

Olney authorized no other Sherman Act cases. During the Pullman strike, District Attorney George J. Denis at Los Angeles took the unusual step of serving an injunction on officials of the Southern Pacific Railroad in order to force them, as he said, "to move mails and interstate commerce, which they can do, but are afraid of losing their own men after the strike is quelled."[9] About a week later, Denis and his special assistant, Joseph Call, reported

[4] Letter from Olney to Walker, Sept 24, 1894, in Lindsey, *The Pullman Strike* 289-20 (1942).

[5] United States v. Debs, 64 Fed. 724 (C.C.N.D. Ill. 1894) (finding the defendants guilty of contempt).

[6] James, *Richard Olney and his Public Service* 57.

[7] Oral Argument of Attorney General, p. 2, *In re* Debs, 158 U.S. 564 (1895).

[8] *In re* Debs, 158 U.S. 564 (argued March 25, 26, 1895; decided May 27, 1895).

[9] Telegram from Denis to Olney, July 8, 1894, in 1896 Appendix 29.

to Olney that the strike was over in their district and that the strikers were "falling over each other to get back to work." But, having begun with assurance that everything was under control, they continued: "The situation, in our opinion, demands enforcement of act of July 2, 1890, against unlawful combines of railroads and transportation companies, and we respectfully suggest bringing suit in name of Government to enforce that law."[1] Olney, thinking that the "situation" was a continued refusal of the Southern Pacific to run trains, authorized "any appropriate suits." He soon discovered, however, that Denis and Call had filed suit to dissolve the Southern Pacific Company, which they alleged was a corporation comprising thirty-five railroads combined to restrain interstate commerce.[2] Olney immediately assured the newspapers that this was not at all what he had meant to authorize.[3] Informed by newsmen of Olney's comment, Denis stated that, considering the authorization of the Attorney General and the notoriety of the Southern Pacific, he and Call "could see no more appropriate time to enforce this all-but-forgotten law. . . . I am absolutely sure that [the Attorney General] . . . will approve of my course when he has an opportunity to read my report of facts to him." [4] Call wrote to Olney in a similar vein, urging that the strike had left "slumbering discontent," and that nothing had "done so much to alienate the people of the Pacific Coast from the Government of the United States as the oppressions of [the Southern Pacific] monopoly upon these people."[5] Olney still replied that the complaint was indefensible and must be dismissed. The Sherman Act was "prospective in its operation; could not, if it undertook to do so, make crimes out of transactions long passed and not criminal when they occurred." He made one concession: Denis might, "after acquiring adequate knowledge of the facts and making

[1] Telegram from Denis and Call to Olney, July 14, 1894, in 1896 Appendix 33.

[2] Telegram from Olney to Denis, July 14, 1894, in 1896 Appendix 33. The suit was filed on July 16; according to Denis, Olney heard about it from complaining officials of the Southern Pacific. See N.Y. *Times* p. 5, col. 4 (July 19, 1894).

[3] Dispatch from Washington, dated July 17, 1894, reported in N.Y. *Times* p. 4, cols. 4-5 (Aug. 4, 1894).

[4] N.Y. *Times* p. 5, col. 4 (July 19, 1894).

[5] Letter from Call to Olney, July 18, 1895, in 1896 Appendix 34-35.

careful study of the law and decided cases," prepare a new bill, but he must submit it to the Department before filing it in court.[6] Denis countered by arguing that the question of retroactive application of the law did not arise, since his bill in equity sought not to punish the defendants for their past actions but to invalidate certain of their present contracts.[7] Nevertheless, he dismissed the bill [8] and did not prepare a new one.

On another occasion, R. B. Glenn, the district attorney in Winston,[9] North Carolina, reported a "terrible clamor" for prosecuting the American Tobacco Company and submitted for approval a proposed indictment. At first Olney thought it best to delay for a while; "it would seem wholly unwise not to wait until the Supreme Court is heard from." After the Court decided the *Sugar Trust* case, Glenn continued to urge action, maintaining that his case against the tobacco trust was much stronger; but Olney considered the question closed.[1]

The Policy of Attorney General Judson Harmon

In June of 1895, Olney became Secretary of State and was succeeded as Attorney General by Judson Harmon. The basic fact controlling antitrust policy remained the same: the *Sugar Trust* decision stood as a great obstacle to further prosecution. Harmon recognized that, according to the decision, trusts, "although they may unlawfully control production and prices of articles in general use, cannot be reached under this law merely because they are combinations and monopolies, nor because they may engage in in-

[6] Telegram from Olney to Denis, Aug. 1, 1894, in 1896 Appendix 36.

[7] Letter from Denis to Olney, Aug. 2, 1894, in 1896 Appendix 37-40.

[8] Telegram from Denis to Olney, Aug. 4, 1894, in 1896 Appendix 40.

[9] Winston-Salem after the towns of Winston and Salem were consolidated in 1913.

[1] Letters from Glenn to Olney, Aug. 6, 1894, Dec. 4, 1894, March 14, 1895; Letter from Olney to Glenn, Dec. 12, 1894; all in Thorelli, *Federal Antitrust Policy* 338. Thorelli conveys the impression that Olney finally vetoed the project during a conference which took place "more than a year" after Glenn first raised the subject, that is, more than a year after August 6, 1894. Thorelli does not supply a more precise date for the conference but, certainly, if it was held on or after August 6, 1895, Olney was not involved, for he resigned the attorney generalship on June 7, 1895.

terstate commerce as one of the incidents of their business."[2] This principle, he felt, largely tied his hands, but not altogether, for the Act might yet be held applicable to combinations the heart of whose business was in interstate commerce. Certainly, it would be worth testing the possibility by an appeal. Soon after arriving in Washington, therefore, he looked through the docket to select, in his words, "a number of cases to argue myself." He found the *Trans-Missouri Freight Association* case, in which the circuit court had held that the Sherman Act was inapplicable to railroads, and the court of appeals, without questioning the lower court's judgment, had gratuitously added that the Act did not prohibit an agreement regulating, but not suppressing, competition. The case had impressed Harmon a few months earlier when, in a private suit he was then conducting, it was cited as authority against him. He was convinced at once that the decision was incorrect, and decided as Attorney General to test his view in the Supreme Court.[3]

Before the Supreme Court heard the *Trans-Missouri* appeal, however, Harmon was forced to begin a new suit involving a similar railroad pool. Senator William Eaton Chandler of New Hampshire, who had become a vigorous antagonist of railroad abuses, wrote to Harmon in August 1895 to complain about an agreement that was then being negotiated among the leading eastern railroads. The Joint Traffic Association which they proposed to form would establish uniform rates, allocate traffic, and distribute earnings; surely, wrote Chandler, the Attorney General should prevent the formation of "the most gigantic trust and combination the world has ever known."[4] Harmon answered that proceedings against the Association, as he gathered from newspaper accounts, would raise the same questions as the *Trans-Missouri* case. "I presume," he continued, "that the present arrangement, whatever it is, has been

[2] *Att'y Gen. Ann. Rep.* 13 (1895).

[3] Letter from Harmon to Macfarlane, Jan. 2, 1896, D.J. Instr. Bk. No. 60, at 448. Harmon made the decision to appeal before August 24, 1895. See Letter from Harmon to Chandler, Aug. 24, 1895, in Senate Committee on Interstate Commerce, *Hearing in Relation to the Agreement of the Joint Traffic Association,* 55th Cong. 1st Sess., S. Doc. No. 64, 33 (1897); United States v. Trans-Missouri Freight Ass'n, 53 Fed. 440 (C.C.D. Kan. 1892), *aff'd,* 58 Fed. 58 (8th Cir. 1893), *rev'd,* 166 U.S. 290 (1897).

[4] Letter from Chandler to Harmon, Aug. 19, 1895, referred to in Letter from Chandler to McKenna, March 27, 1897, D.J. File 759-1887.

carefully brought within the lines of the decision of Judge Sanborn in that case."[5] Although Harmon was on firm ground in refusing to institute a new action until the appeal was settled, he failed to make his position clear to Chandler. Instead of carefully explaining his views and offering to investigate, he said only that the Association agreement was probably within the law and that, "until the pending case is decided and the law settled in the Supreme Court, it does not seem to me that there is anything for this Department to do in the matter." Chandler, having received a similar reply from the Interstate Commerce Commission, wrote to Harmon:

The promptitude with which you have assumed, in behalf of the railroad conspirators, that their coming trust combination is a successful violation of the criminal laws of the United States is only equaled by the celerity with which Commissioner Morrison has decided that the Interstate Commerce Commission knows nothing whatever about the notorious pooling agreement and cannot find out anything until it has gone into operation.[6]

Chandler spent the next four months reminding the President, Attorney General, and Commission of the forthcoming iniquity, which, as he repeated with increasing anger, they were doing nothing to forestall.[7]

In time, William Morrison, chairman of the ICC, began to investigate the matter. He asked railroad officials to inform him of their exact plans; after much prodding, they sent a copy of the completed agreement[8]—which arrived on December 24, eight days before it was to become effective. On December 26, Morrison officially requested Harmon to institute proceedings against the Asso-

[5] Letter from Harmon to Chandler, Aug. 24, 1895, in Senate Committee on Interstate Commerce, *Hearing,* 55th Cong. 1st Sess., S. Doc. No. 64, 33.

[6] Letter from Chandler to Harmon, in Richardson, *William E. Chandler, Republican* 497 (1940). Although Richardson does not give the date, the letter is probably the one sent on August 30, 1895, and referred to in Letter from Chandler to McKenna, March 27, 1897, D.J. File 759-1887.

[7] The voluminous correspondence between Chandler and the ICC is reprinted in *Letter of the Chairman of the I.C.C. Respecting an Agreement to Form a Joint Traffic Association,* 54th Cong. 1st Sess., S. Doc. No. 39 (1895). Richardson, *William E. Chandler, Republican* 497, cites five letters from Chandler to Cleveland, written between August 20th and November 27th.

[8] See *Letter of the Chairman,* 54th Cong. 1st Sess., S. Doc. No. 39, 16-19.

ciation under the Interstate Commerce Act: "This contract, agreement, or arrangement is, we believe, in conflict with the Act to regulate commerce and cannot be carried into effect without violating the provisions of said Act."[9] The ICC decision, seemingly reached in great haste during the day or two after the Commissioner first saw the articles of agreement, was actually not so spontaneous. A few days earlier, the Senate had passed a resolution directing the Commission to report on the entire matter.[1] Morrison had submitted a report which emphasized the difficulties of taking any action, and had then discussed the matter with Harmon. Both of them apparently felt that senatorial pressure required some positive action on their part, no matter how doubtful the outcome. As Harmon wrote to the district attorney whom he put in charge of the case, "we both agreed that as this contract was undoubtedly drawn with great care by able counsel who doubtless believe that it is not contrary to law, the only proper course which can now be pursued is to test the lawfulness of the agreement by civil proceedings."[2] In other words, since the administration was forced to take action against its better judgment, it would use the mildest process it could. Having reached this decision in consultation with Harmon, Morrison returned to his office and wrote the letter officially requesting enforcement, which all five commissioners formally approved.[3] Harmon forwarded the ICC request to the district attorney in New York City, Wallace Macfarlane, with the suggestion that, though he himself had given the applicability of the Sherman Act "no thorough consideration," Macfarlane should look into the problem and report his conclusions.[4]

Subsequently, Macfarlane communicated his opinion that the Association agreement probably violated both the Interstate Com-

[9] Letter from Morrison to Harmon, Dec. 26, 1895, D.J. File 759-87, in *Letter of the Chairman,* 54th Cong. 1st Sess., S. Doc. No. 64, pt. 2, at 1 (where, however, the date is erroneously given as Dec. 27th).

[1] 28 *Cong. Rec.* 253-54 (1895).

[2] Letter from Harmon to Macfarlane, D.A., S.D.N.Y., Dec. 27, 1895, D.J. Instr. Bk. No. 60, at 344.

[3] Senate Committee on Interstate Commerce, *Hearing,* 55th Cong. 1st Sess., S. Doc. No. 64, 24.

[4] Letter from Harmon to Macfarlane, Dec. 27, 1895, D.J. Instr. Bk. No. 60, at 344.

merce Act and the Sherman Act, but he wondered about the effect of the *Trans-Missouri* decision.[5] Harmon agreed that the decision might cause trouble, but observed that it was being appealed and that nothing more could be done. "If, on the strength of it, the other side succeeded in defeating an application for a preliminary injunction the responsibility will be on the court and not on us. . . ."[6] The suit was authorized, and the bill was filed on January 9, 1896. The proceedings were delayed, however, when all but two of the judges in the circuit disqualified themselves because they owned stock or bonds of the defendant railroads.[7] The case was finally heard in April, the court deciding both that the Government had no power under the Interstate Commerce Act to restrain the railroads' agreement, and that their agreement, according to the *Trans-Missouri* decision, did not violate the Sherman Act.[8] Macfarlane planned to ask the court of appeals simply to affirm the decision formally, in order to avoid unnecessary labor and delay in bringing the case before the Supreme Court. But since the members of the Senate Committee on Interstate Commerce were highly displeased that the Government should, as they thought, practically confess the weakness of its position, the case was eventually argued before the court of appeals, which, in a memorandum decision, immediately affirmed the lower court.[9] The *Joint Traffic* case came before the Supreme Court in March 1897, just before that Court published its opinion in *Trans-Missouri*.[1]

In the meantime, although the *Trans-Missouri* decisions obstructed attacks on railroad pools and the *Sugar Trust* decision impeded action against manufacturing monopolies, the Attorney

[5] Letter from Macfarlane to Harmon, Dec. 31, 1895, D.J. File 18467-1895.

[6] Letter from Harmon to Macfarlane, Jan. 2, 1896, D.J. Instr. Bk. No. 60, at 448.

[7] Senate Committee on Interstate Commerce, *Hearing*, 55th Cong. 1st Sess., S. Doc. No. 64, 4-6.

[8] United States v. Joint Traffic Ass'n, 76 Fed. 895 (C.C.S.D.N.Y. 1896), *aff'd mem.*, 89 Fed. 1020 (2d Cir. 1897), *rev'd*, 171 U.S. 505 (1898).

[9] Senate Committee on Interstate Commerce, *Hearing*, 55th Cong. 1st Sess., S. Doc. No. 64, 12-13. The case was argued on March 18-19, 1897. See N.Y. *Times* p. 12, col. 2 (March 19, 1897); p. 12, col. 1 (March 20, 1897). The memorandum decision, United States v. Joint Traffic Ass'n, 89 Fed. 1020 (2d Cir. 1897), *rev'd*, 171 U.S. 505 (1898), was published March 19, 1897.

[1] United States v. Trans-Missouri Freight Ass'n, 166 U.S. 290 (1897).

General could still feel free to operate against combinations "in restraint of trade." An indictment brought against a combination of coal merchants in Salt Lake City had the easy success that seemed specially ordained for actions of this sort from the *Jellico Mountain Coal* case onward.[2] An injunction was sought against livestock dealers who had formed the Kansas City Live-Stock Exchange, and this too was successful in the lower court.[3] Finally, at the urging of James Bible, district attorney at Chattanooga, Harmon authorized a suit against a combination of manufacturers of cast-iron pipe.[4] His response to Bible on this occasion shows clearly the lines of his policy. After apologizing for delay in answering, he wrote:

> I have no objection whatever to your proceeding against the people who are engaged in operating the pipe trust, but, on the contrary, highly approve such action—if you can find the proof to make it successful. The way the law has been construed, especially by Judge Jackson [in] *in re* Greene, and by the Superior Court in U.S. vs. Knight, has made it pretty hard to accomplish anything. . . . I leave the whole matter to your own judgment, with full authority and discretion, only I would be careful not to shoot until I was sure of my aim.[5]

The caution Harmon advocated and practiced eventually yielded a rich harvest. The results began to appear soon after the Cleveland administration left office in March 1897. Less than three weeks later, the Supreme Court overruled the *Trans-Missouri* decision, and perpetually enjoined the operation of the pool.[6] Harmon proudly claimed the decision as a personal victory, while railroad companies, surprised and disconcerted, quickly broke away from the various associations they had come to con-

[2] United States v. Moore, C.C.D. Utah, Nov. 1896 (indictment, under §3 of the act, returned Nov. 4, 1895; defendants found guilty and Moore fined), *rev'd,* 85 Fed. 465 (8th Cir. 1898) (holding that the circuit court no longer had jurisdiction after Jan. 4, 1896, when Utah was admitted to the Union).

[3] United States v. Hopkins, 82 Fed. 529 (C.C.D. Kan. 1897) (bill filed Dec. 31, 1896). On appeal, 84 Fed. 1018 (8th Cir. 1897), the case was certified to the Supreme Court, which reversed the decree. 171 U.S. 578 (1898).

[4] United States v. Addyston Pipe & Steel Co., 78 Fed. 712 (C.C.E.D. Tenn. 1897), *rev'd,* 85 Fed. 271 (6th Cir. 1898), *aff'd,* 175 U.S. 211 (1899).

[5] Letter from Harmon to Bible, Dec. 2, 1896, D.J. Instr. Bk. No. 74, at 573.

[6] United States v. Trans-Missouri Freight Ass'n, 166 U.S. 290 (1897).

sider normal facilities of their business.[7] The Court's subsequent decision that the Joint Traffic Association also was illegal came as something of an anticlimax.[8] Early in 1898, the Sixth Circuit Court of Appeals issued a perpetual injunction against the defendants in the *Addyston Pipe* case.[9] What little Harmon had done had turned out exceedingly well.

In 1896, however, when Cleveland was summing up the achievements of his administration, these successes were not foreseen. It therefore seemed necessary to offer excuses for a poor record. Accordingly, the President's last annual message contained a passage, closely following a memorandum prepared by Olney, which asserted that the antitrust laws "thus far have proved ineffective, not because of any lack of disposition or attempt to enforce them, but simply because the laws themselves as interpreted by the courts do not reach the difficulty." Further legislation might help, the message suggested, but perhaps any Federal law would encounter the same constitutional impediment, and the problem might ultimately be solved only if the states exercised their powers also.[1]

Harmon offered a rather different explanation. Although he, too, was bound to notice the obstacles raised by adverse decisions, he believed some of these could be overcome if Congress would amend the act. It ought to prevent unlawful combinations from shipping goods among the states, define "monopoly" and "restraint of trade" more precisely, prevent witnesses from refusing to testify on grounds of self-incrimination, and add as a rule of evidence that the merging of competitors would, *prima facie,* demonstrate an attempt to monopolize. Finally, the chief administrative problem, the one to which Harmon referred repeatedly throughout his report, was the difficulty of collecting evidence. "If the Department of Justice is expected to conduct investigations of alleged violations . . . it must be provided with a liberal appropriation and a force properly selected and organized. The present appropriation for the detection of crimes and offenses

[7] N.Y. *Times* p. 12, col. 2 (Mar. 24, 1897); p. 5, col. 1 (Mar. 25, 1897).

[8] United States v. Joint Traffic Ass'n, 171 U.S. 505 (1898).

[9] United States v. Addyston Pipe & Steel Co., 85 Fed. 271 (6th Cir. 1898), *aff'd,* 175 U.S. 211 (1899), *reversing* 78 Fed. 712 (C.C.E.D. Tenn. 1897).

[1] Richardson, *Messages & Papers of the Presidents,* IX, 745 (1900).

is very small, and the time of the examiners is fully occupied by the present important duties assigned to them." He added that the work should be done by a special agency outside the Department of Justice.[2] Several years passed, however, before Congress adopted his recommendation or made any attempt to correct this oversight in the original legislation.

Disuse of the Act under President McKinley

The Republican platform of 1896, unlike those of the preceding two elections, said nothing about trusts, and the subsequent activities of President McKinley's Attorneys General suggest that the omission was not an oversight. A few weeks after the election, the newspapers published a letter—supposedly from Mark Hanna to an important Republican—saying that Bryan had found support among those who considered McKinley to be the candidate of the trusts and that, in order to "counteract the impression," McKinley would "assume a dignified attitude of antagonism" toward the combinations.[3] Although Hanna immediately denounced the letter as spurious, it described reasonably well the course McKinley followed. In his inaugural address, he quoted phrases from the Republican platform of 1888 to show that the party had opposed trusts in the past. He promised that this policy would "be steadily pursued, both by the enforcement of the laws now in existence and the recommendation and support of such new statutes as may be necessary to carry it into effect." [4]

The Attorneys General who served under McKinley did virtually nothing to fulfill his pledge. Joseph McKenna, the most active, authorized two suits during his nine months in office. The first was a companion piece to Harmon's suit against the Kansas City livestock dealers and had been prepared in large part during the previous administration.[5] The second suit was instituted

[2] 54th Cong. Ist. Sess., H.R. Doc. No. 234 (1896), reprinted in *Att'y Gen. Ann. Rep.* 3-5 (1896).

[3] N.Y. *Times* p. 4, col. 1 (Nov. 23, 1896).

[4] Richardson, *Messages and Papers of the Presidents,* XIV, 6240.

[5] United States v. Anderson, C.C.W.D. Mo., bill filed June 7, 1897; 82 Fed. 998 (1897); 171 U.S. 604 (1898). The prior case was United States v. Hopkins; see note 3, p. 135 above.

through the efforts of a group of coal consumers and retailers in San Francisco who objected to a combination of coal wholesalers. They hired an attorney who drafted a bill in the name of the Government; and, at the request of the local district attorney, McKenna approved the bill and appointed the private lawyer as special counsel to plead the case for the Government.[6] Dealing with a set of facts which by now had become familiar, the court promptly granted an injunction against the combination.[7]

Even these rather passive efforts exceeded those made by McKenna's successor. John W. Griggs was remarkable for the assiduity with which, during his three years in office, he declined every opportunity except one for enforcing the Sherman Act. To George Rice, who continued to urge that his ancient enemy, the Standard Oil Company, ought to be prosecuted under the Sherman Act, Griggs replied that there was nothing in Rice's letter to indicate that the business "of the alleged combination against which you complained, is of an interstate character." [8] To another correspondent who suggested a suit against the beef trust, Griggs answered that he "must avoid entering upon a discussion with a gentleman who takes six pages of typewritten legal-cap to express his views." [9] The Solicitor General, John K. Richards, to whom Griggs delegated much of the antitrust work, followed a similar course. He allowed a district attorney in Galveston to investigate an alleged shipping trust, but refused the attorney's request for permission to sue. And when a private complainant suggested a suit against the United Fruit Company, Richards indicated that the Department would not proceed unless presented with all the necessary evidence.[1]

In explaining his failure to act, Griggs never tired of referring to the *Sugar Trust* decision. In an annual report he explained that the Department, when considering a complaint, was "governed only by a sincere desire to enforce the law as it exists and to avoid

[6] Thorelli, *Federal Antitrust Policy* 405-6.

[7] United States v. Coal Dealers' Ass'n, 85 Fed. 252 (C.C.N.D. Cal. 1898); *Decrees and Judgments, 1890-1918* 49, 51.

[8] Letter from Griggs to Rice, March 14, 1899, D.J. Misc. Bk. No. 36, at 469, in Thorelli, *Federal Antitrust Policy* 408 n.192.

[9] Letter from Griggs to Cooke, Sept. 21, 1899, D.J. Misc. Bk. No. 39, at 216, in Thorelli, *Federal Antitrust Policy* 409 n.193.

[1] Thorelli, *Federal Antitrust Policy* 407 n.188.

subjecting the Government to useless expense and the law officers of the Government to humiliating defeat by bringing actions where there was a clear want of jurisdiction under the well-defined limits of Federal jurisdiction so clearly laid down by the Supreme Court in cases already decided."[2] That he so completely overlooked the possibilities of building an active enforcement program on the recent and favorable decisions in the *Trans-Missouri, Joint Traffic,* and *Addyston Pipe* cases, indicates that what Harmon considered an impediment Griggs used as an opportune barrier.[3]

Meanwhile, a great series of mergers was creating more and larger combinations than had been formed during the years between 1887 and 1890. The depression that began in 1893 was followed after 1897 by exceptional prosperity, and the unusually active market for securities provided rewarding opportunities for professional promoters who engaged in organizing new monopolies and reinforcing old ones. The wave of consolidations began in earnest during 1898, though for a while the Spanish-American War diverted attention from it. In the following year, the movement reached a peak, producing, according to a contemporary estimate, eighty-seven new consolidations, each capitalized at an average of over twenty million dollars.[4] Newspapers, civic leaders and reformers, lawyers, economists, and bankers suddenly took notice of this remarkable phenomenon and of the evils it threatened. Special conferences were organized in Chicago by the Civic Federation and in St. Louis by the governors and attorneys general of the states; addresses were presented at conventions of various bar associations, at the American Economic Association meetings, at the International Commercial Congress, and at People's Institutes throughout the country; the United States Industrial Commission, a Federal agency created to study eco-

[2] *Att'y Gen. Ann. Rep.* 29 (1899).

[3] The only antitrust action initiated by Griggs, United States *ex rel.* Griggs v. Chesapeake & O. Fuel Co., 105 Fed. 93 (C.C.S.D. Ohio 1900), was affirmed, 115 Fed. 610 (6th Cir. 1902).

[4] Conant, "Industrial Consolidations in the United States," *Publctns. of the Amer. Stat. Ass'n.,* VII, 207, 218 (1901); cf. Markham, "Survey of the Evidence and Findings on Mergers," in Nat'l Bur. of Econ. Research, *Business Concentration and Price Policy* 141 (1955). See also Nelson, Ralph L., *Merger Movements in American Industry* (1959).

nomic conditions, collected evidence on the situation and its presumed causes. By the end of the year, President McKinley himself broke a three-year silence about trusts and, though he did not suggest that more vigorous efforts be made to enforce the existing law, observed that the new combinations were "justly provoking public discussion, and should early claim the attention of Congress."[5] Still, Griggs was quite unmoved. When asked why he did not bring suits against the new combinations, he answered only: "As a matter of fact all the companies which you refer to as now organizing for the purpose of securing complete or partial monopoly of different branches of manufacture, are similar to the sugar combination and are not within the jurisdiction of the federal courts."[6]

Whatever had been their thoughts in 1896, the Republican Party managers could not overlook the need for an antitrust plank during the campaign of 1900. The platform statement, which Hanna himself composed, constituted the first party endorsement of the distinction between "good" and "bad" combinations, a distinction congressmen had often made during the debate on Senator Sherman's antitrust bills but which was not adopted as an explicit guide to enforcement policy until after Theodore Roosevelt became President. The Republican pledge read:

> We recognize the necessity and propriety of the honest cooperation of capital to meet new business conditions, and especially to extend our rapidly increasing foreign trade; but we condemn all conspiracies and combinations intended to restrict business, to create monopolies, to limit production, or to control prices, and favor such legislation as will effectively restrain and prevent all such abuses, protect and promote competition, and secure the rights of producers, laborers, and all who are engaged in industry and commerce.[7]

[5] McKinley, Third Annual Message, Dec. 5, 1899; Richardson, *Messages and Papers of the Presidents,* XIV, 6360.

[6] Letter from Griggs to J. C. Bowadaile, March 21, 1899, in N.Y. *Herald* p. 5, col. 6 (March 22, 1899) and Thorelli, *Federal Antitrust Policy* 409 n.195. Letter from Griggs to Gov. Pingree of Michigan, in N.Y. *Times* p. 14, col. 2 (Sept. 27, 1899).

[7] McKee, *National Conventions and Platforms* 342-43 (4th ed. 1901); Croly, *Marcus Alonzo Hanna* 306-07 (1912).

But this change in the party's program did not bring with it any change in practice during the six months of McKinley's second term. His new Attorney General, Philander C. Knox, did nothing that foreshadowed his later vigor in enforcing the Act, and McKinley showed no sign of increased interest. By September of 1901, when McKinley was assassinated and Theodore Roosevelt took the oath of office, the Sherman Act had gone practically unenforced for five years.

The explanation that Griggs and others offered concerning the weakness of the Sherman Act was accepted by many critics who therefore attributed the poverty of antitrust policy before 1903 to the *Sugar Trust* decision and, more generally, to the supposed hostility of judges. But judges cannot, without declaring a law unconstitutional, absolutely prevent its enforcement. For judicial action to have this effect, the Attorney General must consider himself constrained by the judges' interpretations. If he believes that the courts have enervated a statute, as Olney had reason to believe before, and especially after, the *Sugar Trust* decision, he may well refrain from using it. If, on the other hand, he wishes to expand its scope, he may, even in the face of obstacles, test the precedents by appeal and explore untried aspects of the law, as Harmon did. But once the courts have handed down a series of decisions which suggest that the statute is, after all, applicable in some degree, a striking absence of enforcement must be attributed to government policy. What was prudence and reasonable self-restraint before the Supreme Court decided the *Trans-Missouri, Joint Traffic,* and *Addyston Pipe* cases was bound to seem laxity afterward.

There may or may not have been adequate reasons for the McKinley administration's failure to use the Act after 1899. In any event, only the two or three years of inactivity following that date can plausibly be attacked in the way that the entire early administration of the Act so often has been. It may be that when Edmunds wrote in 1903, "What is needed is not, so much, more legislation as competent and earnest administration of the laws that exist," he was on firmer ground than when he made a similar statement in 1892. Perhaps even in 1903, however, he weakened his position by adding a vital qualification. The Sherman Act could control the trusts, he said, "if the officers of the Government having charge of the enforcement of law understand their duty and are willing to do it, being, of course, supplied with sufficient means to put it into force." [8]

[8] Letter from Edmunds to Sleicher, Jan. 2, 1903, in 36 *Cong. Rec.* 1901 (1903).

CHAPTER FIVE

INTERPRETING THE SHERMAN ACT

1890-1899

As the first effort to control the economy at large, the Sherman antitrust law posed special problems for judges. Antitrust cases required more thorough and delicate analysis of economic issues than had ever been needed in resolving questions under the older branches of law. In some instances, they called for a fuller understanding of monopolistic and competitive behavior than economic theory could offer then—or can now. Controversies involving large companies and the complex structure and widespread activities of whole industries made it necessary to deal with voluminous records. But the greatest difficulty, especially pressing through the early years, was not so much to determine the facts of a case as to discover the meaning of the statute. When the difficulties of arriving at a cogent interpretation of the Sherman Act are considered, it is surprising that the courts were able, in less than a decade, to formulate the fundamental rules of law that have since governed that statute's application.

The gravest problems of interpretation arose from ambiguities in both the legal theory and language of the act. It was based on the common law, and judges generally agreed that it should be interpreted according to the common law; yet they varied widely in their opinions of what the precedents dictated. Their views could easily differ both because contradictory tendencies existed within American case law and because English common law had steadily been diverging from the more typical American precedents. The language of the Act aggravated the problem of interpretation. The first section of the Act declared illegal: "every contract, combination . . . or conspiracy, in restraint of trade. . . ." Congress had intended by this concise formula to outlaw three sorts of agreement known to the common law, each having a proper common-law name: contracts in restraint of trade, combinations in restraint of trade, and conspiracies in restraint of trade. The phrase, "or commerce among the several states," was appended to assert the constitutional power on which the Act rested. But the entire formula, commendable for its brevity, was for that very reason dangerously equivocal. For one thing, it could be read as condemning "every . . . conspiracy, in restraint of . . . commerce among the several states," though many agreements that might be so described—for instance a malicious compact to derail a locomotive—would not have violated the common-law rules against monopoly. The word "every" also created doubts, for it could be taken to mean that the act went beyond the common law, which did not forbid "every" restraint of trade but only "unreasonable" restraints. Uncertainty about the word "every" was contagious; judges who disagreed about its significance were apt to differ next about the technical meaning of the succeeding words, "restraint of trade." All these ambiguities had somehow to be resolved before the Act could be given a workable meaning.

The Common-Law Doctrine of Early Cases

The persistent difficulty of interpreting the Act's common-law foundations did not arise in the first antitrust suit brought by the Government, largely because the defendants in the *Jellico Mountain Coal* case[1] were joined in a combination of quite traditional form. A group of coal dealers and mine operators had organized the Nashville Coal Exchange, the mines agreeing to trade only with dealers in the Exchange, the dealers promising in return to buy only from member mines; the Exchange set prices at which all members were to sell and provided penalties for any disobedience. The court did not hesitate to find that the arrangement violated the Sherman Act. Since the combination would confine the sale of coal to members and prevent them from selling cheaply, it clearly restrained trade. And since, according to the by-laws of the ex-

[1] United States v. Jellico Mountain Coke & Coal Co., 43 Fed. 898 (C.C.M.D. Tenn. 1890) (preliminary injunction refused), 46 Fed. 432 (C.C.M.D. Tenn. 1891) (issued).

change, the established prices would not apply to coal sold to manufacturers and steamboats "until all mines tributary to this market shall become members of the exchange, or until the exchange can control prices to govern coal used by manufacturers," [2] the group was clearly engaged in an "attempt to monopolize"—expressly proscribed by section 2 of the Act. The heart of the decision therefore, was reached merely by comparing the words of the statute and the words of the agreement.

In writing his opinion, Judge Key did not refer to precedents or offer much explanation, and he disposed with equal dispatch of the defendants' further arguments. They maintained, first of all, that the Act was unconstitutional because, while it created criminal offenses, it authorized the Government to proceed by suits in equity, thus denying a defendant's right to trial by jury in criminal cases. They argued secondly that the agreement did not affect interstate commerce: since all the coal mines were located in Kentucky and all the dealers in Tennessee, the agreement to fix prices at the mines concerned commerce within one state and the agreement to fix retail prices concerned commerce within another. Finally, they contended that the prices charged in Nashville were justified by the costs. The judge declined, however, to discuss the constitutionality of the act. He easily found the requisite effect upon interstate commerce in the transportation from the mines in Kentucky to the dealers in Tennessee; and he attached no weight to evidence about whether or how much the combination had actually raised prices of coal, for the statute condemned the "attempt to monopolize," and he held that the Exchange agreement was in itself such an attempt.

This easy conclusion was illusory. The application of the Sherman Act to particular sets of facts required, after all, a more subtle process, as the whisky trust cases of 1892 showed. The early stages of the proceedings dealt with procedural matters. The original indictment charged that certain offenses had been committed by the officers of the Distilling and Cattle Feeding Company, popularly known as a trust, but in fact a corporation chartered by the state of Illinois. These officers, having bought or leased seventy-eight

[2] 46 Fed. 434.

distilleries that produced about three-quarters of the spirits sold in the United States, had offered certain dealers in Massachusetts rebates if they would buy only from the trust. All this was done with the clear intent to monopolize. But since the indictment, because of error or oversight, did not assert that these actions illegally affected interstate commerce or violated the Sherman Act, the court quashed it as "insufficient," that is, as failing to meet the requirement that defendants in criminal prosecutions be given a clear statement of the charges against them.[3]

When these defects were corrected in a new indictment, three courts in various districts were asked to decide whether the defendants could be forced to appear for trial in Boston. The judges then had to render summary judgments based on the meaning of the Sherman Act. In the first of these proceedings, *In re Corning*,[4] Judge Ricks decided that the new indictment did not attribute any crimes to the trust. The Act prohibited "restraints of trade" and "monopolizing," but the indictment did not describe any particular actions corresponding to those terms. Thus, although the indictment charged the defendants with buying up seventy distilleries, it did not assert that the defendants obliged the sellers to refrain from building other distilleries or to give up the business of distilling. And, though it alleged they offered rebates to any dealer who would buy only their goods and sell only at their prices, it did not allege that dealers were bound to those conditions by contract. Accordingly, the court decided that the indictment did not accuse the whisky trust of making any agreements of the sort traditionally recognized by the common law as contracts in restraint of trade. Nor did the indictment allege that the trust had made any agreement with independent distillers to limit output, control prices, or circumscribe markets. In short, it did not accuse them of forming with their competitors in what the common law traditionally identified as a combination in restraint of trade. Judge Ricks added that according to the common-law meaning of "monopoly" the indictment did not support a charge on that ground: the allegation was that the trust had accumulated a great deal of property, not that it had done so in an illegal manner. Ricks therefore refused to

[3] United States v. Greenhut, 50 Fed. 469 (D. Mass. 1892); see pp. 111-12 above.

[4] 51 Fed. 205 (N.D. Ohio 1892).

order the defendants to stand trial in Boston. His decision was closely followed by Judge Lacombe, who heard the second case of the series, and delivered a short opinion adding only one explanatory note—the statute did not prohibit "the actual restraint of trade" but "the making of a contract in restraint of trade." [5]

JACKSON'S OPINION IN THE *Greene* CASE

The doctrine implied by Ricks and Lacombe—that a business might be a monopoly in fact yet not a monopoly at law, if it had become the sole producer of a commodity without having done anything illegal to achieve or retain its control—was stated explicitly by Judge Jackson. In the third whisky trust proceeding, *In re Greene,*[6] the crux of his opinion was that monopoly, as defined by the common law and by the statute (Coke and Blackstone serving as authorities on the former and Senators Edmunds and Hoar on the latter), consisted of two necessary elements: an exclusive right enjoyed by the monopolist, and restrictions imposed on others to prevent them from infringing on his privilege. Under this definition of "monopoly" the whisky trust would not monopolize even if it raised its output from three-quarters of the total liquor sold to the whole—unless in the process it restrained others. But the indictment, Jackson continued, did not allege any particular instances in which the trust had tried to curtail others in producing or selling. The rebate offered to dealers who would deal exclusively with the trust was not a restraint but an inducement; it did not bind the dealers, and there was nothing to prevent other producers from offering the same or greater rebates.[7] Even if the offer were construed as a contract, it would not be a contract in *general* restraint of trade, of the sort judged unlawful by common-law courts, bur rather a *partial* restraint. As such, it would be valid if it were reasonable, that is, if the restraint was not "more injurious to the public than is required to afford a fair protection to the party in whose favor it is secured." [8]

[5] *In re* Terrell, 51 Fed. 213 (C.C.S.D.N.Y. 1892).
[6] 52 Fed. 104 (C.C.S.D. Ohio 1892)
[7] But see note 3, p. 149 below.
[8] 52 Fed. 118.

To support his view that the rebate agreement gave the trust only "a reasonable protection in their business," Jackson now turned to a number of common-law authorities, above all the recent English decision in the *Mogul Steamship* case.[9] There, an association of shipowners had offered to give merchants in China a rebate at the end of six months if during that time they exported tea only on ships belonging to members of the association. The Mogul Steamship Company, which did not participate in the association, had maintained that its business was injured by the exclusive dealing arrangement, but had lost its suit for damages. This struck Jackson as a conclusive precedent. Although the rebate system was no doubt similar in the two cases, Jackson was nevertheless mistaken when he said that in the *Mogul* case "the question (almost identical with that under consideration) was presented whether the combination and arrangement adopted by the association to secure the exclusive transportation of tea trade was in any way unlawful."[1] The question in the English decision was really a different one—not whether the agreement was "in any way unlawful," but, specifically, whether it did unlawful damage to the plaintiff; and, although the House of Lords denied that the association had unlawfully injured the plaintiff, it had no doubt that a common-law court would regard the association as illegal in itself and would refuse to enforce the agreement as between the parties. In the whisky trust case, on the other hand, the pertinent question was whether the defendants had violated a statute that made criminal offenses out of actions merely void at common law; and the *Mogul* decision—bearing only on the damage issue—did not assert that the combination was valid. Moreover, even if the similarity of the two cases had been as close as Jackson thought, the *Mogul* case was not an altogether convincing precedent for an American court. It had been decided two years after the Sherman Act was passed and, as a Federal judge observed in an opinion delivered a few months later, the English common law on monopolies had for some years been drifting toward greater leniency while "in the United States there is a tendency to revive, with the aid of legislation, the strict rules of the common law against all forms of mo-

[9] Mogul S.S. Co. v. McGregor, Gow & Co., [1892] A.C. 25 (1891). See above, pp. 49-51.

[1] 52 Fed. at 119.

nopoly or engrossing."[2] And finally, it is not certain that the rebate arrangement was as innocuous as the *Mogul* decision and Jackson maintained.[3]

In arriving at his decision, Jackson rejected the main point of the Government's pleadings, which was that the trust violated the Act by its mere existence, for, though in form a single corporation, it was in fact a combination to set prices and regulate the output of what had once been seventy competing firms. He conceded that the arrangement might evidence an intent to monopolize, but the intent itself—even if accompanied by actual pre-eminence in the industry as well as by any incidental power that the trust might derive from its great size—was not illegal, and would only become so if the trust tried to realize the intent by, for instance, imposing restraints on others. Supplementing this fundamental argument, he suggested a constitutional consideration, that the Federal Government could not regulate the property of a corporation created by a state.[4] He contended also that, since the trust was formed before the Act was passed, to construe its formation as illegal would be to give the act an *ex post facto* effect.[5] (One might

[2] Oliver v. Gilmore, 52 Fed. 562, 566 (C.C.D. Mass. 1892) (Putnam, J.).

[3] The rebate in both cases was available only to those who during some long period did all their business with one supplier. Now if a buyer has the choice of taking an equal rebate from any one of several sellers, he will regard the choice as indifferent *only if each seller is equally able to supply goods whenever they are demanded.* In the circumstances of the *Mogul* case this condition probably did not prevail, for at any moment the combine could send many more ships to the tea ports than the single independent line could. Consequently, the probability that an exporter would regularly get shipping space just when he needed it was greater if he dealt with the combine. If the exporter had to wait for space, he would incur storage charges or losses, which would to that extent reduce the value of a rebate. Similarly, in the whisky case, if the retailer could not be supplied as quickly or regularly by independent distillers as he could by the trust, the value to him of an independent's rebate—even if the independent offered the same percentage as the trust—would always be less than the value of the trust rebate, since the independent's rebate would have to be discounted for the possibility of lost sales and extra storage charges. Jackson's argument that the independents could offer a larger rebate than the trust paid does not meet the basic problem, since it merely suggests that the independents could, if they chose, put themselves at the disadvantage of incurring greater costs than the trust, and to that extent reduce their chances of surviving the competition.

[4] 52 Fed. at 112-13.

[5] 52 Fed. at 112.

have thought, however, that to continue a combination would be an illegal act even if to form it was not.)

FURTHER APPLICATIONS OF JACKSON'S RATIONALE

Jackson's theory of the case reflected a widespread economic attitude of optimistic confidence in the working of competition, and rested on the belief that monopolies cannot maintain themselves simply by virtue of their economic position. This reasoning assumes that a monopoly cannot drive out competitors through such measures as price-cutting, exclusive dealing arrangements, and price discrimination. Jackson was convinced that independent producers could just as easily destroy a monopoly by using these techniques, for, he said, nothing prevented the whisky trust's competitors from offering larger rebates. If the state did not create or protect monopolies, and if it refused to enforce the restrictive agreements by which monopolies seek to protect themselves, enough competitors, actual or potential, would always be available to destroy the monopoly or limit its power to set prices. This belief led him to interpret the Sherman Act as an attempt to prohibit only those methods by which monopolies could hope to survive in the face of competition, and disposed him to judge that, because it did not restrict its competitors, the whisky trust could not be violating the Act. Jackson's view was immediately accepted as authoritative and it exercised a decisive influence for several years.

Indeed, in the next antitrust case, *United States v. Nelson,*[6] Jackson's doctrine that there could be no monopolizing without restraining was carried to even greater lengths. In a short opinion, Judge Nelson sustained the demurrer of a group of lumber merchants indicted for combining to raise prices, though he said nothing more about the merits of the case than that the defendants could not really raise the prices as they intended. He was convinced on general principles that "competition is not stifled by such an agreement, and other dealers would soon force the parties to the agreement to sell at the market price, or a reasonable price, at least."[7] This observation, insofar as the judge was concerned, dis-

[6] 52 Fed. 646 (D. Minn. 1892).
[7] 52 Fed. at 647.

posed of any need to differentiate between the case before him and contrary common-law precedents as well as the facts of the *Jellico Mountain Coal* case. He simply overlooked the conflict between his view—that an attempt to raise prices was not illegal if unsuccessful—and the opinion of Judge Key in the *Jellico* decision—that the Sherman Act prohibited the attempt, successful or not. Moreover, although he was following Jackson, Nelson did not see that the facts in the case before him were different in one crucial respect from those in the whisky trust proceedings. There, the combining firms had become the property of a single corporation, and precedents provided a basis for deciding, as Jackson did, that the parts of any single firm, no matter how large the whole, might act in concert without constituting a combination. In contrast, the *Nelson* combination was made up of independent firms and, although their agreement might not be restraining anyone else, it was unquestionably restraining them.

The outlines of Jackson's doctrine were followed again—this time to the detriment of the defendants—in a case heard shortly afterwards, *United States v. Patterson*.[8] Judge Putnam, in upholding the major portion of an indictment against officers of the cash register trust, seemed most impressed by the coercive methods the trust had used to restrain trade. It had attempted to intimidate its competitors by beating or bribing their employees, employing spies, inducing breach of contract, threatening suits for patent infringement, and so forth.[9] The mere fact that the trust had come to control much of the cash register business, or even that it deliberately intended to control all of the business, did not in itself violate the Act, but since, in addition, the trust had used violence, it could be guilty of monopolizing. Violence, Putnam said, was equivalent to restrictive legal arrangements, might indeed be used to impose them on competitors, and was therefore an unlawful attempt to exclude competition.[1]

The *Patterson* decision illustrated the strength of Jackson's rationale. Those who asserted that competition would automatically destroy pacific monopolies, though perhaps correct in fact, were denying that the Act should be used to hasten the automatic de-

[8] 55 Fed. 605 (C.C.D. Mass. 1893).

[9] 55 Fed. at 606.

[1] 55 Fed. at 641.

cay or that Congress had intended it to be used for that purpose. But as the *Patterson* decision showed, by adopting this position, they were not rendering the Act impotent. On the contrary, they insisted that the Act prohibited any attempt to impede the process of competition, whether by violent or contractual methods. This rule, as stated most fully by Jackson and followed in most cases before 1893, directed the attention of judges to overt acts, and thereby established a clear criterion of illegality. If it narrowed the scope of the Act, it defined that scope precisely. The criterion it established—later expressed in the dictum, "size alone is not a violation of the Act"—slowly evolved into a principle that has since been used in interpreting antitrust law: control of an industry is not unlawful even though it gives the defendant power to do harm; what the Act prohibits is the abuse of that power by the actual doing of harm.

THE *Trans-Missouri* CASE

Some judges went much further than Jackson and assumed not only that enough competition would naturally exist to counteract monopolies, but that in some industries there might at times be too much competition. And, whereas Jackson believed that the common law did not invalidate peaceful combinations and that the law in general need not, these other judges believed that the law positively endorsed combinations whose sole purpose was to do away with excessive competition. Their view was clearly demonstrated in the first two trials of the *Trans-Missouri Freight Association* case.[2] The defendants were a number of railroads that had united to fix uniform rates and terms for freight carriage. They had established a scheme whereby a member of the association could deviate from the established rates only by following an elaborate, time-consuming procedure, obviously designed to make him keenly aware of his colleagues' displeasure. This arrangement, said District Judge Riner (who decided the case on its first hearing), contained not a "single element of monopoly" because the defendants had no exclusive right to carry freight by rail.[3] On the other hand, the

[2] United States v. Trans-Missouri Freight Ass'n, 53 Fed. 440 (C.C.D. Kan. 1892), *aff'd,* 58 Fed. 58 (8th Cir. 1893), *rev'd,* 166 U.S. 290 (1897).

[3] 53 Fed. at 452-53.

agreement was certainly a contract in restraint of trade. But an extensive review of the precedents convinced Riner that such contracts were void only if the restrictions they imposed were unnecessarily broad and "publicly oppressive."[4] In other words, the common law did not aim to preserve competition as such, but only a desirable amount of competition. "Undoubtedly all contracts which have a direct tendency to prevent healthy competition are detrimental to the public, and, therefore, to be condemned; but when contracts go to the extent only of preventing unhealthy competition, and yet at the same time furnish the public with adequate facilities at fixed and reasonable prices, and are made only for the purpose of averting personal ruin, the contract is lawful."[5] The difficulty of determining whether the public enjoyed "adequate facilities" at "reasonable prices" did not arise, for the framing of the issue on the pleadings required Riner to assume the truth of the defendants' assertions, and they had said that the combination was formed in order to maintain "just and reasonable rates."[6] He concluded that the restraint was reasonable, and that it benefited the public by eliminating excessive competition among the railroads and thus contributing to their prosperity.

This opinion might seem to have depended on an appraisal of economic order very different from Jackson's, and it did for the first time introduce into antitrust law a precedent expressing some doubt as to the unlimited merits of competition. Yet, in a broader sense, Riner and Jackson were at one, for each felt that a judge obliged by statute to follow the common law might approve an arrangement whose effect, or at least immediate effect, was to reduce competition. No doubt there was authority in common-law cases for Riner's decision, since courts had often indicated that they would approve railroad pools designed to eliminate "ruinous" competition.[7] There could be no doubt, moreover, that Riner based his decision in part on the fact that the contracting parties

[4] 53 Fed. at 451.
[5] 53 Fed. at 451.
[6] 53 Fed. at 451.
[7] Manchester & L.R.R. v. Concord R.R., 66 N.H. 100, 20 Atl. 383 (1890); see Chicago, St. L. & N.O.R.R. v. Pullman So. Car Co., 139 U.S. 79 (1891); Wiggins Ferry Co. v. Chicago & A.R.R., 73 Mo. 389 (1881); Dewey, "The Common-Law Background of Antitrust Policy," 41 *Va. L. Rev.* 759, 782-83 (1955), and cases cited therein.

were railroads, for, in closing his opinion, he held that the Sherman Act did not apply to these defendants in any event as they were already regulated by the Interstate Commerce Act.[8]

The Eighth Circuit Court of Appeals, which reviewed the *Trans-Missouri* case a year later, affirmed the decision on substantially the same principles.[9] The appellate court held that, as the defendants were not joined in a monopoly of necessities or in a pool, their association was not prima facie illegal. It was a combination, and as such was lawful or unlawful by common-law criteria, depending on whether it merely "regulated" or actually "suppressed" competition—that is, on whether it was "reasonable."[1] Moreover, another standard reinforced the common-law conclusion. Conceding that the Association "checked" competition among the member railroads and had been formed for this sole purpose, the court went on to maintain that Congress, in passing the Interstate Commerce Act, had itself adopted the policy of reducing competition among railroads, and that railroads which did for themselves what the law proposed to do for them could not be convicted of acting contrary to public policy.[2] The only question left to decide was whether the defendants had gone too far in executing a plan that was unexceptionable in itself. On examining the agreement, the court determined that it would not necessarily or probably "suppress" competition. Nor did the evidence establish that the defendants had in fact charged unreasonable rates. The court accordingly upheld Judge Riner's opinion that a railroad combination was reasonable and legal if it charged "reasonable" prices.

In 1896, when District Judge Wheeler dismissed a bill brought against a similar arrangement in the *Joint Traffic Association* case,[3] he too set forth as the ultimate test of a railroad combination's legality whether it charged "reasonable" prices.

The effect of these very early antitrust decisions, then, was to establish the doctrine that the Sherman Act should be interpreted

[8] 52 Fed. at 454-56.

[9] United States v. Trans-Missouri Freight Ass'n, 58 Fed. 58 (8th Cir. 1893), *rev'd,* 166 U.S. 290 (1897).

[1] 58 Fed. at 69, 73.

[2] 58 Fed. at 74-77.

[3] United States v. Joint Traffic Ass'n, 76 Fed. 895 (C.C.S.D.N.Y. 1896), *aff'd mem.,* 89 Fed. 1020 (2d Cir. 1897), *rev'd,* 171 U.S. 505 (1898).

according to the common law, and the common-law rule most often invoked was that combinations were illegal only if they restrained trade unreasonably, that is, by using restrictive agreements or physical coercion, or by excessively raising prices.

The Broader Interpretation of the Act in the Labor Union Cases

The judges who heard early labor cases arising under the Sherman Act could not so easily find a common-law tradition to guide them. It was clear, despite what the common-law rules had once been, that, since early in the nineteenth century, American courts had ceased to classify unions as unlawful combinations in themselves. And, after the decision of *Commonwealth v. Hunt* in 1842,[4] strikes were no longer regarded as illegal, provided they were intended to force the strikers' own employer to raise wages and were conducted peaceably. The mere establishment of unions and the organizing of an uneventful strike therefore appeared permissible under the Sherman Act if common-law rules were to be followed. The status of other union activities was more doubtful.

THE FIRST LABOR ANTITRUST CASE

The nature of the problem became apparent in the first antitrust case involving a union, *United States v. Workingmen's Amalgamated Council.*[5] The defendants were conducting a general strike in New Orleans. The Government sought to end it, and District Judge Billings issued a temporary injunction on the ground that the strike violated the Act. While conceding that Congress had been moved to enact the antitrust laws by "the evils of massed capital," he nevertheless held that, in the course of debate, "the subject had so broadened in the minds of the legislators" that they had decided to interdict "every contract or combination in the form of trust, or otherwise in restraint of trade or commerce," whether organized by businessmen or by laborers.[6] Was this strike illicitly "in restraint

[4] 45 Mass. (4 Met.) 111 (1842).
[5] 54 Fed. 994 (C.C.E.D. La.), *aff'd,* 57 Fed. 85 (5th Cir. 1893).
[6] 54 Fed. at 996.

of trade"? Billings conceded that unions as such were lawful and, in effect, accepted the defendants' argument that ordinary strikes were lawful as well.[7] And he did not maintain that the Council's strike would be illegal at common law, though he did point out, in summarizing the evidence, that the strikers had practiced violence and intimidation.[8] Therefore, in order to show that the strike violated the Sherman Act, Billings had to conclude that, despite the common law, it was a "combination . . . in restraint of trade." The only authority he offered was a somewhat remote New York precedent, *People v. Fisher.*[9] Decided in 1835, it was one of the last to forbid an ordinary strike involving no violence. Moreover, the particular remark quoted by Billings as authoritative was *obiter dictum.* Chief Justice Savage of New York had written that certain strikes, including general strikes, "would be productive of derangement and confusion, which certainly must be considered 'injurious to trade.' "[1] The justice wrote "would be" rather than "are" because his remark was an afterthought that did not concern the events of his case, a peaceful strike of shoemakers. Finally, even this aged dictum was not very suitable for Billings' purposes. The quotation marks that had surrounded "injurious to trade" when Savage used the words, and that vanished when Billings repeated them,[2] were no mere affectation, for the words occurred in the New York statute invoked in *People v. Fisher,* a statute that outlawed conspiracies "injurious to trade."[3] But Billings quietly overlooked all these defects in his precedent and reasoned that, since a general strike had once been said to "injure" trade, it must now be judged to "restrain" trade. Forgetting also that the words "restraint of trade" in the Sherman Act were intended to be given their common-law, rather than their literal, meaning, he was able to deduce that the New Orleans general strike violated the act. It would not, perhaps, have been much more difficult to reason that a gang of train-robbers would violate the antitrust statute, for they too would be a combination and would "restrain trade" if they halted a train.

[7] 54 Fed. at 999.
[8] 54 Fed. at 1000.
[9] 14 Wend. 9 (N.Y. Sup. Ct. Jud. 1835).
[1] 14 Wend. at 19.
[2] 54 Fed. at 1000.
[3] 14 Wend. at 14.

The Circuit Court of Appeals for the Fifth Circuit soon affirmed, or appeared to affirm, Billings' decision.[4] In fact, the court upheld only the technical propriety of the proceedings and said little about the substance of the opinion, since the lower court had not yet concluded its hearings: "On this appeal from an interlocutory order, which we affirm, we deem it unnecessary to anticipate the further progress and final hearing of this case by an expression of our views as to the full scope and sound construction of this recent and important statute."[5] But as the lower court never held final hearings, its original decision stood as the only substantial precedent in the field when the Pullman strike cases came before the courts a year later. The judges in those cases relied on Billings' opinion and regarded the decision of the court of appeals as greatly enhancing its authority.[6]

THE PULLMAN STRIKE LITIGATION

The most important labor antitrust case during this period, *United States v. Debs,*[7] began when the leaders of the American Railway Union disobeyed injunctions ordering them to cease conducting the Pullman strike. Their attorneys responded to the contempt proceedings that followed by questioning the jurisdiction of the courts, the vailidity of the injunctions, the assertion that they had been disobeyed, and so on. Although none of these arguments persuaded Judge Woods, who heard the case in the circuit court at Chicago, two of them seemed to impress him. The first raised the same question that had been the chief problem for Judge Billings in the *Workingmen's Council* case. How, Debs's attorneys asked, could the union be said to have violated the Sherman Act? It was not a "combination in restraint of trade"; even supposing that its activities had injured or restrained trade, there was a vast legal

[4] Workingmen's Amalgamated Council v. United States, 57 Fed. 85 (5th Cir. 1893).

[5] 57 Fed. at 86.

[6] See, *e.g.*, United States v. Cassidy, 67 Fed. 698, 705 (N.D. Cal. 1895) (charge to jury); United States v. Eliot, 62 Fed. 801, 803 (C.C.E.D. Mo. 1894); *In re* Grand Jury, 62 Fed. 840, 841 (N.D. Cal. 1894) (charge); Thomas v. Cincinnati, N.O. & T.P. Ry., 62 Fed. 803, 821 (C.C.S.D. Ohio 1894).

[7] 64 Fed. 724 (C.C.N.D. Ill. 1894).

difference between injuring or restraining trade and being "in restraint of trade." Woods's resolution of this difficulty, more sophisticated and complex than Billings', rested on a novel reading of the statute. The first section of the Act, as Judge Woods interpreted it, defined three distinct categories: contracts in restraint of trade, combinations in restraint of trade, and conspiracies. The distinctness of the three or, more particularly, of the third in relation to the first two, was emphasized by the Act's title, which stated that the Act was designed to prohibit "unlawful" contracts and combinations in restraint of trade—the sort that had been considered illicit at common law. But the qualification implicit in the title obviously did not attach to conspiracies, which are by definition unlawful. The question then arose, what sort of conspiracies did the Sherman Act forbid? Not "Conspirac[ies] . . . in restraint of trade," for no such category was known at common law; nor, Woods insisted, only those conspiracies involving contracts or combinations in restraint of trade.[8] The answer was to be found by interpreting the phrase "conspiracy . . . in restraint of trade or commerce" as equivalent to "conspiracy to restrain trade or commerce." Since "conspiracy . . . in restraint of trade" did not, to be sure, have a well-established meaning at common law, the Woods construction did not stretch the language of the Act as radically as had Billings' manipulation of "combination . . . in restraint of trade." Woods argued that "to restrain" was not more different from "in restraint of" than "drinking house" was from "tippling house," and that courts had in the past treated the latter two as synonymous. This much established, the course of his argument required him next to insist that "trade" and "commerce" were not synonyms. He had no difficulty in establishing that "commerce" as used in the Sherman Act meant "commerce" as used in the Constitution to define the regulatory power of Congress. And this completed the foundations of the principle he now announced: the Sherman Act prohibited conspiracies to injure or restrain interstate commerce.[9]

Having proceeded so far by reasoning from the language of the

[8] 64 Fed. at 748. Contrary to Woods's assertion, there are several common-law cases of conspiracy in restraint of trade: see p. 48 above.

[9] 64 Fed. at 747-52.

Act, Woods now turned to its policy. He observed that various decisions had narrowed the scope of the statute until it apparently applied only to commodities in the course of transportation among the states, or to agreements "intended to engross or monopolize the market." He concluded that the Act should be broadened by his interpretation. "Why should it not be construed to embrace all conspiracies which shall be contrived with intent, or of which the necessary or probable effect shall be, to restrain, hinder, interrupt, or destroy interstate commerce?" [1] By this process, Woods tried to reinforce Billings' test; but he apparently recognized the extreme weakness of the *Workingmen's Council* decision, for, although he cited it as one of the precedents establishing that a court of equity had jurisdiction over such cases, he did not mention it as an authority for his interpretation of the substance of the law.[2]

It still remained for Woods to dispose of another argument which Debs's attorneys advanced—perhaps to exploit a gap in Billings' opinion. They insisted that many conspiracies, even though they interfered with interstate commerce, could not reasonably be supposed to violate the Sherman Act. Taking as their text the argument advanced by the defendants in *United States v. Patterson,* Debs's counsel maintained that, if the Act were interpreted as prohibiting *any* interference with interstate commerce, it would have to be applied—contrary to its obvious purpose—to any conspiracy to commit "an act of murder, robbery, forgery, shop-breaking, store-burning, champerty, or maintenance, which in fact has a natural, though unintended, result of interference with interstate commerce." [3] Woods dismissed this assertion by denying that members of a conspiracy to murder could be considered members of a conspiracy to restrain interstate commerce, if the restraint were an unintended consequence of the murder. They

[1] 64 Fed. at 752.

[2] 64 Fed. at 754.

[3] 64 Fed. at 752. The words as they appear in text apparently are quoted by the court from the brief for Debs; they correspond only roughly with the words used in the brief for Patterson, United States v. Patterson, 55 Fed. 605, 632 (C.C.D. Mass. 1893). For example they do not explicitly say, as Patterson's attorney did, that in view of the decisions that would otherwise result, the act must be interpreted as requiring a specific intent to interfere with interstate commerce.

would, he stated, be responsible for the murder as conspirators and for the incidental restraint as individuals.[4] This principle, though it answered the defendants' objection, might have created new difficulties for Woods, since it obliged him to show that the defendants had interfered with interstate commerce directly and not merely incidentally. This problem he overcame by holding that Pullman cars were "instrumentalities of commerce," that Debs and his colleagues engaged in a conspiracy to interfere with commerce when they ordered the boycott, and that they became liable as individuals for the criminal results that ensued. Moreover, when they sought to enforce the boycott by calling a strike against railroads that continued to carry Pullman cars, "the original conspiracy against the use of Pullman cars became a conspiracy against transportation and travel by railroad." [5]

The theory devised by Billings and reinforced by Woods became the basis of decisions in other cases arising out of the Pullman strike. In *United States v. Elliott,* a circuit court in Missouri issued a preliminary injunction against officers of the union and used Billings' decision as authority for its interpretation of the Sherman Act.[6] A few weeks later, in overruling the defendants' demurrer in that same case, Judge Philips explained that, in the Sherman Act, "the term 'restraint of commerce' was used in its ordinary, business understanding and acceptation"; he proceeded to give a literal definition of "restraint," and concluded that it justified the injunction.[7] In *Thomas v. Cincinnati, N.O. & T.P. Ry.,*[8] a private suit turning on whether a strike leader had unlawfully interfered with a receiver appointed by the court to administer the railroad, Judge William Howard Taft held the interference unlawful on several grounds. Although he seemed to regard the Sherman Act violation as the least important of these grounds, he did not hesitate to cite the *Workingmen's Council* decision in support of his holding or to allude to the fact that a number of judges had followed Billings' decision in enjoining the Pullman strike.[9] Again,

[4] 64 Fed. at 752-53.
[5] 64 Fed. at 765.
[6] 62 Fed. 801, 803 (C.C.E.D. Mo. 1894).
[7] United States v. Elliott, 64 Fed. 27, 30 (C.C.E.D. Mo. 1894).
[8] 62 Fed. 803 (C.C.S.D. Ohio 1894).
[9] 62 Fed. at 821-22.

Judge Morrow, in his charge to a grand jury investigating the strikers' activities in California, cited Billings' decision which, he said, established the principle that a strike accompanied by violence and intimidation was proscribed by the Sherman Act. Morrow stressed, moreover, that the Fifth Circuit Court of Appeals had affirmed this view.[1] Later, when a number of strikers were tried, Morrow instructed the jury by again referring to the Billings opinion, now further reinforced by Woods's decision in the *Debs* case.[2]

When the *Debs* case came before it, the Supreme Court neither endorsed nor rejected the Billings-Woods-Morrow theory of the Sherman Act. The Court based its decision instead on an argument advanced by Attorney General Olney—that the Government did not need to invoke the Sherman Act, since it had common-law authority to obtain injunctions against disturbances amounting to a public nuisance. The Court said nothing about Woods's interpretation of the Act; however its silence must not be taken to mean disagreement.[3] Woods's literal reading of the statute therefore continued to stand as precedent for a method of interpretation that extended the scope of the Act.

Jurisdictional Problems and the Knight *Case*

Though many congressmen had feared that the weakest point in the Sherman Act would be its constitutional basis, and though its opponents had constantly urged that it certainly was unconstitutional, no court had been forced to face this issue before 1895. As yet, no judge had failed to find that the defendants before him were engaged in interstate commerce and acting so as to affect it. The mine owners in the *Jellico* case had traded with dealers in another state; the whisky trust had supplied out-of-state merchants; the railroads in the *Trans-Missouri* and *Joint Traffic* cases were unquestionably engaged in interstate commerce; and Debs could not deny that he had conducted a strike against interstate carriers. To be sure, in the *Greene* case Judge Jackson had asserted that the Federal Government lacked power to interfere with the lawful

[1] *In re* Grand Jury, 62 Fed. 840, 841-42 (N.D. Cal. 1894).

[2] United States v. Cassidy, 67 Fed. 698, 705 (N.D. Cal. 1895).

[3] *In re* Debs, 158 U.S. 564, 600 (1895).

use of property by citizens of the states and corporations created by a state,[4] and he had expressed some doubt as to the interstate character of the sales recounted by the indictment,[5] but these views were not essential to his decision.

The sugar trust case, *United States v. E. C. Knight Co.*,[6] was the first to turn on the question of interstate commerce. The Government's attorneys had not foreseen the difficulty—understandably, since none of the previous decisions warned them. They confidently asserted that, in buying up four of its five remaining competitors, the trust had combined and conspired with the erstwhile competitors to restrain and monopolize interstate commerce. Evidently the Federal attorneys never imagined that any question could arise as to whether the trust engaged in interstate commerce. But the strategy adopted by the Government unfortunately emphasized the very aspect of the trust's activities that was not "commercial" in the constitutional sense. The chief remedy sought was cancellation of the contracts by which the trust had acquired its competitors' plants, a solution reasonable enough in the circumstances, particularly since sound reasons existed for preferring a suit in equity to a criminal indictment.[7] Nevertheless, the proposed remedy called attention to the trust's manufacturing activities, which necessarily went on within states rather than among states. Perhaps still more inauspicious, as it happened, was the fact that all four of the purchased plants were located in the same state and, indeed, in the same city, Philadelphia. District Judge Butler seized on this as the central fact that disposed of the entire issue. "The contracts and acts of the defendants," he held, "relate exclusively to the acquisition of sugar refineries and the business of sugar refining, in Pennsylvania. They have no reference and bear no relation to commerce between the states or with foreign na-

[4] *In re* Greene, 52 Fed. 104, 112-13 (C.C.S.D. Ohio 1892).

[5] 52 Fed. at 117.

[6] 60 Fed. 306 (C.C.E.D. Pa.), *aff'd*, 60 Fed. 934 (3d Cir. 1894), *aff'd*, 156 U.S. 1 (1895).

[7] The whisky trust defendants had complained that criminal action was in effect persecution, and District Judge Ricks, in one of the whisky trust cases, had suggested that the courts would be more receptive to civil suits, *In re* Corning, 51 Fed. 205, 212-13 (N.D. Ohio 1892). In any event, settled rules of interpretation required courts to construe a criminal statute narrowly.

tions." [8] It followed that the contracts and acts could not be prohibited by a Federal statute.

In the chief lines of his argument, Butler followed Judge Jackson's reasoning in the *Greene* case, but without fully understanding it. The essential question, Butler said, had been "fully considered" by Jackson ("now of the Supreme Court") in an opinion that was "clear and satisfactory." [9] Despite its clarity, however, Butler did not quite appreciate its implications. He maintained that the sugar trust's monopoly of manufacture did not give it a monopoly of commerce because commerce was "untouched, unrestrained and open to all who choose to engage in it." [1] This was certainly Jackson's test of monopoly, but Jackson would not have made the initial concession that the trust had a monopoly of manufacture; for he would have found that the trust had done nothing to close manufacturing to any who might "choose to engage in it." Oddly enough, Butler did take the trouble of listing among the material facts proved by evidence "that the contract of sale in each instance left the sellers free to establish other refineries and continue the business if they should see fit to do so." [2] Clearly, if he was using Jackson's criterion of monopoly, then this fact established that the trust had no monopoly of manufacturing; and, if he was not using Jackson's criterion, the fact was immaterial. Butler moved to more solid ground when he considered whether the trust had a secondary monopoly of commerce. He maintained that, even if it had one, the trust restrained commerce only incidentally and therefore did not violate the Act, which could only prohibit "direct" interference with commerce.[3] The Third Circuit Court of Appeals upheld Butler's decision and emphasized the core of the argument by insisting that "the questioned conduct of the defendants"—that is, the contracts to purchase competitors' plants—did not concern interstate commerce.[4]

The Government's appeal in the *Knight* case was decided by the

[8] 60 Fed. at 309.
[9] 60 Fed. at 310.
[1] 60 Fed. at 309.
[2] 60 Fed. at 307.
[3] 60 Fed. at 309-10.
[4] United States v. E. C. Knight Co., 60 Fed. 934 (3d Cir. 1894).

Supreme Court early in 1895.[5] Chief Justice Fuller, in affirming the decisions of the lower courts, at the same time further clarified the central problem and disposed of the collateral issues. He began his opinion by insisting that the suit turned solely on whether the contracts to buy up competitors were valid. He then briefly dismissed each of the other questions raised by the parties and by Butler's opinion. It did not matter, he said, whether monopoly meant only a privilege granted by the state or a power acquired by the private efforts of individuals. It did not matter whether the case involved a combination, or whether Butler was correct in thinking that no combination could be shown here because the trust had made a separate bargain with each of the four competitors. Nor was it significant, as Butler thought, that the trust lowered the price of sugar, for low prices did not relieve "the objection to concentration of power." Finally—and most important in view of Butler's treatment of the case—it made no difference that the contracts were not in restraint of trade, though the Chief Justice obviously did not believe that the absence of restraint could be deduced from the fact that "others were theoretically left free to go into the business of refining sugar, and the original stockholders of the Philadelphia refineries after becoming stockholders of the American Company might go into competition with themselves, or, parting with that stock, might set up again for themselves." [6]

From the way Fuller disposed of the implications of Butler's "material facts," it is clear that he did not accept Jackson's theory that competition would inevitably destroy the trusts. His reference to "concentration of power," his sarcastic treatment of the possibility of new competitors entering or old competitors re-entering the industry, his refusal to distinguish between a monopoly in fact and a monopoly at law—all these indicate a sharp disapproval of the sugar trust's position and practices. Nevertheless he insisted that the fundamental legal question was "whether conceding that the existence of a monopoly in manufacture is established by the evidence, that monopoly can be directly suppressed under the Act of Congress in the mode attempted by this bill." [7] This way of putting the case stressed two parts of the question: first, whether

[5] United States v. E. C. Knight Co., 156 U.S. 1 (1895).
[6] 156 U.S. at 9-11.
[7] 156 U.S. at 11.

the Sherman Act could destroy a monopoly of manufacture, and, second, whether attempt to dissolve the contracts involved in this case was an appropriate way to invoke this Act against these defendants. Fuller answered the first half of the question by holding that the monopoly of manufacture only "incidentally and indirectly" affected commerce and that it therefore was not amenable to Federal statutes based on the commerce clause.[8] The second part he answered by suggesting that, had the Government concentrated its attack on the trust's commercial activities, the decision would have gone differently. To assail the trust for acquiring manufacturing plants was inevitably to make the trust's commercial activities appear secondary; but if its commercial activities had been emphasized in the bill, no constitutional question could have arisen. This suggestion appears in his first summary of the case as well as in his closing remark that "there was nothing in the proofs to indicate any intention to put a restraint upon trade or commerce, and the fact, as we have seen, that trade or commerce might be indirectly affected was not enough to entitle complainants to a decree."[9]

Many other signs in Fuller's opinion suggest that but for this defect in the Government's strategy, the Court would have decided in its favor. In discussing what Butler called the material facts of the case, Fuller implied that the trust really had imposed restraints on other parties, albeit hidden restraints, so that, even under Jackson's doctrine, they might have been condemned. But the Court was apparently ready to go further than Jackson in presuming that a monopoly was illegal. "[A]ll the authorities agree," Fuller wrote, "that in order to vitiate a contract or combination it is not essential that its result should be a complete monopoly; it is sufficient if it really tends to that end and to deprive the public of the advantages which flow from free competition."[1] Significantly, Fuller's opinion did not approve or even mention Jackson's opinion in the *Greene* case. The Chief Justice's attitude throughout shows that the decision of the Court depended strictly on the facts of the case. It did not lay down the rule, often ascribed to the *Knight* decision, that manufacturers as such are immune from the Sherman Act,

[8] 156 U.S. at 12.
[9] 156 U.S. at 17.
[1] 156 U.S. at 16.

but rather held that manufacturing was immune, and therefore that manufacturers were subject to the Act only insofar as their activities constituted interstate commerce or directly affected it.

Justice Harlan's dissent in the *Knight* case, although it denied at each critical point the conclusions of the majority, really rested on the assumption that the Court had authority to treat the case in a broader fashion than that proposed by the Government. Along with its prayer for a decree annulling the contracts of sale (and in the traditional style of bills in equity), the Government had prayed for such other relief as the Court might see fit to grant. Fuller had answered that the Court would not heed the more general prayer unless it found cause to grant the specific and principal remedy requested. Harlan, on the other hand, insisted that the general remedy could be provided even though the specific one was not.[2] If one assumed, as Harlan did, that the case ought to be viewed as an attack on the sugar trust as such, rather than on the four contracts alone, the rest of Harlan's position would have been difficult to dispute. He pointed out that the sugar trust had been organized not only to manufacture sugar but also to sell it; he could quote from the district court's summary of the facts the finding that the sugar trust had bought up its competitors in order to perfect its *"control over the business* of refining *and selling sugar in this country";*[3] and he could insist with obvious accuracy that everyone knew the trust sold sugar throughout the country. Moreover, it was not difficult for him to show that previous decisions of the Supreme Court had held selling to be a part of commerce—indeed, the majority opinion in this very case conceded the point. The way was thus open to conclude that the trust, by its mere existence, had the power to control the sale of sugar—that is, to control part of interstate commerce—in a way forbidden by the Sherman Act. In this view of the case, the contracts to purchase the competitors were important not because they themselves violated the Act but because they showed that the trust violated the Act. In this manner, Harlan showed that the Court could and should have transformed the weak case brought by the Government against the contracts of sale into an overpowering case against the trust. Had it done so, the whole constitutional question would have disappeared.

[2] 156 U.S. at 45-46.
[3] 156 U.S. at 18.

But Fuller and the majority held that it was not for the Court to improve the strategy that the Government had chosen.

Literal Interpretation vs. the Rule of Reason: the Trans-Missouri *Decision*

PECKHAM'S OPINION

The view that the Sherman Act was more than a codification of the common law, foreshadowed in the *Debs* and *E. C. Knight* decisions, achieved full expression when, in 1897, the Supreme Court reversed the lower courts in the *Trans-Missouri Freight Association* case.[4] Justice Peckham took the explicit position that the Sherman Act went beyond the common law: whereas the latter proscribed only unreasonable restraints, the Act in so many words prohibited every restraint. During the next six years, Peckham was the Court's chief spokesman in antitrust cases, and the doctrine he announced generally prevailed.

In the *Trans-Missouri* case, once it was determined that the Sherman Act applied to railroads,[5] the only question was whether the

[4] United States v. Trans-Missouri Freight Ass'n, 166 U.S. 290 (1897).

[5] The pleadings of the Freight Association, endorsed by the decrees of the lower courts, made it imperative that Peckham first dispose of a jurisdictional question—whether the Sherman Act applied to railroads at all. The defendants had advanced a series of arguments denying that it did, chief among them the one that had prevailed below—that the Interstate Commerce Act, 24 Stat. 379 (1887), permitted associations like that before the Court. If the Sherman Act were presumed to prohibit the Association, they maintained, it would be construed as implicitly repealing the Interstate Commerce Act, which no one could suppose to be its purpose. Peckham, however, saw the relation between the two statutes in quite another way. He held that, although the Commerce Act did not prohibit such associations, neither did it authorize them. The Sherman Act, which did prohibit them, was therefore not in conflict with the Commerce Act, and both acts could consistently apply to railroads. 166 U.S. at 314-16. Moreover, the Sherman Act's very language indicated that the statute reached the railroads. "When the act prohibits contracts in restraint of trade or commerce, the plain meaning of the language used includes contracts which relate to either or both subjects." 166 U.S. at 325. This was another way of saying what Woods had said in the *Debs* case: since the Act, read literally, prohibited arrangements in restraint of interstate commerce, a restrictive agreement among interstate rail-

Freight Association violated it. The answer depended, according to the defendants, on whether the Association was illegal at common law, and they supported their view by pointing to the title of the Act, which reads, "to protect trade and commerce against *unlawful* restraints and monopolies." [6] But Peckham, speaking for the majority of the Court, maintained that the title did not refer to restraints and monopolies that were illegal by common-law principles but to those that were "made unlawful in the body of the statute." [7] Contracts in restraint of trade, Peckham reasoned, were a familiar category at common law, and had come to be divided into two classes. "Some of such contracts have been held void and unenforceable in the courts by reason of their restraint being unreasonable, while others have been held valid because they were not of that nature. A contract may be in restraint of trade and still be valid at common law." But the Sherman Act had erased this distinction.

When, therefore, the body of an act pronounces as illegal every contract or combination in restraint of trade or commerce among the several States, etc., the plain and ordinary meaning of such language is not limited to that kind of contract which is in unreasonable restraint of trade, but all contracts are included in such language, and no exception or limitation can be added without placing in the act that which has been omitted by Congress.[8]

Although the "plain language" of the Act decided the issue at trial as far as he was concerned, Peckham went on to discuss the hypothetical question of whether the Association would have violated the Act had the statutory prohibitions been construed as being no broader than those at the common law. The common law, he asserted, had come to tolerate contracts that included a restraint of trade collateral to the sale of a business—the sort of arrangement by which the seller of a shop might agree not to open a com-

---

ways would certainly be within its scope. Adopting another argument advanced by Woods, Peckham maintained, moreover, that inasmuch as the *Knight* decision excluded manufacturing from the scope of the Act, to exclude railroads as well "would leave little for the act to take effect upon." 166 U.S. at 313, 326.

[6] Emphasis added.

[7] 166 U.S. at 327.

[8] 166 U.S. at 328.

peting business in the same neighborhood. And then, surprisingly, Peckham added that such contracts "might not be included, within the letter or spirit of the statute."[9] His next sentence explained this apparent contradiction by implying that judges may carve exceptions from the letter of the law in order to bring its effect closer to the legislators' intent. But Peckham, unlike some other judges, would not go so far as to assert that all reasonable restraints should be excepted on the same principle.

He turned now to the merits of the arguments by which the defendants tried to show that the Association constituted a reasonable restraint and was formed to achieve purposes which Congress could not have meant to declare illegal. They urged that competition among railroads is always excessive and, if unrestrained, would lead to bankruptcy and ruin. A combination designed to prevent this result by restricting excessive competition and establishing reasonable rates could not be supposed contrary to public policy. Peckham was inclined to agree that railroads always stood in danger of ruinous competition,[1] but he rejoined that many commentators took the opposite view—that full competition not only benefited the public but, in the long run, did not injure the railroads.[2] Moreover, he asserted, it would be impossible to determine whether rates set by a combination were reasonable, and recognition of this difficulty might well have prompted Congress to prohibit all agreements in restraint of trade, whether reasonable or not.[3] It might even be true, he conceded, that the Association was valid at common law. The argument to the contrary was "not entirely conclusive."[4] But, in any event, Congress had refused to distinguish in the body of the Act between reasonable and unreasonable restraints, and the Court would decline "to read into the act by way of judicial legislation an exception that is not placed there by the law-making branch of the Government."[5] Thus, every inquiry led Peckham back to the same essential rule, that the Act must be given its literal meaning.

[9] 166 U.S. at 329.
[1] 166 U.S. at 331, 340.
[2] 166 U.S. at 338.
[3] 166 U.S. at 331-32.
[4] 166 U.S. at 335.
[5] 166 U.S. at 340.

WHITE'S DISSENT

Peckham's opinion called forth a strong dissent, written by Justice White, which is memorable as the first statement of the doctrine later known as the "rule of reason." All of the majority's errors White summarized as "unreasonable." The word runs like a refrain through his opinion. While the common law invalidated only unreasonable restraints on trade, the present agreement between the defendants was reasonable—so much, White said, was conceded by the majority.[6] The contract, therefore, was reasonable according to the common law, or, as White put it, according to "general principles of law." But the Act, as Peckham construed it, condemned the contract. In other words, it condemned a reasonable contract. Therefore, White concluded, the Act must be unreasonable. If so, Congress was unreasonable in passing it, and the courts could not avail themselves of reason in interpreting it.[7] Having identified this as a logical difficulty in Peckham's opinion, White moved on to an argument from precedent. Was it true, as Peckham asserted, that the common law considered any contract which in fact restrained trade a "contract in restraint of trade"? Could a "contract in restraint of trade," as Peckham asserted, be either valid or invalid at common law? White answered no. He maintained that the term "contract in restraint of trade" had always been reserved for illegal contracts and had never been used, except in a loose and imprecise way, to describe permissible contracts. Only those contracts that unreasonably restrained trade were illegal and properly known as "contracts in restraint of trade." The source of confusion, White explained, was that, originally, every contract which restrained trade had been interpreted by the courts as a "contract in restraint of trade," that is, as an illegal contract. But, in time, more and more contracts that restrained trade were judged by the courts to restrain it "reasonably," and these contracts were therefore excluded from the proscribed class of "contracts in restraint of trade."[8] It followed that the Sherman Act, in prohibiting

[6] 166 U.S. at 343-44. This was a slight exaggeration; the majority conceded the point about the common law, but merely assumed for the sake of argument that the agreement was reasonable. 166 U.S. at 335.

[7] 166 U.S. at 344.

[8] 166 U.S. at 346-52.

"every contract in restraint of trade," did not prohibit every contract tending to restrain trade but only those contracts which restrained it unreasonably and which had been prohibited at common law as "contracts in restraint of trade."

Having stated his chief objection to the majority's interpretation and presented his own view of the Act, White added some reflections on the impolicy of the majority position. For one thing, he pointed out, a rigorous application of Peckham's rule would render illegal every contract in restraint of trade which was collateral to a sale of property. Peckham was inconsistent in holding first that "every" meant what it said and then that collateral restraints might be permissible. But if "every" were taken as all-inclusive and "contract in restraint of trade" were regarded as describing any contract that in fact restrained trade, then the Act would prohibit trade—or at least that part of trade comprising sales of property to which restraining conditions were attached. The result would be that a statute designed to free trade would, unreasonably, be enforced so as to restrain it. Nor was this the most dire result he foresaw. By denying the rule of reason and destroying the security afforded by the rule's flexibility, Peckham's interpretation would subject liberty of contract and freedom of trade "to the mere caprice of judicial authority." [9] He offered little hope that the fabric of civil society could be preserved unless the courts returned to the rule of reason and interpreted the Sherman Act as prohibiting only unreasonable restraints of trade.

It may seem curious that the same case should have evoked these two extreme principles of interpretation. The appearance of these divergent opinions at this moment depended to some extent on the coincidence that Peckham and White were members of the Court at the same time. But it also reflected a more permanent division of ideas in the Court, a disagreement that had probably existed before 1897 but had never before had occasion to be expressed. Since the *Knight* decision had gone off on a constitutional issue and the *Debs* case on general principles of common law and equity, the *Trans-Missouri* case was the first in which the Supreme Court was called on to interpret the substance of the Act. The split might have been expected, because the ambiguity of the Act al-

[9] 166 U.S. at 355.

lowed interpretation to vary according to the diverse views that Justices entertained about the meaning of the common law and its relation to the statute. But, for the moment, and indeed for over a decade, the majority of the Court preferred Peckham's approach to the rule of reason.

The Common Law Reconsidered: Taft's Addyston Pipe *Decision*

Just at this moment, when the courts seemed to have settled on a literal interpretation of the Sherman Act, a decision was rendered which suggested a way to view the common law so as to give the Act an almost identical interpretation. This analysis appeared in the opinion that William Howard Taft, then sitting on the Sixth Circuit Court of Appeals, wrote in the *Addyston Pipe* case.[1]

The case had been heard by the trial court in 1897,[2] just a month before the *Trans-Missouri* decision, and had been decided—for the defendants—according to the prevailing doctrines. It involved six cast-iron pipe manufacturers, producing between one-fifth and one-third of the nation's supply,[3] who had organized an association and a complex pooling system. When large users of pipe, chiefly municipalities and utility companies, advertised for bids, the association's executive committee would decide on the price to be asked and would award the privilege of bidding to whichever of the six member companies offered to pay the highest bonus into the association's treasury. The firm winning the right to bid was "protected" by its fellow members, who, for the sake of appearance, submitted bids slightly higher than its own. This system, which prevailed on large special orders, was augmented by the requirement that members pay fixed bonuses on goods sold in the ordinary course of business, as well as on all sales in "reserved cities"—

[1] United States v. Addyston Pipe & Steel Co., 85 Fed. 271 (6th Cir. 1898), *aff'd,* 175 U.S. 211 (1899), *reversing* 78 Fed. 712 (C.C.E.D. Tenn. 1897).

[2] United States v. Addyston Pipe & Steel Co., 78 Fed. 712 (C.C.E.D. Tenn. 1897).

[3] 78 Fed. at 714. The six firms had a total daily capacity of 650 tons, while two groups of unassociated competitors had capacities of 835 and 1550 tons daily. According to Taft, the Association had nearer one-third of the national capacity. 85 Fed. 271, 277 (6th Cir. 1898).

places assigned to each company as its exclusive market. Bonuses were not due, however, on goods sold in "free territory," the twelve New England and Middle Atlantic states where the association faced intense competition. Accumulated bonuses were periodically distributed among the members according to predetermined proportions. The Government contended, and proved to the satisfaction of the trial court, that the purpose of the arrangement was to reduce competition among the defendants and permit them to raise the price of pipe. The trial court held, nevertheless, that the association had not violated the Sherman Act.

The primary basis of the trial court's decision was that, since the defendants were manufacturers who affected interstate commerce only indirectly, they were exempt from the Sherman Act under the rule of the *Knight* case. The lower court implied, moreover, that even if it had considered the Act applicable, it would have found the association lawful. The judges attached considerable weight to affidavits presented by the defendants' customers in which the customers expressed satisfaction with the prices they had been charged. The lower court was convinced that the defendants had not been able to "raise or maintain prices above what is reasonable" or, rather, that "in some instances prices have been above what was probably fair or reasonable, but the proof fails to show that the average prices have been so."[4] All of which meant that, the *Knight* principle aside, a combination to set reasonable prices was reasonable at common law and therefore legal under the Sherman Act.

By the time the *Addyston* case came up on appeal the Supreme Court had handed down the *Trans-Missouri* decision, which undermined the position that the pipe dealers' combination was lawful because its prices were reasonable. In reversing the lower court in the *Addyston* case, however, the circuit court of appeals did not rely very heavily on Peckham's reasoning. To be sure, Taft did open his opinion by questioning the defendants' assertion that they had not violated the Act because they had done nothing contrary to common law. "It might be a sufficient answer to this contention," he wrote, "to point to the decision of the supreme court of the United States in U.S. v. Trans-Missouri Freight Ass'n . . . in which it was held that contracts in restraint of interstate transportation were

[4] 78 Fed. at 714-15.

within the statute, whether the restraints would be regarded as reasonable at common law or not." [5] But the way Taft phrased Peckham's decision shows that he was uncertain about its application. He said it "might be," not that it definitely was, a "sufficient answer"; he represented the rule of the *Trans-Missouri* case as applying to "transportation" rather than to the broader subject, "commerce"; and he thought that some credit might be due the suggestion that Peckham's decision was more stringent because the defendants were quasi-public corporations than it would have been had ordinary private companies been involved.

Taft preferred to rest the decision on other grounds. An examination of the common law convinced him, as it had Peckham, that "collateral" or "ancillary" restraints of trade were valid. According to Peckham, this was a ground for excepting them from the general operation of the Sherman Act as literally interpreted. But Taft emphasized the obverse—that all nonancillary restraints were void at common law—and in effect concluded that the Sherman Act need not be thought to go beyond the common law to be given an interpretation as broad as Peckham's.

He therefore devoted the core of his opinion to showing that an agreement like that among the pipe manufacturers was invalid at common law. His review of the precedents began with White's historical generalization: in the beginning the common law prohibited all restraints of trade; later, becoming more flexible, it permitted some. But, Taft said—and here he diverged from the usual analysis—the exceptions to the rule were all of one sort. They involved contracts in which the restraint was ancillary to some other main object, such as the sale of a business or property, the founding or dissolution of a partnership, or the employment of an apprentice or agent. Such contracts had been upheld when they were reasonable, "reasonableness" being measured in relation to the legitimate object of the contract; so that a restraint attached to the sale of a business, for instance, would be regarded as reasonable and unexceptionable if it offered the buyer only as much protection as was necessary to preserve the goodwill of the business.[6] Taft's interpretation of the cases implied (contrary to the views of many commentators and especially of English judges) that the common law had not

[5] 85 Fed. at 278.
[6] 85 Fed. at 280-82.

withdrawn its favor from free competition in order to bestow it upon free contract, but had instead promoted the "free purchase and sale of property" while defending with undiminished zeal the freedom to compete. For, Taft maintained, reasonable ancillary restraints did nothing to diminish competition; a buyer who undertook to observe such a restraint "was not reducing competition, but was only securing the seller against an increase of competition of his own creating." [7]

His view was supported, Taft said, by the fact that the common law regularly invalidated the other category of contracts in restraint of trade, those "where the sole object of the parties . . . is merely to restrain competition." [8] The restraints imposed by such contracts could not be reasonable because these contracts had no lawful main purpose to justify the restraint or to serve as a measure of its reasonableness. If courts undertook to distinguish among them, the only standard they could apply would be "the vague and varying opinion of judges as to how much, on principles of political economy, men ought to be allowed to restrain competition." [9] The fact nevertheless remained that, in a few cases, some courts had sanctioned nonancillary contracts in restraint of trade, and Taft now proceeded to show that, in assuming "the power to say . . . how much restraint of competition is in the public interest," these courts had mistaken the common-law rules and "set sail on a sea of doubt." [1]

Of the precedents that the defendants in this case and judges in previous antitrust cases had relied on as authoritative, but that Taft believed erroneous, he first considered *Wickens v. Evans*.[2] There the court had approved an agreement among three trunk makers to partition England into districts in which each would be the exclusive supplier. The court reasoned that the restraint left the trade open to entry by all other persons. The principle of the decision was the same which Jackson had espoused in the *Greene* case, and perhaps Taft regarded this as an additional reason for refuting an argument that would, he said, "validate the most complete local

[7] 85 Fed. at 281.
[8] 85 Fed. at 282.
[9] 85 Fed. at 283.
[1] 85 Fed. at 284.
[2] 3 Y. & J. 318, 148 Eng. Rep. 1201 (Ex. 1829).

monopoly of the present day."[3] Not that he denied competition would sooner or later prevail over monopolies, but he insisted that the law could not idly wait for the eventual outcome.

> It may be, as suggested by the court, that local monopolies cannot endure long, because their very existence tempts outside capital into competition; but the public policy embodied in the common law requires the discouragement of monopolies, however temporary their existence may be. The public interest may suffer severely while new competition is slowly developing.[4]

In any event, he added, the decision in *Wickens v. Evans* could not be reconciled with later cases, English as well as American.

Similar reasons prevailed against the other precedents that were supposed to show that the common law approved as reasonable some outright restraints of trade.[5] An English decision, upholding a combination among stevedore companies, was refuted by an American case suppressing a similar combination. A Canadian decision favoring a combination of salt manufacturers was outweighed by the contrary decision of an Ohio court. A Wisconsin decision was dismissed on account of its age. And a New York decision was disqualified because, resting on the principle "that competition is not invariably a public benefaction,"[6] it wrongly left the court discretion to decide how much competition was beneficent. It also diametrically opposed a Kentucky decision.

The *Mogul Steamship* case, Taft insisted, did not properly belong among the other seemingly contrary decisions, although the defendants sought to place it there. The courts, he said, had not upheld the legality of the steamship combination; they had only held that it did not illegally damage its competitors. Furthermore, several of the judges had said that they would have refused to enforce the agreement if the case had come up on that issue. The *Mogul* decision, therefore, like all the decisions except those few in which judges had mistakenly strayed, supported the proposition that any agreement made for the sole purpose of restricting competition was illegal at common law. And if the Sherman Act followed the common law, it too condemned all such agreements—all unreasonable

[3] 85 Fed. at 284.
[4] 85 Fed. at 284.
[5] 85 Fed. at 284-87.
[6] 85 Fed. at 286.

ancillary restraints and all direct restraints whatsoever, or, in other words, all unreasonable contracts in restraint of trade and all combinations in restraint of trade.

Once the decision was grounded on the illegality of all restraints except ancillary restraints, many of the defendants' arguments became irrelevant. In particular, their plea that the pipe manufacturers' combination must be deemed reasonable because it charged reasonable prices, and the affidavits to that effect, were of no avail; for Taft held that, by forming the association, they had acquired the power to charge unreasonable prices, whether or not they had thus far chosen to exercise it. But, Taft added, "if it were important, we should unhesitatingly find that the prices charged in the instances which were in evidence were unreasonable"; they were far above the cost of production and transportation plus a reasonable profit.[7]

The question yet remained whether this combination, illegal at common law, was constitutionally subject to the Sherman Act. The defendants strongly urged that it was not, maintaining that, as pipe manufacturers, they much more nearly resembled the sugar refiners of the *Knight* case than the railroads in the *Trans-Missouri* case. Taft flatly rejected this argument. The *Knight* case, he held, had been decided for the defendants because the contracts in question "related only to the manufacture of refined sugar, and not to its sale throughout the country."[8] The Supreme Court had not meant that any contract between manufacturers was immune, but only such contracts as related exclusively to manufacturing. "The obstacle in the way of granting the relief asked in U.S. v. E. C. Knight Co. was (to use the language of the chief justice) that 'the contracts and acts of the defendant related exclusively to the acquisition of the Philadelphia refineries, and the business of sugar refining in Pennsylvania, and bore no direct relation to commerce between the states or with foreign nations.' "[9] The contracts in this case were of a quite different sort. They concerned the sale in one state of goods to be delivered in another, and were "interstate commerce in its strictest and highest sense."[1] Indeed, they were of

[7] 85 Fed. at 293.
[8] 85 Fed. at 296.
[9] 85 Fed. at 298.
[1] 85 Fed. at 295.

the exact kind that Chief Justice Fuller had designated as most certainly subject to Federal regulation, "contracts to buy, sell, or exchange goods to be transported among the several states." [2] No doubt existed, then, that the defendants had violated the Sherman Act.

Taft's pruning operation cut away the irregular branches of the common law and showed that its outlines were very similar to those which Peckham attributed to the statute. Meanwhile, however, the Supreme Court persisted in Peckham's analysis of the act.

The Rule of Competition

During 1898 and 1899, Justice Peckham had the opportunity to restate his doctrine in four more antitrust opinions. In each of these, though he continued to maintain that the Act went beyond the common law, he retreated from the extreme position he had taken in the *Trans-Missouri* case by clarifying his definition of "restraint of trade."

The severity of the *Trans-Missouri* rule came under serious question in *United States v. Joint Traffic Association,*[3] the first of this group of cases. The defendants argued that if Peckham's interpretation were to prevail, the Act would prohibit a great variety of contracts in restraint of trade that were admittedly necessary and beneficial. This result, defendants urged, would unconstitutionally interfere with freedom of contract. In short, either Peckham's interpretation was erroneous or the Sherman Act was unconstitutional. They listed, as among these useful and commendable contracts or combinations in restraint of trade, labor unions, partnerships or corporations formed by persons already engaged in the same business, common selling agencies, an agreement by which the vendor of a business promised not to compete, and a covenant restricting the use of real estate. To this, Peckham answered, first, that as none of the contracts listed was like the defendants' association, their argument was somewhat beside the point. Moreover, he went on to say, the argument was not well founded. For instance,

[2] 85 Fed. at 297.
[3] 171 U.S. 505 (1898).

the formation of partnerships and corporations had "never, to our knowledge, been regarded in the nature of a contract in restraint of trade or commerce."[4] It seems odd that Peckham should have made this appeal to precedent when he explicitly denied that the common law was an appropriate basis for interpreting the Act; this and similar passages show, however, that he did sometimes invoke common law as a guide to the meaning of "restraint of trade." Characteristically, he found guidance in a more literal reading of the statute a moment later when he said, "It might also be difficult to show that the appointment by two or more producers of the same person to sell their goods on commission was a matter in any degree in restraint of trade." This statement implicitly reasserted that the proper method to determine whether a contract restrained trade was not to refer to the common law but rather to decide by a process of reasoning whether a practice actually restricted the exchange or movement of goods. Later on, Peckham did outline the nature of restraints, but for the present he was content to continue his refutation of the argument that the Act, under his interpretation, would prohibit desirable restraints. Taking up another of the defendants' examples, he pointed out that the sale of a business with a collateral covenant not to compete was permissible; this type of contract had been explicitly discussed in the *Trans-Missouri* opinion and described there as outside the spirit of the Act.[5]

Having given particular reasons why some contracts were not within the statutory proscription, Peckham now turned to the general principle which assured that his interpretation would not render illegal all sorts of other indispensable and beneficial contracts and combinations. The principle, discussed at length in another antitrust opinion delivered on the same day, *Hopkins v. United States,*[6] was a slightly modified version of the rule that had governed the *Knight* case: Peckham held that the Act applied only to contracts "whose direct and immediate effect" was to restrain interstate commerce. This meant, he said, that "an agreement entered into for the purpose of promoting the legitimate business of an individual or corporation, with no purpose to thereby affect or restrain

[4] 171 U.S. at 567.
[5] 171 U.S. at 568.
[6] 171 U.S. 578 (1898).

interstate commerce, and which does not directly restrain such commerce, is not, as we think, covered by the act." [7] The Act was still to be interpreted without reference to common law, but the literal reading would henceforth be moderated by interpreting "restraint" as "direct and immediate restraint." In this way Peckham was using a constitutional criterion to do the same work accomplished by the common-law distinction between reasonable and unreasonable restraints. A restraint attached to a sale of property would be lawful under the Act, according to Taft, because it was reasonable and ancillary at common law, and, according to Peckham, because it had no direct or immediate effect on commerce. A restraint imposed by a combination of pipe manufacturers was prohibited by the Act, in Taft's view, because it was not ancillary, and therefore not valid at common law, and, in Peckham's opinion, because it directly and immediately affected commerce. Although the content of the rules was different, they might often, and usually did, lead to the same conclusions. The extent of Peckham's retreat from the extreme position of the *Trans-Missouri* opinion is shown by a passage in the *Hopkins* decision, which Peckham considered so important that he quoted it in the *Joint Traffic* opinion: "The act of Congress must have a reasonable construction or else there would scarcely be an agreement or contract among businessmen that could not be said to have, indirectly or remotely, some bearing upon interstate commerce, and possibly to restrain it." [8]

The opinions written by Peckham in the Supreme Court's last four antitrust cases of the century—*Joint Traffic, Hopkins, Anderson,* and *Addyston Pipe*—provided a clearer view of how he determined whether an agreement "directly and immediately" restrained commerce. To interpret restraint of commerce quite literally, as any reduction in the physical quantity of goods moving among the states, might lead to ludicrous results. A shipowner who scrapped a ship, a manufacturer who closed his plant, a laborer who retired—all of these and many more would appear to have violated the Act. Peckham therefore asked whether the combination complained of actually reduced competition and thus tended toward monopoly. The Joint Traffic Association was condemned

[7] 171 U.S. at 568.

[8] Hopkins v. United States, 171 U.S. 578, 600 (1898), quoted in 171 U.S. at 568.

for this reason. "An agreement of the nature of this one which directly and effectually stifles competition, must be regarded under the statute as one in restraint of trade." [9] The association in the *Anderson* case did not reduce competition and, hence, was lawful.[1] The *Addyston Pipe* combination, like that in the *Joint Traffic* case, was unlawful, however, and Peckham once again stated the rule:

> We have no doubt that where the direct and immediate effect of a contract or combination among particular dealers in a commodity is to destroy competition between them and others, so that the parties to the contract or combination may obtain increased prices for themselves, such contract or combination amounts to a restraint of trade in the commodity, even though contracts to buy such commodity at the enhanced price are continually being made.[2]

Although Peckham had begun by insisting that the Act meant what its plain language said, the necessity of applying the statute to concrete situations had forced him to interpret the plain words. Constitutional considerations and reflection on the legislative intent suggested the proper interpretation, and he now understood "every contract in restraint of trade or commerce among the states" to mean in effect "every contract that directly and immediately restricts competition and directly affects commerce among the states." This formula in the main controlled the interpretation of antitrust cases for the following decade.

[9] 171 U.S. at 577.

[1] Anderson v. United States, 171 U.S. 604, 614 (1898).

[2] Addyston Pipe & Steel Co. v. United States, 175 U.S. 211, 244 (1899).

CHAPTER SIX

THE SHERMAN ACT REACHES MATURITY

1901-1904

The coming to age of the Sherman Act was marked by the *Northern Securities* case. This birthday gala was in every way a stirring performance. The fame of the defendants alone was enough to arouse popular interest. Among them were three major railroads of the Northwest—the Northern Pacific, Great Northern, and Burlington, and the largest holding company yet established—the Northern Securities Company, a holding company formed to control the three railroads. And yet those institutional giants were upstaged by two human defendants who might have been delegated to personify the popular idea of Big Business and High Finance: James J. Hill, the swashbuckling railroad man who had built the Great Northern, the only one of the transcontinental railroads erected without heavy Federal subsidies; and J. Pierpont Morgan, the Goliath of bankers. Each was accompanied by a host of supporting minor moguls. It was the first antitrust case in which those cast as villains were celebrities.

On the other side the personalities were less vivid, although behind the Government's attorneys lurked the romantic and excitable figure of Theodore Roosevelt, partly stage manager and script writer, partly protagonist. But what the Government's corps, led by Attorney General Philander Knox, lacked in spontaneous enthusiasm, it made up for by the most precise and painstaking craftsmanship. The drama was staged, indeed, as a conflict between Reason and Extravagance, between the respectable requirements of the common good and the wilfulness of colorful, but dangerous, buccaneers.

The performance was in the end so stagy that even the Supreme

Court was infected with histrionic urges. It split five to four, but the majority required two separate opinions to express its views and the minority required two more—indicating a degree of idiosyncrasy that was more rare in the Court then than it has since become. Holmes, writing his version of the dissenting view, almost bluntly expressed his resentment over the dramatics of the case in the famous epigram, "Great cases like hard cases make bad law." This, like others, was a "great case" because of an "accident of overwhelming interest which appeals to the feelings and distorts the judgment"—in this instance the presence on stage of Morgan and Hill and, in the wings, of Harriman. The imagination of the observer was too likely to be carried away by the clash of great and stormy battles, his mind prevented from concentrating coolly on the single, isolated justiciable issue.

Holmes's complaint was above all a criticism of Roosevelt's management, and Roosevelt resented it as such. It was, in one sense, a fair criticism, for Roosevelt was nothing if not showy, and it is easy to believe that he very much wanted to create just the sort of public spectacle that Holmes considered out of order. In another sense, however, Holmes's objection may have been irrelevant. Roosevelt conceived his role as that of head political tutor to the American people. Every teacher knows that teaching is in some degree a dramatic art, for schoolboys must be seduced into learning, and the effort of thought sometimes makes them sleepy. Roosevelt made a production of the *Northern Securities* case in order to shock the voters into recognizing the nature of the trust problem. Roosevelt was arousing support for a policy of improving the technology of antitrust action, the policy he pursued in his own curious fashion throughout his tenure of office. Holmes, on the other hand, like any dedicated judge, was bound to be most concerned—for the moment, at least—with the overwhelming problem of trying to accomplish justice, under a given statute, in the particular case before him.

The difference in views between the two men illustrates a conflict that often arises between law and politics, most vividly in what are called political trials, but sometimes also, if more subtly, in major antitrust suits. Whether a judicial proceeding ought to be treated by government as an instrument for educating the electorate; whether the end of instituting a new policy is compatible with the end of administering justice even-handedly between the parties—these are problems whose character is illustrated in the history of the *Northern Securities* case.

Formation of the Northern Securities Company

The case arose from one of those titanic struggles, comic-opera style, that makes the commercial history of the turn of the century read like the work of a storyteller whose sole aim is to excite small boys and terrify lovesick maidens.

The foundation was serious enough. In 1900, four main railroads connected the Pacific Coast with the Mississippi Valley. Of these, the southernmost, the Southern Pacific, was most advantageously located, for it could run trains, on its own tracks, from the port of San Francisco to the port of New Orleans, from whence goods were easily carried by water through the Gulf into the Atlantic, and up the Mississippi into the heartland of the continent. None of the other three could do as well. The central line, the Union Pacific, was landlocked at both ends, Ogden (Utah) at the west, Omaha and Kansas City at the east. The two northern lines, the Northern Pacific and Great Northern, both reached the Pacific at Seattle, but had no better access to the East than Duluth, the westernmost port on the Great Lakes, and no handier debouch into the Mississippi than their common terminal at St. Paul. To Chicago and St. Louis, the eastern outlets that would have been more advantageous economically, none of the three great lines had right-of-way along its own tracks.

These deprivations did not, of course, prevent the northern two or the Union Pacific from accepting freight for shipment between any point on their own lines and any other part of the country. To carry out such orders, they had only to arrange a through rate with whatever railroads made end-to-end connections with their own tracks. But the cooperation of those adjoining railroads was always in doubt and might be utterly refused them if the connecting railroad were acquired by a competitor—not to mention the fact that in the absence of substantial competition, the connecting railroad might, because of whim or policy determined by accidental variations in business, decide at any moment to demand an extortionate fee for its irreplaceable services. Having had long experience of all this, James J. Hill had for some time been trying to acquire a railroad connecting the end of his Great Northern line at St. Paul with the more desirable end-point of Chicago.

The possibility of his doing so was enhanced, in about 1900, by a combination of circumstances. The first was that although the Northern Pacific appeared to be in competition with Hill's Great Northern, and although it was a separate corporation, it was in fact under Hill's control. It had been very distinctly a competitor, a threatening one, during the 1880's, while Henry Villard was rapidly (and perhaps wastefully) extending it to the Pacific Coast. But in 1893 it had been forced into bankruptcy, and during the course of the next three years it was reorganized under the auspices of Morgan, acting for the former bondholders, represented by J. P. Morgan & Co. and the Deutsche Bank of Berlin. Morgan and Hill agreed that competition between the two lines would suit the interests of neither, and that the sort of "community of interest" which represented to Morgan the heights of Industrial Statesmanship should replace it; moreover Morgan rightly admired Hill's ability to run a railroad and hoped that Hill could make the reorganized Northern Pacific show profits. Morgan, Hill, and the various English and German principal parties had therefore drawn up a so-called "London agreement," in May 1895, in which the Great Northern undertook to guarantee an issue of Northern Pacific mortgage bonds up to $175,000,000, in return for which it should take one half of the Northern Pacific's capital stock and nominate five of the nine directors of the Northern Pacific for a stipulated period. That agreement was, however, held unlawful by the U. S. Supreme Court, in March 1896,[1] on the grounds that the Great Northern, a Minnesota corporation, was violating a statute of Minnesota prohibiting railroad mergers in these terms: "No railroad corporation shall consolidate with, lease or purchase, or in any way become owner of, or control any other railroad corporation, or any stock, franchise, or rights of property thereof, which owns or controls a parallel or competing line."

But what the Great Northern Railroad was prohibited from doing in its corporate capacity, its principal owners could accomplish privately. A second "London agreement" was therefore

[1] Pearsall v. Great Northern, 161 U.S. 646 (1896).

drawn up in 1896, whereby Hill and his associates were sold about $16,000,000 of Northern Pacific stock, or about 10 per cent of the total issue. The effect of this substantial minority holding, when coupled with the block of shares under Morgan's control, was to give them effective joint control of the Northern Pacific. The intended effect of all this was shown by a letter that Hill sent Morgan two years later, in which he wrote:

> The sole object of myself and friends in signing the London agreement with your house and the Deutsche Bank was to bring together as nearly as possible the general policy of the Northern Pacific and the Great Northern, so that both companies could be operated on such lines of general policy as would preserve their mutual independence and allow each one to discharge all its duties to itself and to the public in such a manner as to avoid unnecessary expenditure of money either in building new lines or in the operation of existing lines. We believed this could only be done by the holding of a large and practically a controlling interest in both companies by the same parties.[2]

In buying a connecting line extending eastward from the common terminus of the Great Northern and Northern Pacific at St. Paul, Hill could therefore use the joint resources of the two lines and could depend on additional financial backing from Morgan.

The other circumstance favorable to Hill's plans was that in 1900 the best of the several lines that might have served his purpose became available for purchase. It was the Chicago, Burlington and Quincy—the Burlington Road—which had the great advantage of connecting St. Paul not only with Chicago, but also with St. Louis, Kansas City, Omaha, Denver, and much more. Hill found out that the directors were willing to recommend that the shareholders accept a generous takeover bid. Negotiations were completed by April 1901. The Great Northern, together with the Northern Pacific, bought almost the whole capital stock of 1,800,000 shares, at a negotiated price of $200 per share, each railroad taking title to half the shares. In payment they gave bonds which they issued jointly and which were secured by collateral consisting of the Burlington stock which they now owned. Hill—or, more precisely, the two northern railroads—had achieved the eastward access they wanted. As Hill wrote to his friend and

[2] Pyle, *Life of James J. Hill*, II, 3-29 (1917).

financial associate, Lord Mount Stephen, president of the Bank of Montreal:

> The best traffic of the Great Northern and Northern Pacific is the cotton and provisions west[-bound] and the lumber and timber east-bound. The San Francisco [i.e., Southern Pacific] lines run through the cotton country from New Orleans through Texas and Arkansas. The great provision centres are Kansas City, St. Joseph, Omaha, Chicago, and St. Louis, none of which are reached directly by the Great Northern or Northern Pacific. Both companies have to divide the through rate with some other line to reach these important points. . . . The Burlington lets us into all these districts and commercial centres, over better lines and with better terminals than any other road.[3]

This success did not gladden the heart of E. H. Harriman, president of the Union Pacific Railroad. He had reason to congratulate himself on other accounts, for a few months earlier his Union Pacific group had taken over working control of the Southern Pacific system by buying about $75,000,000 worth of the Southern Pacific's total capital stock of $200,000,000.[4] Yet this coup did not yet give his railroads any convenient route into the Northeast. The Burlington deal was therefore doubly rankling. It was bad enough that his northern competitors could now, should they choose, deny him service on one of the main feeder lines connecting Omaha and Kansas City with the East Coast; it was worse that by controlling a line which paralleled his tracks in much of Kansas, Nebraska, and Colorado, they could engage him in direct competition. Although caught by surprise, Harriman had not let the take-over go utterly by default. During the spring of 1900 he and his colleagues had bought a large block of Burlington stock, about $10,000,000 worth, or about 10 per cent of the total, but finding it difficult to buy much more of the stock they gave up the attempt and sold out their holdings before the end of the year.[5] Then they suddenly discovered that Hill and Morgan had virtually captured the Burlington. Whereupon, Edward Harriman, to adopt the chaste language of a Federal court, "applied to James J. Hill and J. Pierpont Morgan . . . to permit the Union Pacific Company to join and share with them in the purchase of the Burlington system,

[3] Pyle, *Life of James J. Hill,* II, 119 f.
[4] 72 *Comm. & Fin. Chron.* 242, 284 *et seq.* (Feb. 2, 9, 1901).
[5] Kennan, *E. H. Harriman,* I, 290 ff. (1922).

but his application was denied." [6] As the more romantic story has it, Harriman went, in "a towering rage," to accuse Hill of having negotiated for the Burlington "secretly"; offered to buy one-third of the line; was refused; and left saying, "Very well, it is a hostile act and you must take the consequences." [7]

The consequences were vivid. Thwarted in his attempt to join courteously in the ownership of the subsidiary, Harriman decided to buy control of one of its parents, the Northern Pacific. This modest undertaking required him to take up a majority of the voting stock of 1,550,000 shares—800,000 common and 750,000 preferred—then selling near their par value of $100 each, that is, to buy a majority of issues then valued in the market at about $155,000,000.

Harriman and his colleagues—chief among them Jacob Schiff, senior partner of Kuhn, Loeb and Co.—launched their campaign quietly, in April 1901. By the beginning of May, they had succeeded in acquiring a clear majority of the stock, over 780,000 shares, of which 370,000 were common stock and 410,000 preferred.[8]

Their success was made easier by the fact that Morgan and Hill were absent from the scene. Morgan had gone off to Europe for a rest, having just completed arrangements for forming the United States Steel Corporation. Hill was in Seattle. That much is known; the rest is hazier.

The received account becomes at this point most dramatic. Harriman's heavy purchases were sending up the price of Northern Pacific. Hill, in Seattle, felt that all this boded no good. He ordered the superintendent of the Western division of the Great Northern to schedule a special train for him "with unlimited right of way over everything," and sped to New York in record time, arriving on the afternoon of Friday, May 3. He rushed in to see Schiff, who told him that Harriman and he had indeed been buying Northern Pacific: "You secretly bought the Chicago, Burlington, & Quincy and refused to give us a fair share; now we're going to see if we can't get a share by purchasing a controlling interest in the Northern Pacific." Confounded, Hill rushed off with the bad news to Morgan and Company, where he told it to

[6] Minn. v. Northern Securities Co., 123 Fed. 692, at 695 (1903).
[7] Kennan, *Harriman,* I, 296.
[8] 123 Fed. at 695.

Robert Bacon, one of Morgan's partners. Bacon was astonished. After quick consultation with other partners, he cabled Morgan for authority to buy 150,000 shares of Northern Pacific common stock, and during the weekend Morgan cabled his approval.[9]

It might seem curious, since the Harriman group had already captured the majority of Northern Pacific shares, that the Morgan-Hill group should go to the trouble of reinforcing their minority holdings. It was worth the effort, however, because Harriman's control was somewhat impermanent. The preferred stocks, armed as they were with full voting rights, could be disarmed quickly enough: the railroad company had the power, at its option, to retire the preferred stocks by buying them in at $100 per share on the first day of any year. More precisely, that power was lodged in the board of directors of the railway company, and in May 1901, the board of directors was controlled by the Morgan-Hill group. Harriman's ownership of the preferred stock—and the majority of all votes it gave him—could therefore be nullified by an action of the board of directors controlled by Hill and Morgan. Once that was done, control of the company would fall into the hands of those who held a majority of the 800,000 shares of common stock. Now, as of Friday, May 3, neither the Harriman nor the Morgan-Hill group held a clear majority of the common stock, Harriman being short of it by about 30,000 shares, Morgan by considerably more. There was, accordingly, still room for conflict.

On Saturday, May 4—so the received version continues—Harriman had a definite advantage. He was closer than the Morgan group to having captured a majority of the common stock; he was ready to move ahead, whereas his opponents were immobilized, awaiting the message from Morgan. Harriman, "stricken ill and confined to his home" on that Saturday, nevertheless summoned the strength to telephone Kuhn, Loeb's offices, and place an order to buy 40,000 shares more of Northern Pacific common stock, enough to give him a clear majority. But, so goes Frederick Lewis Allen's version of the story, Harriman's order "couldn't be executed because Schiff, a devout Jew, was at the synagogue."[1] That was

[9] The prime source for the romantic version of the episode is Josephson, *Robber Barons* (1934), esp. pp. 435 ff.

[1] Allen, *The Great Pierpont Morgan* 212 (1949); another version of the tale is in Josephson, *Robber Barons* 437 ff.

the beginning of the end. On Monday, Morgan's cable arrived; by Wednesday Morgan's men had bought what they needed, and Harriman's attack was decisively beaten off.

As usual, however, the legend is too neat on the surface, and too full of gaps at its foundation. For instance, Hill is supposed to have been alerted to the raid by the way the prices of Northern Pacific stocks rose during April. In fact he should have been surprised had they not risen as they did, for the prices of all stocks and especially of railroad stocks rose quite steadily from June of 1900 through April of 1901.[2] As to the price of Northern Pacific common stock, it rose during April with exceptional regularity but with not enough speed to give away Harriman's secret; the high prices for daily sales reached $99 during the first week of April, $100 during the second week, $106 during the third week. It is true enough that on Monday, April 29, the high price jumped to $120, a figure that might have agitated Hill, but then on Tuesday, Wednesday, and Thursday, the high prices leveled off at $117, on Friday the high was down to $115, and on Saturday to $110.[3] Perhaps Monday's high price was enough to agitate Hill; but that it need have done so is far from obvious.

Again, as the story has it, Hill stormed straight into Schiff's office. Why Schiff? Even if Hill suspected a raid on Northern Pacific, there were other potential raiders to suspect. Moreover, if Schiff were the raider, why should Hill have expected Schiff to confess the fact?

A more satisfactory explanation is available, if less colorful. A week later, when the crisis was over, and the Harriman-Schiff group told their side of the story, the *Commercial and Financial Chronicle* reported as follows: "Last week they [the Union Pacific group] had purchased or contracted to purchase 43 per cent of the outstanding shares, and so notified the Morgan-Hill interests, and again asked for such an arrangement [about the Burlington] as would protect the interests of the Union Pacific." The Hill-Morgan group responded to the news by buying Northern Pacific stock,

[2] An index of 20 rails prices, which averaged about 75 in June 1900, rose to 90 in Dec. 1900, 100 in March 1901, and 110 in April; Standard and Poor, *Security Price Index Record* (May, 1960).

[3] 72 *Comm. & Fin. Chron.* 661, 709, 760, 808, 859, 922.

and their orders "were followed by renewed buying on the part of the Union Pacific interests."[4]

The important difference between this account and the blood-and-thunder version is that Harriman and Schiff *notified* Hill and Morgan as soon as they had acquired a sizeable minority interest. This fact, if fact it is, destroys the conception of the whole affair as a secret fight to the death, full of alarms and excursions. It fits much better into the generally conciliatory and compromising spirit in which the issue was resolved, as well as into the spirit of gentlemanly "community of interest" that Morgan and the financial community at large had long been trying to sponsor. The heroic version is anachronistic because it tells a story of 1901 in the style more pertinent to financial mores and manners of the 1870's and 1880's. By 1900, the leaders of finance had become civilized and statesmanlike.

In view of all this, the notion that the climax occurred when Schiff refused to turn from his prayers must be treated as poor fiction. No doubt Schiff, being devout, may have been at the synagogue; but Kuhn, Loeb and Company was a business firm, that kept its doors open on Saturday whether the partners were or were not at synagogue, and which (it is hard to believe otherwise) was capable of executing a buying order for some $4,000,000, Saturday or not. Besides, the senior partner of a great banking house would not normally have taken any personal part in executing such an order; he or his brokers would keep their man on the floor of the New York Stock Exchange—which in those days was open for business on Saturday mornings—to do the simple routine of placing orders to buy. Great bankers may pray at appointed hours, as other folk do; great bankers forget things and hire employees who forget things on their behalf; but a man does not become a great banker by letting business slide while he prays nor by overlooking orders worth millions, orders placed by his prime customers and closest associates.

Indeed, according to the Union Pacific statement,[5] when their

[4] 72 *Comm. & Fin. Chron.* 936 (May 11, 1901). This report is borne out by a letter from Schiff to Morgan, May 16, 1901, in Adler, *Jacob Schiff*, I, 102 ff. (1928).

[5] 72 *Comm. & Fin. Chron.* 936 (May 11, 1901).

offer to bargain was refused and the Morgan-Hill group began instead to buy Northern Pacific common stock, the Harriman-Schiff group also went to market for more of it. The price of the stock showed the effect of this last buying spree. On Monday, May 6, it jumped to $133, on Tuesday to $150, on Wednesday to $180, and on Thursday, May 9, it sold for $700 up to $1000. In fact, on Thursday it was hardly selling at all; a "corner" had occurred, that is, the sellers, some of them selling short, had contracted to sell more of the stock than could be had. In the rush to acquire shares with which to honor their contracts, they bid the prices up to fantastic levels; in order to pay the tremendous prices, they were forced to sell out other securities at distress prices; and banks, frightened of the whole affair, refused to make short-term loans, or made them only at interest rates that rose to 60 per cent.[6] Moreover, the substantial fall in prices of most stocks other than Northern Pacific led brokers and bankers to call for additional funds from stockholders who had bought on margins, and this produced further distress selling. The outcome was a stockmarket break known as the "Northern Pacific Panic."

At this point, statesmanship reasserted its benign influence. Morgan had a great deal to lose by "demoralization" of the money market. He would not be able to sell securities in large new enterprises such as U. S. Steel, nor would borrowers be able to repay outstanding loans, were a wave of bankruptcy to set in. He therefore directed that $6,000,000 of his firm's funds be made available for immediate loan at about 6 per cent, thus augmenting the effort of a consortium of New York banks that made $20,000,000 of their funds available at the market rate of interest.[7] And his firm immediately reached an agreement with Harriman and Schiff whereby those short-sellers who were unable to fulfill their Northern Pacific contracts would be permitted to settle the contracts at $150 per share.[8]

Harriman and Schiff had their own reasons for preferring a settlement on any congenial terms. Schiff's desire, as a banker, for a stable or rising stock market was identical with Morgan's. But he had an additional reason: he and Harriman had been en-

[6] 72 *Comm. & Fin. Chron.* 900 (May 11, 1901).
[7] 72 *Comm. & Fin. Chron.* 900 (May 11, 1901).
[8] 72 *Comm. & Fin. Chron.* 901.

gaged on a second front. During the week ending April 27, an uncommon degree of activity had been observed in Union Pacific stocks. The feverish purchases might have been merely speculative, but rumor had it that they represented an effort by someone to wrest control of the Union Pacific system from Harriman. That someone, it was at first conjectured, might be the Vanderbilt group, acting in their capacity as principal owners of the Chicago, Northwestern Railroad and of the Chicago, Milwaukee, and St. Paul Railroad. These two lines, competitors of the Burlington, had been threatened by the Burlington acquisition, which meant to them that they could no longer have their shipments carried on favorable terms by the Northern Pacific and Great Northern; they felt, so it was said, that they must now bring under their own control some route leading to the West Coast. They were therefore, rumor had it in late April, trying to take over the Union Pacific.[9] During the following week, the prices of Union Pacific stock showed even more frenzied activity. On Monday, April 29, the high price was 120; by Wednesday, May 1, it was 130.[1]

Later on, after the fight between Harriman and Hill over the Northern Pacific had become public knowledge, there were many who surmised that the attempt to take over the Union Pacific was made not by Vanderbilt at all, but by Hill, as a counterattack against Harriman; but both sides "authoritatively denied" this interpretation; and indeed the details of timing do make it seem unlikely. Nevertheless, whatever its explanation, there is no doubt that enough was happening about Union Pacific to worry Harriman and Schiff and to force them to increase their holdings of Union Pacific stock.[2] Since each of these separate games was being played with stakes in hundreds of millions of dollars, the players, for all that they commanded vast resources, must have been approaching their limit. And this fact, as well as a general aversion to sheer chaos, must have urged Harriman and Schiff, as it did Morgan and Hill, toward some peaceable settlement. It took the form of concession to the Harriman group of a strong representation on the Northern Pacific's board of directors. The compromise was formally ratified in an Arbitration Agreement

[9] 72 *Comm. & Fin. Chron.* 794.
[1] 72 *Comm. & Fin. Chron.* 842.
[2] 72 *Comm. & Fin. Chron.* 936.

of May 31, 1901, Schiff issuing a public statement for the occasion to the effect that "complete and permanent harmony will result under the plan adopted between all interests involved." [3]

One aspect of that new-found harmony was illustrated a few weeks later by the announcement that a vice-president of the Southern Pacific Company had been charged by Harriman with the duty of coordinating freight rates on all parts of the Union Pacific system and Southern Pacific system—charged, that is, with the role of preventing any rate competition between the various railroads that made up the great group. The New York *Evening Post* added that James Hill had appointed an officer to do the same work for his railroads, and moreover that Harriman's man and Hill's man were to act together, "not as advocates of their respective former interests, but as trustees, in a sense, for all the Pacific lines." [4] The Burlington dispute had, in effect, been resolved by the formation of a larger and more stable railroad pool than ever before.

Shortly after all this activity, Hill, Morgan, and their colleagues began to make the arrangements that led to the incorporation, that autumn, of the Northern Securities Company, a holding company organized under New Jersey laws and brought into existence to acquire ownership of the Great Northern and Northern Pacific railroads. The Northern Securities Company was incorporated on Nov. 12, 1901, with an authorized capital of $400,000,000. It soon acquired most of the capital stock of the two railroads, paying with its own stock.

According to sworn testimony of the promoters, they had been thinking of setting up some such holding company during the seven or eight years preceding. It is suggestive, nevertheless, that they should have created it, in fact, immediately after the Harriman incursion. One explanation of the coincidence is that the two railroads being joined, the total value of the holding company's common stock would be considerably greater than that of either railroad separately, and a raid like Harriman's would be that much more difficult to carry off. Instead of $78,000,000, the raiders would need to invest over $200,000,000 to buy a clear majority

[3] 72 *Comm. & Fin. Chron.* 1081 (June 1, 1901).

[4] 72 *Comm. & Fin. Chron.* 1207.

of the Northern Securities Company's stock. In short, for Morgan and Hill, who wanted to maximize the amount of control they could accomplish with a given supply of capital, a holding company with enormous total assets was an aid to achieving moderately secure control while holding only minority of the stock. As Hill himself said: "We were particularly anxious to put a majority of that stock where it could not be raided again as it had been." [5] There may have been—there almost certainly were—additional reasons for forming the Northern Securities Company.

But the one reason that can hardly have weighed heavily was any desire to combine the Great Northern and Northern Pacific into a monopoly. As the history of the entire background makes plain, both railroads were sufficiently owned and controlled by the Hill and Morgan group. As their joint purchase of the Burlington Road shows, the two railroads were already coordinating their policies before the Northern Securities Company was created. Indeed, the Northern Securities Company itself—despite the legal fiction which made *it* appear to be buying *them*—was their joint creature or, to put it quite literally, was a device propagated by the same group of men who owned both railroads together. In short, for some years before the Northern Securities Company was created, its owners were in a position to allow just as much or as little competition between the two railroads as suited their purposes. Their policy as to competition was made public and formal by establishment of the holding company, but it was not in any other way altered.

President Roosevelt's Antitrust Policy

On September 6, 1901, while the lawyers were drawing up the Northern Securities charter, an anarchist in Buffalo shot President McKinley. Eight days later he died, and the next evening, at a friend's house in Buffalo, Theodore Roosevelt took the oath of

[5] Pyle, *Hill*, II, 164. Morgan said he wanted to put the stock of both railroads into "a company with capital large enough that nobody could ever buy it. . . ." Record in United States v. Northern Securities (193 U.S. 197) 335 f.; quoted in Oral Argument of the Attorney General for the United States (Sup. Ct.), 35.

office. With the new President a new set of policies, chief among them a new antitrust policy, entered. Since in time Roosevelt's antitrust policy, symbolized by his phrase "The Big Stick," became one of the more famous pieces of his political garb, it might be thought that he brought it into office with him ready made. Nothing could be further from the truth.

Not only had Roosevelt no clear or detailed antitrust policy when he took office, but even his fundamental attitude toward the problem had been too recently defined to be entirely his. He had, as yet, merely adopted the opinion of certain others.

Roosevelt's search for an opinion is documented step by step in his correspondence. The beginning of the search is marked by a letter from Roosevelt to Herman Kohlsaat—a close friend of McKinley, an important Republican leader, and publisher of the Chicago *Times-Herald,* which he used as a platform for advocating his pet policies, protective tariff and gold standard. In the summer of 1899, when Roosevelt was beginning to think about his second annual message as Governor of New York, and to think as well about his chances for national office, he asked Kohlsaat for some advice.

> How about trusts? I know this is a very large question, but more and more it seems to me that there will be a good deal of importance to the trust matter in the next campaign. . . . During the last few months I have been growing exceedingly alarmed at the growth of popular unrest and popular distrust on this question. It is largely aimless and baseless, but there is a very unpleasant side to this overrun trust development, and what I fear is, if we do not have some consistent policy to advocate, then that multitudes will follow the crank who advocates an absurd policy, but who does advocate something.[6]

All Roosevelt had decided, at this point, was that he and his party needed to advocate something about the trusts. His language allows the inference that he had also decided that the "something" should not be as "aimless and baseless" as a radical attempt to outlaw all trusts on the supposition that all were bad.

The only limit that Roosevelt so far had defined for the "consistent policy" he sought was that it should not be founded on what he identified as a superstitious denial of facts. This is made

[6] Aug. 7, 1899; *Roosevelt Letters,* II, 1045.

clear by a passage in a letter written a few days later to his intimate, Henry Cabot Lodge:

> The agitation against trusts is taking an always firmer hold. It is largely unreasonable and fanned into activity by the Bryan type of demagogue. . . . But when there is a good deal of misery and injustice, even though it is mainly due to the faults of the individuals themselves, or to the mere operation of nature's laws, the quack who announces he has a cure-all for it is a dangerous person. . . .[7]

"Misery"—presumably, poverty—being "mainly" due to the faults of the poor and the operations of the market, ought not to be blamed exclusively on the trusts. But although the explanation Roosevelt offered of poverty was cast in the language of *laissez faire* and "rugged individualism," he was not the sort of man to readily recognize any limitation imposed by Nature on what government could accomplish.

Yet the question remained: Granted government could do whatever might be necessary, what should government do about trusts? Roosevelt was far from ready to answer. Writing to another Midwestern Republican politician and editor, Charles Frederick Scott, he repeated his plea:

> . . . would you mind giving me a hint about trusts? I have been in a great quandary over them. I do not know what attitude to take. I do not intend to play a demagogue. On the other hand, I do intend to, so far as in me lies, see that the rich man is held to the same accountability as the poor man. . . .[8]

The fundamental difficulty was that Roosevelt knew little and understood little about economics. Uncle Joe Cannon, Speaker of the House throughout Roosevelt's presidency, arrived at that conclusion,[9] and if Cannon's testimony is taken as dubious, because both he and Roosevelt were too hard and rough to have meshed without friction, it is testimony confirmed by Roosevelt himself. In a letter to Elihu Root, he wrote: "I am quite honest in saying that I think you would have made a better [Governor of New York than I], for in just such matters as trusts and the like you have the ideas to work out whereas I have to try to work out what

[7] Aug. 10, 1899; *Roosevelt Letters,* II, 1048.
[8] Aug. 15, 1899; *Roosevelt Letters,* II, 1060.
[9] Busbey, *Uncle Joe Cannon* 209-13 (1927).

I get from you and men like you."[1] Whether Roosevelt did in fact "work out" much is doubtful, but take advice he most certainly did; more than that, he chose advice, taking it exclusively from men who thought that trusts ought to be somewhat regulated, though not very strictly, but ought not at all to be outlawed, representing as they did the wave of the future.

His chosen advisers made an interesting group. There were renowned economists, A. T. Hadley, then President of Yale, Prof. Jeremiah Jenks of Cornell, and Prof. E. R. A. Seligman of Columbia. There were eminent lawyers, Elihu Root, William Cohen, who had just finished a term as Justice on the Supreme Court of New York, and James B. Dill, a famous corporation lawyer who had drafted a still more famous law, the statute of New Jersey authorizing the incorporation of holding companies. There were also Roosevelt's political supporters in New York politics, Senator T. C. Platt, and N. N. Stranahan, a leader of the state senate; and there were members of the national administration—Root, just appointed Secretary of War, and perhaps also Attorney General Griggs. At least, Griggs was asked for his opinion because, as Roosevelt wrote, "I feel that when I touch such a delicate matter as trusts I should be in some kind of relations with the National administration." What that group of advisers had in common was a belief that the way to deal with the trusts was first to investigate them—an activity in which Jenks, for instance, was already involved as an expert for the U. S. Industrial Commission—and second, to publicize their activities, in the hope that exposure would destroy their power to succeed by deception.[2]

Not surprisingly, then, Roosevelt's message of January 3, 1900,[3] reflected strongly the views of his advisers. In that message, Roosevelt began his discussion by defining trusts as "those vast combinations of capital, usually flourishing by virtue of some monopolistic element, which have become so startlingly common a feature in the industrial revolution which has progressed so rapidly during recent years." He went on in an eminently reasonable way to assert that some of the trusts produced deleterious effects, some beneficial effects, others still, mixed effects. He clearly im-

[1] Dec. 15, 1899; *Roosevelt Letters,* II, 1110.

[2] *Roosevelt Letters,* II, 1060, 1105, 1110, 1114.

[3] Roosevelt, *Works,* XV, 42-47 (Nat'l Ed. 1926).

plied that the beneficial effects were the economies proceeding from advanced technology and production on a large scale. As to the abuses, he listed them at some length: misrepresentation of financial data in order to deceive buyers of stocks and collectors of taxes, excessive profits to promoters, "overcapitalization," "unfair competition," monopolistic pricing, and monopsonistic wage-setting. This distinction between the good and bad effects of trusts led him to a general principle of policy. "We do not wish to discourage enterprise. We do not desire to destroy corporations; we do desire to put them fully at the service of the State and the people." In other words he aimed at, or at least hoped for, a policy that would at the same time enable the community to enjoy the economic efficiency attributable to large organizations without suffering the privations imposed by unscrupulous promotion and monopoly practices.

It was a laudable intention, could it only be achieved. Roosevelt sketched a program that he hoped would achieve it. The first step, he made clear, was to place little or no reliance on the antitrust laws, since they were futile or worse because they would destroy the possibility of preserving the increased efficiency of large firms. "Very many of the antitrust laws which have made their appearance on the statute-books of recent years have been almost or absolutely ineffective because they have blinked the all-important fact that much of what they thought to do away with was incidental to modern industrial conditions, and could not be eliminated unless we were willing to turn back the wheels of modern progress. . . ." Again, "much of the legislation not only proposed but enacted against trusts is not one whit more intelligent than the medieval bull against the comet, and has not been one particle more effective."

His own program, therefore, to preserve the benefits of modern industrial organization while eliminating its incidental abuses, would begin with an attack on the depredations of promoters. "The first essential is knowledge of the facts, publicity," to be accomplished by amendment to the corporation laws. Publicity would protect the public in its role as investors. Happily, publicity would also protect the public in its role as consumers. If the State had the power to investigate and publicize the financial condition of trusts, "then, if there are inordinate profits, competition or public sentiment will give the public the benefit in lowered prices; and if not, the power of taxation remains." And this brought him immediately to the end of his statement. "It is therefore evident that publicity is the one sure and adequate remedy which we can now invoke. There may be other remedies, but what these others are we can only find out by publicity, as the result of investigation. The first requisite is knowledge, full and complete."[4]

When, during the following summer, the Republican National Convention nominated Roosevelt for Vice President, his letter of acceptance briefly summarized, in its section on trusts, the view he had expressed as Governor. The only addition was a note appropriate to his new political scope: the trust problem could be handled by the States, if they used their powers, but "where they decline to co-operate the National Government must step in."[5] It was with this policy that Roosevelt entered the Vice Presidency, and within the year, the Presidency.

Roosevelt became President in September 1901. Eight weeks later the formation of the Northern Securities Company was announced. The first effect was a considerable clamor. The corporate charter, issued by the state of New Jersey under its holding company statute, was dated November 12, 1901. One week later Governor Van Sant of Minnesota invited the governors of the other Northwestern states to a conference to determine on joint action; and by January 7, 1902, the Attorney General of Minnesota had placed an application before the Supreme Court of the United States, the first step in a suit to dissolve the Northern Securities Company.[6]

Roosevelt, in keeping with his announced policy, left the matter to the states at first. But presently he moved the Federal Government to intervene, though in a manner still perfectly in keeping with his announced policy. On December 20, 1901, the Interstate Commerce Commission, acting presumably on Roosevelt's orders, had adopted a resolution to investigate "consolidations

[4] Roosevelt, *Works,* XV, 42-47.
[5] *Roosevelt Letters,* II, 1400.
[6] Meyer, *History of the Northern Securities Case* 242 ff. (1906).

and combinations of carriers . . . including the method of association known as the 'community of interest' plan," the investigation to begin with hearings in Chicago on January 8, 1902.[7]

During January the Interstate Commerce Commission gathered evidence; meanwhile, in Washington, the Supreme Court heard oral arguments in the case of *Minnesota v. Northern Securities Company*.

Then quite suddenly, on February 19, 1902—before the I.C.C. had published its testimony, before the Supreme Court had handed down its decision on Minnesota's application—Attorney General Knox announced that the Federal Government would shortly take the Northern Securities Company to court. His statement was released, with great delicacy, after the Stock Market had closed for the day.

The decision, as Knox described it, had been made by Roosevelt. "Some time ago the President requested an opinion as to the legality of this merger, and I have recently given him one, to the effect that in my judgment it violates the provisions of the Sherman Act of 1890; whereupon he directed that suitable action should be taken to have the question judicially determined."[8] Not only had Roosevelt made the decision, but he had apparently made it quite alone, or at least without consulting his cabinet and especially his revered adviser on such matters, Elihu Root. So it appears from a comment that Taft is said to have made some years later:

Root was very bitter both at Knox and Roosevelt, because he had not been informed as to [the Northern Securities] suit, and he had never

[7] Interstate Commerce Commission, *In the Matter of Consolidations and Combinations of Carriers* (1902).

[8] 74 *Comm. & Fin. Chron.* 428 (Feb. 22, 1902). The precise date on which Roosevelt asked Knox for an opinion is of some importance in interpreting his policy. Knox, in his statement, said "some time ago." But the *Commercial and Financial Chronicle* (vol. 74, p. 95) reported as early as Jan. 11 that Roosevelt had ordered Knox as well as the I.C.C. to investigate. On the other hand, the same journal, in commenting on Knox's announcement, said, "It seems that President Roosevelt *some days since* asked Attorney General Knox for an opinion . . ." (vol. 74, p. 398, emphasis added). As "some days since" looks like a gloss on Knox's "some time ago," however, it does not help very much. The scattered bits of evidence make it seem likely that Roosevelt asked Knox about the case in January.

forgiven Knox and still feels some resentment toward Roosevelt. I think he believes that Knox, for some personal reason, pledged Roosevelt to withhold all knowledge from him.[9]

The announcement was greeted everywhere with surprise, and in some places with dismay. One of Roosevelt's correspondents, H. V. Jones, the publisher of the Minneapolis *Commercial West*, wrote to criticize "the announcement of the suit without a public warning." Roosevelt quite reasonably answered:

What we did was just exactly to give this public, instead of private warning . . . How could we give "public warning" otherwise than in the way we did? I am sure it is unnecessary to say to you that our action was taken purely upon our own responsibility and without any reference to the State authorities of Minnesota. I am rather inclined to think it was as much of a surprise to them as to anyone.[1]

His answer shows that he had inferred from Jones's complaint two unstated grounds of objection: that he should have given the defendants a private warning and that he should not be using Federal power to back the action of Minnesota.

The notion that the President ought to give prospective defendants private notice might seem to impose on him too heavy a burden of chivalry. But J. P. Morgan too is said to have felt that this would have been the decent thing for Roosevelt to have done. At least, one story has it that when Morgan was interrupted at dinner to be told of Knox's announcement, he turned to his guests to complain of Roosevelt's unfairness. Roosevelt ought to have told him, ought to have given him an opportunity either to reshape the Northern Securities Company or to dissolve it voluntarily. "He had regarded Roosevelt as a gentleman. . . ."[2] He still had some hope apparently that Roosevelt would fulfill the promise of his breeding, for three days later he went to call on the President, having been preceded on two days earlier by J. J. Hill, and on the day preceding by his own partner and Roosevelt's friend, George Perkins.[3] Morgan complained of his discourteous treatment, to which Roosevelt—if the unofficial account

[9] Butt, *Taft and Roosevelt,* II, 690 (1930).

[1] Letter from Roosevelt to H. V. Jones, Feb. 26, 1902, in *Roosevelt Letters,* III, 236.

[2] Allen, *Morgan* 220.

[3] *Roosevelt Letters,* IV, 1349.

can be believed—answered that advance warning had been out of the question. Morgan responded in an immortal line: "If we have done anything wrong, send your man to my man and they can fix it up." Roosevelt declined the offer of a negotiated peace.[4] Despite the social ties that existed between him and Morgan, he felt no obligation of courtesy on this score.

Although such complaints against the secrecy and indelicacy of the suit can be disregarded, a much larger question does arise. Roosevelt had repeatedly said that publicity was the best way to deal with the trusts and that, if it came to prosecution at all, the states were amply armed with statutory authority for it. Now, suddenly, just when publicity was being prepared by the I.C.C., and the State of Minnesota was embarked on a prosecution, Roosevelt had suddenly reversed himself and initiated a Federal suit. Why?

The action was taken secretively enough so that no direct evidence remains in Roosevelt's or Knox's papers or in the Department of Justice files. But it is possible to surmise Roosevelt's reasons. For one thing, it appears that he had changed his mind fairly quickly about the efficacy of action by the states. This had become clear in his first annual message as President, which was dated December 3, 1901, but which he had begun to prepare almost immediately on taking office to serve as a substitute for an inaugural address. As early as September he was discussing the principal theses with friends and experts, and two comments from his letters at the time show against what resistances his own views were formed.

To Douglas Robinson, his brother-in-law, he wrote on October 4:

> I am very fond of [George] Perkins. He is one of the men whom I most respect. But, to be perfectly frank, he did not appear to advantage in the talk he had with me on the evening in question. This is no reflection on him. He was occupying exactly the same attitude that Bob Bacon occupies on this question, and of Bob Bacon I am even fonder. Both of them are men of the highest character, who are genuine forces for good as well as men of strength and weight. But on this particular occasion they were arguing like attorneys for a bad case, and at the bottom of their hearts each would know this if he were not personally in-

[4] Allen, *Morgan* 220.

terested; and especially if he were not the representative of a man so strong and dominant a character as Pierpont Morgan. In plain English, what Perkins wanted me to do was to go back on my messages to the New York Legislature and on my letter of acceptance of the nomination for the Vice-Presidency, as well as on my Minneapolis speech, which was by no means as strong as either the messages or the letter. Now if I felt convinced that I had been wrong in what I had hitherto said, or even if I were doubtful about it, I should not have the slightest hesitation in announcing that I had changed my mind; but as a matter of fact I was right. I intend to be most conservative, but in the interests of the big corporations themselves and above all in the interest of the country I intend to pursue, cautiously but steadily, the course to which I have been publicly committed again and again, and which I am certain is the right course. I may add that I happen to know that President McKinley was uneasy about this so-called trust question and was reflecting in his mind what he should do in the matter. Perkins wanted me to do nothing at all, and say nothing except platitudes; accept the publication of what some particular company chooses to publish, as a favor, instead of demanding what we think ought to be published from all companies as a right.[5]

Other similar pressures were being exercised within the party: Hanna, when he saw a draft in November, also objected to aspects of the statement on the trusts, and Roosevelt made some adjustments to soften it.[6]

The passage on trusts, in the final version of the message, had altogether a tone of moderation that made it prey to satire. This tone, of course, had constantly been present in Roosevelt's statements of the problem, but was more pronounced this time because Roosevelt took more care than ever to establish that his intentions were neither as socialist nor anarchist as his flamboyant career made some sober Republicans fear. A long preamble, therefore, spelled out the lessons of such texts as: "The captains of industry who have driven the railway systems across this continent, who have built up our commerce, who have developed our manufactures, have on the whole done a great good to our people," and "The mechanism of modern business is so delicate that extreme care must be taken not to interfere with it in a spirit of rashness or ignorance." Nevertheless, this preamble obviously was leading up to a great "But," which came in the statement, "All this

[5] *Roosevelt Letters,* III, 159 f.

[6] Pringle, *Theodore Roosevelt* 244 (1931).

is true; and yet it is also true that there are real and grave evils, one of the chief being overcapitalization because of its many baleful consequences; and a resolute and practical effort must be made to correct these evils." He then proceeded, as always before, to say that "Publicity is the only sure remedy which we can now invoke." Other remedies, less sure, he vaguely suggested in the phrase, "combination and concentration should be, not prohibited, but supervised and within reasonable limits controlled. . . ."[7] The performance as a whole was not altogether unfairly summarized by Mr. Dooley: " 'Th' trusts,' says he, 'are heejoous monsthers built up be th' enlightened intherprise iv th' men that have done so much to advance progress in our beloved country,' he says. 'On wan hand I wud stamp thim undher fut; on th' other hand not so fast.' "[8]

But Dooley and many others did not notice a shift—small, but vital—in Roosevelt's views on what the states could or could not accomplish by themselves. Before, he had said that they could do much, if they chose to. Now he said:

> The large corporations, commonly called trusts, though organized in one State, always do business in many States, often doing very little business in the State where they are incorporated. There is utter lack of uniformity in the State laws about them; and as no State has any exclusive interest in or power over their acts, it has in practice proved impossible to get adequate regulation through State action. Therefore, in the interest of the whole people, the nation should, without interfering with the power of the States in the matter itself, also assume power of supervision and regulation over all corporations doing an interstate business. This is especially true where the corporation derives a portion of its wealth from the existence of some monopolistic element or tendency in its business.[9]

What this national regulatory statute should be, however, he did not say and probably had not yet worked out, except to say that it should be framed in light of "the experience gained through the passage and administration of the Interstate Commerce Act." Evidently he had in mind something like what eventually became the Federal Trade Commission. Nevertheless, he had apparently

[7] Roosevelt, *Works,* XV, 87-93.

[8] Pringle, *Roosevelt* 245.

[9] Roosevelt, *Works,* XV, 92.

come to believe—or at least had for the first time openly declared —that the trust problem was by its nature a problem that the states could not solve and the Federal Government alone must.

Despite his change of mind, it is strange that Roosevelt should have urged or allowed Knox to announce a Federal suit on February 19, 1902, just at the moment that the states were certainly not inactive nor had been shown to be ineffective. Indeed, the decision in Minnesota's proceedings was expected on the following Monday, February 24. Had Roosevelt strongly desired to leave antitrust action to the states, he could easily have waited until the beginning of the next week to see what success Minnesota might encounter. This implication was certainly recognized by contemporaries. The New York *Sun,* for instance, greeted the announcement with great surprise, and added: "The shock was the more pronounced because of the fact that the Supreme Court, before which the application of the State of Minnesota . . . is still undetermined, reconvenes early next week." [1]

The timing of Knox's announcement indeed suggests that Roosevelt quite deliberately chose to make it clear that the Federal Government's action was in no way bolstering the initiative of Minnesota. His comment to Jones, that "our action was taken purely upon our own responsibility and without any reference to the State authorities of Minnesota" was probably exact to the letter.[2]

Still, even if he had decided that the Federal Government must step in, why should he have hurried to court? What of investigation and publicity? The answer may be, quite simply, that those means had already been used. The I.C.C. had held its hearings; Hill, Harriman, and others had testified; but as the *Commercial and Financial Chronicle* laconically remarked, "no new facts appear to have been elicited." [3] The fortunes of the Northern Securities Company had not yet been visibly injured by the publicity.

More important, however, than the apparent failure on this occasion of his pet antitrust tactic (which could never in any event have entirely suited his personality and political style), may have

[1] N.Y. *Sun* (Feb. 21, 1902).
[2] See p. 202 above.
[3] 74 *Comm. & Fin. Chron.* 268 (Feb. 1, 1902).

been a desire on Roosevelt's part to test the Sherman Act before he began planning any new legislation. Could the Sherman Act, he might well have wondered, be depended on at all, even to outlaw flagrant abuses? Here was an opportunity to discover the answer. More, here was an opportunity to teach the public the answer, by launching a case that could not fail to be noticed. The educational effect would be great, no matter what the outcome. If Morgan, Hill, and Harriman won, the public would readily understand that the Sherman Act must be superseded. If the Government won, that would do no political harm at all, and the argument that the Sherman Act ought to be augmented by a regulatory commission could still be made, without the need to face complaints from firebrands that the Government should enforce the existing law before it added new laws. The only persons who might be alienated by the suit were Morgan, his colleagues, and their sympathizers, but they were captives of the Republican Party in any event, and might be placated sooner or later by the belief which Roosevelt often expressed and sincerely held, that it was not the wealthy but wrongdoers who should be repressed. In short, by bringing the Northern Securities Company to court, Roosevelt could not fail to win—in the long run, the short run, or both.

Attorney General Knox's Strategy in the Northern Securities *Case*

The Federal attack on the Northern Securities Company was organized with the precision of a military drill by the Attorney General, Philander Knox. He and McKinley had met as students and become close friends. Knox had gone on to establish himself as a leading corporation lawyer in Pittsburgh; in 1899 McKinley had offered him the position of Attorney General, which Knox refused then because he was just in the middle of drawing up the organization of the Carnegie Steel Company. In April 1901, when the offer was renewed, Knox agreed to become John Griggs's successor; Roosevelt, on his accession in September, continued Knox in his cabinet. Later, during the four years after 1908 when Knox served as Taft's Secretary of State—or, as some said, his Prime

Minister—his personality became better known. Taft himself said, "There is no lack of confidence in Knox"; and Lord Bryce said that Knox had a "certain impatience of temperament" inclining him "to be autocratic and rapid in his decisions." Perhaps because of that, he administered the State Department—if not the foreign policy of the United States—with great skill.[4] In his management of the *Northern Securities* case, the same suddenness of decision and the administrative precision were amply demonstrated. It was the first antitrust proceeding that the government carried through with an air of "modern" efficiency.

Just when Knox first took notice of the Northern Securities affair is not certain. As early as December 1901, however, Roosevelt forwarded to him letters from a Philadelphia lawyer who believed that the Sherman Act should be invoked; a short correspondence with Knox developed.[5] In January 1902, also, the I.C.C. offered to send Knox the testimony it was taking in Chicago; and W. B. Douglas, Attorney General of Minnesota, who had come to Washington to plead his state's application before the Supreme Court, took time to call on Knox for a conference.[6] By mid-February, in any event, Knox had decided to move. His first step was to wire Douglas for information. Douglas immediately sent copies of the papers in his case, as well as in two private suits that had by now been brought in Minnesota courts, and wrote to Knox: "I am very glad indeed that you purpose making a personal investigation of the matter prior to the determination by the Supreme Court of our motion which is still pending, involving the question of jurisdiction. I trust you will see your way clear to institute an action under the Federal anti-trust act."[7] It is, perhaps, as good evidence as any of Knox's decisiveness that within two days of receiving Douglas' letter and information, he issued the statement—which so startled Morgan and

[4] Hill, *Mr. Secretary of State* 48, 127, 62, (1963).

[5] Letters from Emlen Miller to Roosevelt, Dec. 9, 1901, and to A. G., Jan. 23, 1902, in D.J. File 18429-1901.

[6] Letter from Edward A. Moseley (Secretary, I.C.C.) to Knox, Mar. 4, 1902, in D.J. File 18429-1901, 3862-1902. Letter from Douglas to Knox, Feb. 15, 1902, in D.J. File 18429-1901, 2599-1902.

[7] Letter from Douglas to Knox, Feb. 15, 1902, in D.J. File 18429-1901, 2599-1902.

surprised Root—announcing the Government's intention to proceed against the Northern Securities Company.

The evidence shows, moreover, that Knox had already decided just what the crux of the case would be. In answer, apparently, to a question in Knox's telegram, Douglas wrote:

> Bearing upon the pretense of railway companies that contracts entered into by any person or corporation are not subject to control by Congress, I beg to call your attention to the language of Mr. Justice Peckham in the *Joint Traffic Association Case,* 171 U.S. 571; to wit: "The constitutional right of a citizen to make contracts is not inconsistent with the existence of the power of Congress to prohibit a contract of the nature involved in this case." [8]

Knox, it is clear, recognized from the beginning that the Northern Securities Company would defend itself chiefly on the ground that it existed to buy stocks, not to operate railroads, that its business was to make innocent contracts to purchase and sell, not unlawful contracts to restrain trade. His estimate was confirmed by the New York *Sun,* which, when informing its readers on February 25 that the Supreme Court had just declined to hear the case of Minnesota against the Northern Securities Company, outlined the reasoning that the defense would follow in the Federal suit.

> The direct and substantial object of the present transaction was the acquisition by the Securities Company of the shares of the two railroad companies concerned. The results which may follow therefrom will be, according to the company's attorneys, "indirect, remote, incidental and collateral," and not, therefore, bringing the enterprise within the prohibition of the statute.[9]

"The prohibition of the statute," according to the *Sun,* was defined by the rule stated by Justice Peckham in his *Addyston Pipe* opinion: the Act applied only to agreements that "directly and substantially, and not merely indirectly, remotely, incidentally and collaterally, regulate to a greater or less degree commerce among the States." [1]

Knox's estimate of the defense strategy was confirmed, more-

[8] Letter from Douglas to Knox, Feb. 15, 1902, in D.J. File 18429-1901, 2599-1902.

[9] N.Y. *Sun* p. 6, col. 1 (Feb. 25, 1902).

[1] 175 U.S. 211, at 229.

over, by information given out more or less confidentially by the defendants themselves. On February 25, Knox asked William A. Day to gather further information in New York about the Northern Securities Company. Day was no stranger to the affair, having served as special counsel for the I.C.C. in its Chicago hearings during January; the I.C.C. was apparently lending his services to Knox at this point; and in March 1903, Knox appointed him to the newly created position of Assistant to the Attorney General. In his few days in New York, although Day discovered nothing new and important, he heard from an acquaintance on Wall Street the same story, and in almost the same words that the *Sun* used:

> Counsel will contend that the direct and substantial object of the Securities Company was the acquisition by it of the shares of the Northern Pacific and Great Northern Railroads, and that the results which the Attorney General fears, or will allege to flow therefrom, are indirect, remote, incidental and collateral, and not, therefore, within the prohibition of the Anti-Trust Act.[2]

Against this defense, whose character had so quickly become clear, Knox would obviously need to oppose the view that the purposes or direct effect of the Securities Company was to restrain trade. A question that arose immediately was whether the Securities Company owned, or had tried to acquire, a controlling interest in both railways. Knox put this question to Henry L. Burnett, U. S. Attorney in New York City, on February 21. Burnett answered that the Securities Company had distributed a circular to all stockholders of Great Northern inviting them to exchange their shares for Northern Securities shares. But, he was forced to add, he could find no evidence that they had made the same offer to stockholders of Northern Pacific; there were rumors, but they could not be confirmed because, "in the present situation, you can understand both Morgan & Co. and the Northern Securities Co. would be on their guard about furnishing facts of this kind."[3]

In the interval before Knox had announced the Federal action, however, the defendants had been less circumspect. On the contrary, they had succumbed on a number of occasions to the temp-

[2] Letter from Day to Knox, Feb. 28, 1902, in D.J. File 18429-1901, 12313-02.

[3] Letter from Burnett to Knox, Feb. 24, 1902, in D.J. File 18429-1901, 3327-1902.

tation of declaring the truth, that the purpose of the Northern Securities Company was to create industrial peace between the railroads, or, in Morgan's favorite phrase, a "community of interest." When testifying in *Peter Powers v. No. Pacific,* Morgan said he had put Harriman men on the Northern Pacific board of directors to show that he, Hill, Harriman, and their associates "were acting under what we know as a community of interest principle."

Q. What is community of interest?
A. The community of interest is that principle that a certain number of men who own property can do what they like with it.
Q. But they sha'n't fight one another? . . . Is not this community of interest idea one of working in harmony?
A. Working in harmony; yes.
Q. Even though they own competing and parallel lines?
A. No; they own them all.[4]

Indeed some such declaration, however delicately phrased, was essential if the stockholders were to be induced to exchange their familiar shares of known value for shares in a new and untried corporation—the incentive was the monopoly profit that a well-designed merger offered. The financial interests of the promoters and organizers, in short, led them to make pronouncements which in years past had exposed them to no legal danger, but which now, as it turned out, had become indiscreet. But before Knox had announced his intention to sue, the promoters had been fairly frank (though not foolishly so), stimulated to frankness by the powerful alliance of truth and profitability.

So, when the pacts between Hill and Morgan and between them and Harriman had first been made public, and when the authoritative *Commercial and Financial Chronicle* had indicated that the directorate of the Securities Company was to be shared among the Hill group, Morgan group, and Harriman group, it had quickly added:

It is affirmed emphatically, however, that the object of the new company is unity and not division of interests, and that the intent was not to allot so many directors to the Union Pacific, so many to the Great

[4] Testimony in Peter Powers v. No. Pacific, pp. 1365-67; quoted in U.S. v. No. Securities (C.C., Minn.), Abstract of Testimony for Complainant 48 (15-July 1902).

Northern and so many to the Northern Pacific, "but rather to form the strongest and most harmonious combination possible, representing the joint interests involved." [5]

The music of this harmony—which the organizers were happy enough to broadcast—turned within two years into a dirge.

Again, Hill, when testifying in the private suit of *Peter Powers v. Northern Pacific* on February 18—only one day before Knox announced the Federal suit—had more or less readily admitted to the incriminating intent.

Q. . . . At the time when the Northern Securities Co. was formed, was it your expectation and desire that a majority of the common stock of the Northern Pacific Railway Co. should be turned in to the Northern Securities Co. in exchange for the latter company's stock? . . .

A. Yes. . . .

Q. Was it your expectation and desire at the time . . . that a majority of the stock of the Great Northern Railway Co. should also be exchanged for Northern Securities Company stock?

A. I think it was expected that a majority would be exchanged.[6]

The admission did not pass unnoticed; when Knox asked for evidence on intent, Douglas very particularly called his attention to this exchange.

By the end of February the main lines of the attack and defense had been drawn. The Department of Justice turned to preparing its bill in equity, which made three main points. The Northern Pacific and Great Northern Railroads had been "two separate, independent, parallel, and competing lines of railway." By the creation of the Northern Securities Company and its acquisition of stocks in the two railroads "a virtual consolidation under one ownership and source of control of the Great Northern and Northern Pacific Railway systems has been effected." The Northern Securities Company was not an authentic investment company; as it never had *funds* with which to buy stocks, but merely exchanged its stocks for the others, it "is a mere depository, custodian, holder, and trustee of the stocks" of the two railroads—it was, in the colloquial, nothing but a "pool." [7] The fundamental allegation was

[5] 73 *Comm. & Fin. Chron.* 1062 (Nov. 16, 1901).

[6] Quoted in letter from Douglas to Knox, Feb. 26, 1902, in D.J. File 18429-1901, 3583-1902.

[7] Bill in Equity; text given in Northern Securities v. U.S., 193 U.S. 197 at 200 ff.; cf. 202, 209, 211 (Mar. 14, 1904).

the second one, that the purpose or direct effect of the Securities Company was to consolidate two competing railways, thereby restraining trade.

By early March 1902, the Government's bill drawn, Knox was ready to go to court. The manner in which he staged the first step in the legal process is typical of the showiness and precision with which he conducted the whole affair. On March 8 he sent Milton Purdy, the U. S. attorney at St. Paul, the printed bills. Purdy's instructions were most detailed. The moment the bills reached him, he was to telegraph the Attorney General. Knox would thereupon instruct him, by return telegraph, to file the bill in the U. S. Circuit Court. Having signed the bill and filed it, Purdy must serve copies on counsel for defendants. He must keep the Department fully informed of all steps he took. Some of the point of this precision drill was revealed by a sentence in Knox's letter, "At the same time that you are instructed by wire to file the bill, instructions together with the bill itself will be made public in this city." [8] And to make quite certain that the publicity value of this great maneuver would not be jeopardized, Knox even went to the trouble of asking the Postmaster General of the United States to ensure that the postmaster at St. Paul would handle the letter to Purdy with "the greatest caution and promptness." [9] Timing was everything.

Aside from precision, Knox wanted speed above all. This desire showed itself in two chief ways. In the first place, he hoped that the proceedings could be abbreviated by confronting the courts with questions of law only—that is, by excluding all need to determine matters of fact. Thus in May, as soon as the defendants had filed their answers to the Government's bill, he asked T. E. Hutchins, the Department's expert on procedure, whether the case could safely be tried on the bill and answers—that is, whether the defendants had in their answers conceded all the relevant facts, in which case it would not be necessary to spend months taking testimony. Hutchins replied in a long report, pointing out that the Government's case rested on the allegations that

[8] Letter from Knox to Purdy Mar. 8, 1902, in D.J. Instruction Book No. 156, pp. 358-59.

[9] Letter from H. C. Payne (Postmaster General) to Knox, Mar. 8, 1902, in D.J. File 18429-1901, 4340-1902.

the defendants had agreed to transfer control of the two railroads to the Northern Securities Company and to prevent competition between the two railroads. Opinions of the Supreme Court in earlier antitrust cases had established, he said, that it is "not necessary for the Government to make any direct proof of any intention or design to effect either of these results, yet it would seem necessary to show, at least, that such would be the natural and direct result of what was intended or done." It would also be necessary to prove that the Securities Company owned a controlling interest in each of the two railroad companies, because the defendants' answers did not concede this.[1] And, indeed, when he finally came to the point, Hutchins was obliged to say that the Government would need to prove practically every one of its allegations. Knox reconciled himself to the necessity.[2]

But in August the fond hope that the labor of taking testimony and preparing briefs on it could be avoided was renewed. The Solicitor General asked W. A. Day whether the government could safely submit the case on the bill and the answer of the Securities Company, if all the defendants—who had filed separate and different answers—would agree to stipulate the facts as stated in the Securities Company's answer. Day was nearly as discouraging as Hutchins had been,[3] and from then on it was clear that testimony would have to be taken. It was taken, finally, in October; even

[1] They were able to avoid conceding it by a stratagem revealed in the answer of the Securities Company: "This defendant says it has bought and paid for and has caused to be transferred to it upon the records of the Great Northern Company, in accordance with the by-laws of that company, about five-twelfths (5/12) of the shares of that company's stock; and has also negotiated for, but has not yet caused to be presented to the Great Northern Company for transfer upon its records, other shares of the stock of that company aggregating about four-twelfths (4/12) of the total amount of its stock, but has not acquired a right to vote as stockholder of the Great Northern Company on stock not so transferred." (Answer of the Northern Securities Company, 193 U.S. 221, 227.) Hutchins commented in his report to Knox, "the fact that it refrains to have transferred the stock that it has bought and paid for, is strong evidence of the truth . . . that the transfer is withheld in order to prevent successful attacks in the courts upon this combination." (Letter from Hutchins to Knox, June 5, 1902, p. 13; in D.J. File 18429-1901.)

[2] Letter from Hutchins to Knox, June 5, 1902, in D.J. File 18429-1901.

[3] Letter from Day to J. K. Richards (Solicitor General), Aug. 28, 1902, in D.J. File 18429-1901.

then Knox was able to abbreviate the process somewhat by having admitted as evidence in his case testimony that had been taken in February in the case of *Peter Powers v. Northern Pacific*.[4]

The other sign of Knox's desire for speed was the Department's consistent effort to have the Federal court hear the case soon. Thus in December, before the record in the case was printed, the Solicitor General was already urging the U. S. Attorney in St. Paul to get the case on the calendar. The Attorney, C. C. Haupt, said he would try to have it brought on soon after the court convened on January 13, to which the Solicitor General and the defendants' New York lawyers agreed.[5] This agreement was frustrated, however, when David Willcox, one of Morgan's lawyers, fell ill with flu, and his colleague, Francis Lynde Stetson, asked that the hearing be postponed to the latter half of February.[6] The Solicitor General agreed, but it now seemed doubtful whether a hearing could be had even in February, for Judge Lochren of the Federal court at St. Paul followed the practice of disposing of all jury cases at the opening of a session before taking any of the equity cases.[7] It looked as though months might elapse as a result of the usual delays of justice.

Knox, however, had been forearming himself against such delays. When, in the previous October, he had made his first major statement on the trust problem, he had suggested that the need for thorough preparation and speedy trial of antitrust cases could be satisfied only by supplementary legislation.[8] Roosevelt had supported him strongly, exerting a great deal of pressure on Congress to consider a series of bills that Knox had prepared for the pur-

[4] Letter from Knox to C. C. Haupt (U.S. Atty., Minn.), June 21, 1902, in D.J. Instruction Bk. 162, p. 175; Letter from Haupt to Knox, June 30, 1902, in D.J. File 18429-1901, 10703-1902; Letter from Haupt to Knox, Sept. 10, 1902, in D.J. File 18429-1901, 15282-1902.

[5] Letter from Haupt to Solicitor General, Dec. 20, 1902, in D.J. File 18429-1901, 20572-1902; Letter from Sol. Gen. to Haupt, Dec. 23, 1902, in D.J. Instruction Bk. 171, p. 31.

[6] Letter from Stetson to Sol. Gen., Dec. 30, 1902, in D.J. File 18429-1901, 54-1903.

[7] Letter from Haupt to Sol. Gen., Jan. 6, 1903, in D.J. File 18429-1901, 343-1903.

[8] Knox, *The Commerce Clause of the Constitution and the Trusts:* An address . . . before the Chamber of Commerce, Pittsburgh, Pa., on October 14, 1902 (1902).

pose,[9] and threatening that if necessary he would convene an extra session.[1] Among the results was a bill introduced by Senator Hoar and Representative Littlefield, "to expedite the hearing and determination of suits in equity" under the Sherman Act. The bill was introduced on January 7, 1903, reported by the Judiciary Committees of the House on January 9 and Senate in rapid order, amended, passed, and signed by February 11.[2] The Expediting Act provided that in antitrust suits brought by the United States, the Attorney General could certify to the circuit judges[3] that the case was of "general public importance," whereupon the case was to be given precedence over all others. Such cases were to be heard before three or more circuit judges whose decision could be appealed only to the Supreme Court, the appeal to be lodged within sixty days of the decision.

Hardly more than two weeks after the Expediting Act became law, Knox invoked it to speed up the Northern Securities hearing. And in his letter to Henry C. Caldwell, senior judge of the Eighth Circuit, asking that a date be set as soon as possible after March 15, he added that since the Court would not be sitting in bench at St. Paul until May, the government was quite willing to argue before it at its session in St. Louis.[4] The defendants' attorneys at St. Paul made one last effort to delay, pointing out to Caldwell that the suit was instigated by the Government, that the Government had chosen St. Paul and ought to stick to it, that the judges, being busy, would no doubt find it more convenient to hear the arguments in May in St. Paul, and that the defense would be convenienced if the hearing took place after April 1; however, they rounded out their letter by promising to do whatever he thought best.[5] Caldwell decided to hear the case in St. Louis on March 18, 1903.

This emphasis on speed made the last few weeks hectic. In mid-

[9] See p. 240 below.

[1] Letter from Roosevelt to Lawrence Abbott, Feb. 3, 1903, in *Roosevelt Letters*, III, 416.

[2] 32 U. S. Stat. 823.

[3] The circuit court was at that time the Federal court of first instance.

[4] Letter from Knox to Caldwell, Feb. 26, 1903, in D.J. Judges and Clerks Bk. 27, pp. 121 ff.

[5] Letter from Young *et al.* to Caldwell, Mar. 3, 1903, in D.J. File 18429-1901, 3711-1903.

February the Department was still gathering information from the U. S. Attorneys in the Northwest about the state constitutions and statutes relevant to the railroads, and the last of these requests did not go out until March 9.[6] Not until March 11 did D. C. Watson, of the Pittsburgh law firm of Watson and McCleave—whom Knox had retained as special counsel for the case—send the Department the typescript of his long brief on the intent of the defendants.[7]

But the haste that Knox infused into the whole affair infected the Circuit Court as well. Argument opened on March 18 as scheduled, and Watson delivered his last words on Saturday, March 21, whereupon the Court announced its intention to dispose of the case speedily, allowing only three days for the filing of printed arguments—which resulted in a huge overtime charge from the printers.[8] And on April 9, 1903, the Court issued a decree declaring that the defendants had entered into an unlawful combination; enjoining the Northern Securities Company from buying any more stock in the two railroads, voting the stock that they already held, or in any way influencing the two railroads; and enjoining the two railroads from paying dividends to the Securities Company. The decree thus left the Securities Company standing as a corporate entity while destroying its capacity to control or benefit from the two railroads—an outcome more measured than that the Government's bill had prayed for, yet quite strong enough to spike the defendants' guns.[9]

About a year later the Supreme Court affirmed the decree, by the slightest of majorities.[1]

[6] E.g., Letters from Knox to R. V. Cozier (U. S. Att'y, Idaho) Feb. 14, 1903; Cozier to Knox, Feb. 25, 1903, in D.J. File 18429-1901, 3364-1903; Asst. Att'y Gen. to H. K. Butterfield (U. S. Att'y, Milwaukee) Mar. 9, 1903, in D.J. Instruction Bk. 174, p. 440.

[7] Letter from Watson to James M. Beck (Asst. Att'y Gen.) Mar. 11, 1903, in D.J. File 18429-1901.

[8] Letters from Day to Hoyt (Sol. Gen.) Mar. 21, 1903, in D.J. File 18429-1901, 4982-1903; Watson to Day, Mar. 30, 1903, in D.J. File 18429-1901, 5919-1903.

[9] U.S. v. Northern Securities Co., 120 Fed. 721 ff. (Apr. 9, 1903).

[1] *Northern Securities v. United States,* 193 U.S. 197 (argued Dec. 14-15, 1903; decided Mar. 14, 1904).

Judicial Reasoning in the Northern Securities *Case*

OPINION OF THE CIRCUIT COURT

For all the excitement and anger that the *Northern Securities* case aroused, it did not present to the lower court many problems of great importance or many issues about which the judges seemed to feel that the arguments on both sides were almost equally persuasive.

The four members of the Circuit Court, in any event, reached their decision quickly, with no dissent, and as far as one can tell from the opinion of Judge Thayer, with few qualms or unresolved doubts. The opinion followed the general outline of the Government's bill. The Court concluded, as to matters of fact, that the Northern Pacific and Great Northern were competing railroads, and that the controlling shareholders of these railroads, together with the corporate defendants, had been acting in concert to reduce the competition between them. It cited as evidence on the latter point the following facts: first, the two railroads had "united in purchasing" the stocks of the Burlington Road and became "joint sureties" for its bonds; second, certain large stockholders in the two railroads had agreed to create the Northern Securities Company, to turn over to it their stock in the two railroads, and "to use their influence to induce other stockholders" to do so, with the object of putting most or all of those stocks in the hands of the Securities Company; third, by the efforts of the defendants, this goal had been accomplished, the Securities Company then holding 96 per cent of the stock of Northern Pacific and 76 per cent of the stock of Great Northern. As its final conclusion on matters of fact, the Court found that the defendants' "scheme" led "inevitably" to two results: it placed control of the two railroads in the hands of a single person, the Securities Company; and "it destroyed every motive for competition between two roads engaged in interstate traffic, which were natural competitors for business, by pooling the earnings of the two roads for the common benefit of the stockholders of both companies." This last, essential conclusion of fact was not, of course, based on direct evidence produced by the Government. Nor was it based on admissions by the defendants, who, on the contrary, always declared that their only purpose in establishing the Securities Company was to make their railroads immune to another raid like Harriman's. Still, lacking direct evidence, the Court inferred this conclusion of fact from the whole history of the affair, explaining that "according to the familiar rule that every one is presumed to intend what is the necessary consequence of his own acts when done willfully and deliberately, we must conclude that those who conceived and executed the plan aforesaid intended, among other things, to accomplish these objects." [2]

The Court, turning next to questions of law, recited the relevant rules of law established by the Supreme Court in the *Trans-Missouri Freight, Joint Traffic Association,* and *Addyston Pipe* cases. The Sherman Act applied to any combination in restraint of interstate commerce, whether it did or did not take the form of a trust. It applied to interstate railroads, and to corporations as well as individuals. "The words 'in restraint of trade or commerce' do not mean in unreasonable or partial restraint of trade or commerce, but any direct restraint thereof. . . ." An agreement to fix their rates "in concert" "directly restrains commerce by placing obstacles in the way of free and unrestricted competition between carriers who are natural rivals for patronage." [3] Given these rules, the Court continued, "it is almost too plain for argument" that the defendants would have violated the Act had they done just as they did but without creating the Securities Company, that is, had they transferred control of the railroads to a single individual or association of individuals. It was no defense to assert that the two railroads still operated independently in that each still had its own board of directors, since it was well established both in common knowledge and by legal precedents that whoever owns the majority of a corporation's stock controls the corporation; accordingly, if one person owned both railroads, he controlled both, even though he might exercise his control through two separate groups of men. If, then, it would have been illegal to carry out the combination by putting control of the two railroads into the hands of one or several human beings, it must be illegal to do so by a method that was, if anything, more effectual. The Court was reassured, it said, in this conclusion, by the reflection that "the law, as

[2] 120 Fed. at 723 f.
[3] 120 Fed. at 724 f.

administered by courts of equity, looks always at the substance of things—at the object accomplished, whether it be lawful or unlawful—rather than upon the particular devices or means by which it has been accomplished." [4]

Having reached its decision, the Court turned to explain why it had rejected a number of arguments advanced by the defendants. As to the supposed immunity in a Federal court of the corporate charter that the state of New Jersey has issued to the Securities Company, the Court held that the state could not be presumed to have granted a charter authorizing the corporation to violate a Federal law, but that had such a charter been issued, it would have been void "or at least . . . could not be permitted to stand in the way of the enforcement of that act." [5] Defendants had argued that any restraint of trade resulting from the agreement was indirect and therefore not a violation of the Act; the Court responded that the decisions which the defendants cited—the *E. C. Knight, Hopkins,* and *Anderson* decisions—were irrelevant because in this case, unlike those, there was no doubt that the combination restrained interstate commerce and did so directly.[6] Defendants had argued that if the Sherman Act prohibited their activities, then the Act was unconstitutional because it unduly restricted the right to make contracts and to buy and sell property. The Court disposed of this by quoting a passage from the Supreme Court's decision in the *Addyston Pipe* case declaring that the citizen's constitutional liberty to make contracts is limited by the constitutional power of Congress to regulate interstate commerce.[7] In like manner the Court dismissed the argument that the antitrust law was not intended to prohibit the outright or virtual "consolidation" of railroads, refusing to recognize the distinction between a merger and a combination. And it dismissed the argument that the present combination would benefit the public, relying on its finding that the combination—whether beneficial or harmful—was a direct restraint on interstate commerce and therefore unlawful.[8]

[4] 120 Fed. at 726.
[5] 120 Fed. at 727.
[6] 120 Fed. at 728 f.
[7] 120 Fed. at 729 f.
[8] 120 Fed. at 730 f.

In accordance with its findings the Court drew up a decree, enjoining the Securities Company from exercising any control over the two railroads, enjoining the railroads from paying dividends to the Company, and "permitting" the Securities Company to return to the former stockholders of the two railway companies the stocks they had transferred to it. This last, the most surprising part of the decree, was obviously intended to allow the defendants a means by which they could effectively dissolve the Northern Securities Company, in fact if not at law, this dissolution being set as the price the defendants would have to pay before they could start drawing dividends again from the two railroads. The Court could do no more than this, for although, as it had carefully said, the New Jersey charter "could not be permitted to stand in the way of" enforcing the Sherman Act, neither could that charter be declared void by a Federal court judging an issue that arose under a Federal statute. The Court refused, in this, to follow the Government's prayer that it issue a mandatory injunction *requiring* the Securities Company to return the railroad stocks to the former stockholders;[9] but it apparently did so to avoid any suspicion that it was overstepping the boundary between powers of the United States and powers of the states. The Attorney General had not, on any account, grounds to complain of the decision.

For all the clarity of its reasoning, however, the opinion of the Circuit Court was vague or incomplete at three major points. Not surprisingly, it was at those weak points that trouble later entered.

The first of these weaknesses had to do with the initial question of fact: were the two railroads in competition? The Court's answer was ambiguously stated. The two railroads, it said, "*are,* and in public estimation have ever been regarded as, parallel and competing lines. For some years, *at least,* after they were built, they competed with each other actively for transcontinental and interstate traffic."[1] The Court, in other words, had not quite decided whether the two railroads were still competing ("are") or had long ago stopped competing (after "some years, at least"). That the Court was vague on this point is suggested, furthermore, by its invocation of "public estimation," which can hardly have

[9] Government's Bill; 193 U.S. at 213.

[1] 120 Fed. at 722. Emphasis added.

been relevant evidence about a matter of fact disputed by the litigants.

The muddiness of the Court's conclusion on this point may be accounted for by a similar awkwardness in the positions of both parties. The Government's bill, to be sure, declared directly and simply that prior to the formation of the Northern Securities Company the two railroads were "separate, independent, parallel, and competing. . . ."[2] But this essential fact the Securities Company denied in its answer. Day hopefully informed the Solicitor General, "I think the court ought to take judicial notice of that fact."[3] But as the court could not be depended on to be so kind, the Government set out to prove the fact. Thus, James Beck, the Assistant Attorney General, after describing for the Court all the methods by which Hill and Morgan had for years tried to suppress competition between the two lines, went on to say,

> . . . the ink was hardly dry upon the opinion of the Supreme Court in *Pearsall v. Great Northern Railway,* before Mr. Hill and his associates, representing the Great Northern Railway, and acting in the interests of the Great Northern Railway, had acquired from Mr. Morgan stock of the reorganized Northern Pacific to the amount of $26,000,000. Mr. Morgan and his associates, on the other hand, held stock in the Great Northern Railway to a large but unascertained amount. This common interest in ownership sufficed to produce harmony between the railroads, and it is possible that no further attempt to eliminate competition would have taken place. . . .[4]

Beck, in making this point, was effectively arguing that competition had ceased between the Northern Pacific and Great Northern *before* the Burlington affair and Harriman's raid on Northern Pacific; the course of his argument should have led to the conclusion that the Northern Securities Company was not, as he put it, a *"further attempt* to eliminate competition" between the Northern Pacific and Great Northern, but rather a way of insuring that the combination existing between them would be more securely continued. What the Government consistently failed to make clear was the distinction between "competition" and "potential

[2] 193 U.S. at 202.

[3] Letter from Day to Richards, Aug. 28, 1902, in D.J. File 18429-1901.

[4] *Argument of Assistant Attorney-General James M. Beck, for the United States,* In the Circuit Court of the United States for the Eighth Circuit, pp. 18-19.

competition"; the two railroads, in 1902, were not "engaged in competition" and had not been for years, but their geography inevitably made them "potential competitors." The latter fact, which ought to have been critical in the Government's argument, was put in the legally feeble form of a declaration that the two roads were "parallel."

The defendants further confused the question of whether the two roads were competing. They denied, on the one hand, that the two roads "are parallel or competing, except for the short distances and to the limited extent hereinafter mentioned." On the other hand, they said that the Great Northern and Northern Pacific, having built up a great international commerce, each "competes both in this country and on the ocean with the other transcontinental lines (including the Canadian Pacific). . . ."[5] How the lines could each compete with all the other transcontinental lines without being potential competitors of each other the defense did not explain. But the Government was equally caught in the paradox, as a comment by the Solicitor General showed.

> Observe that Morgan speaks of the Union Pacific as a competing line [vis-à-vis the Northern Pacific]. At the same time he thinks the Great Northern is noncompeting. Why? Certainly not because of its territorial location. Territorially considered, the Great Northern was a parallel and competing line to the Northern Pacific to an extent never reached by the Union Pacific. But Hill and Morgan had reached a "community of interests" understanding (tacit, of course), which put an end to the Great Northern being a rival interest.[6]

The Government's best tactic, and certainly the position that would best have cleared the air, would have been to insist that the geography of the two lines inevitably made them capable of competing with each other.

Indeed, this was the position that the Court, when it emerged from the fog indicated by its opening remarks, did take. It said, for instance, that the Securities Company "destroyed every motive for competition between two roads engaged in interstate traffic, which were *natural competitors* for business, by pooling the earnings of the two roads for the common benefit of the stockholders of

[5] Answer of the Northern Securities Company, 193 U.S. at 223, 231.

[6] *Abstract of Testimony for Complainant,* in U.S. v. Northern Securities (C.C., Minn.), July 15, 1902, p. 50.

both companies. . . ."[7] Again, it alluded to the two railroads as "natural rivals for patronage,"[8] But as these rare, incidental comments could not make a great impression, the issue was still clouded when the case went up on appeal.

The second weak point in the Circuit Court's opinion was the great leap it took from the premise, that the defendants had combined to place control of the two railroads into the hands of the Northern Securities Company, to the conclusion, that as "a necessary consequence" competition between the two railroads would now cease. The only argument that the Court put forward to bridge the gap was this, that the combination, "by pooling the earnings of the two roads for the common benefit of the stockholders of both companies" "destroyed every motive for competition." This argument is inconclusive in pure logic, since a pooling of income would not destroy the motive for competition but, rather, would make it totally indifferent to the stockholders whether the railroads competed vigorously or lethargically. It is incomplete in terms of economics, for the most important effect of the joint ownership would be to give the two railroads the power jointly to raise their rates and thus earn monopoly profits, at least on that part of their traffic in which they did not compete with other transcontinental lines. The argument, again, is excessive, for to say that the combination destroyed "*every* motive" was to deny the possibility that the defendants, though armed with the power to suppress competition between the two railroads and aware of the financial incentives for doing so, would nevertheless refrain—their "motive" being to abide by the antitrust law. The Court would have avoided these difficulties had it clearly said that the combination gave the defendants power to fix noncompetitive rates for the two railroads.

Even that form of the statement would however have left unsettled problems, as a decision of the same court four months later nicely illustrates. The defendants were much the same as in *U.S. v. Northern Securities,* but this time the complainant was the state of Minnesota, and the only judge was District Judge Lochren. This was, in fact, the case that the Attorney General of Minnesota had first tried to bring before the Supreme Court, had then

[7] 120 Fed. 721, at 724. Emphasis added.

[8] 120 Fed. 721, at 725.

brought before the state courts of Minnesota, whence it was removed to the United States Circuit Court in Minnesota by joint petition of all the defendants.[9] In view of the outcome of the Federal Government's case, Attorney General Douglas might well have awaited victory with some confidence. In the event, however, Judge Lochren dismissed the state's bill.

One of Lochren's chief reasons for doing so was his refusal to take the great leap that his brethren had taken in their decision on *U.S. v. Northern Securities.*

> To epitomize this decision: It is held that it will be for the interest of the Northern Securities Company to restrain trade by suppressing competition between these two railroad companies, and that by coercing or persuading the two boards of directors, whom it has the power to elect, it will certainly cause them to commit highly penal offenses, by entering into combinations, contracts, and arrangements in restraint of trade, in violation of the anti-trust act, and hence the Northern Securities Company is already guilty of these offenses that have never been committed or thought of by its officers or promoters, so far as appears, and it must be suppressed and destroyed. I am compelled to reject the doctrine that any person can be held to have committed, or to be purposing and about to commit, a highly penal offense, merely because it can be shown that his pecuniary interests will be thereby advanced, and that he has the power, either directly by himself, or indirectly through persuasion or coercion of his agents, to compass the commission of the offense.[1]

The nub of Lochren's critique reappeared, albeit in a shadowy form, in the subsequent dissents of Supreme Court Justices White and Holmes.

The third weak point in the Circuit Court's opinion was the loose way in which it used the statutory terms "contract in restraint of trade" and "combination in restraint of trade." It used them interchangeably throughout to describe the activities of the defendants, a failing that their familiarity with the common-law precedents and their reading of Taft's *Addyston Pipe* opinion[2]

[9] *Minn. v. Northern Securities* (C.C. Minn.), 123 Fed. 692 (Aug. 1, 1903). For additional facts of the case, cf. arguments and opinion on appeal to the Supreme Court, 194 U.S. 48 (Apr. 11, 1904).

[1] *Minn v. Northern Securities,* 123 Fed. at 702 f.

[2] See above, pp. 172-78.

should have warned them to avoid. Holmes made great capital of this piece of carelessness.

HARLAN'S OPINION FOR THE SUPREME COURT

The majority of the Supreme Court, nevertheless, had no difficulty in affirming the decree. Harlan, once the sole dissenter in the *E.C. Knight* case, now spoke for the Court, or at least for four of the five members of the majority. He began by endorsing the Circuit Court's conclusions of fact. Some of these he expressed more bluntly, as for instance when he said that the two railroads "have become, practically, one powerful consolidated corporation, by the name of a holding corporation, the principal, if not the sole, object for the formation of which was to carry out the purpose of the original combination under which competition between the constituent companies would cease."[3] Harlan, that is, came closer to holding that as a matter of fact, rather than by way of necessary inference, as the Circuit Court put it—or "conjecture," as Lochren labelled it—the defendants had displayed the *intent* to eliminate competition.

Harlan then stated the rules that had emerged from the precedents, listing them in the briefest and barest manner. Among them were the "propositions," as he put it, that the Sherman Act "embraces *all* direct *restraints*" on interstate commerce, that Congress "has prescribed the rule of free competition" for those engaged in interstate commerce, and thus "that *every* combination or conspiracy which would extinguish competition between otherwise competing railroads engaged in *interstate trade or commerce,* and which would *in that way* restrain *such* trade or commerce, is made illegal by the act."[4]

Another of the "propositions" which, Harlan maintained, was plainly implied in the precedents was "that the natural effect of competition is to increase commerce, and an agreement whose direct effect is to prevent this play of competition restrains instead of promotes trade and commerce."[5] In this passage, and over and over throughout his opinion, Harlan makes clear his view that the

[3] 193 U.S. at 326 f.
[4] 193 U.S. at 331.
[5] 193 U.S. at 331.

Sherman Act established *competition* as the rule for interstate commerce. In taking this view, Harlan was not expressing a novel and private interpretation of the Act, but following the doctrine expressly laid down in the *Hopkins* and *Joint Traffic* cases.[6]

Having reached his essential conclusion, Harlan turned by way of epilogue to considering the special objections that had been raised to applying the Act in the present case. The list he considered was much like that which the Circuit Court had disposed of in its opinion, and Harlan disposed of them as well. In some instances his treatment showed a degree of irritation or disdain. For instance, he brushed aside the argument that Congress lacked constitutional power to prevent individuals or corporations from disposing of their property or investing their money, such power being reserved to the states. Harlan answered:

> It is unnecessary in this case to consider such abstract, general questions. The court need not now concern itself with them. They are not here to be examined and determined, and may well be left for consideration in some case necessarily involving their determination.[7]

Considering how relevant and concrete an issue this was, in the eyes not only of the defense but also of the dissenting minority, no comment on it could have been more cavalier. But, in fact, having given voice to a sharp expression, Harlan went on to discuss the issue at length, though under other rubrics, such as the congressional power to control *ownership* of stock in interstate businesses, and especially the broad problem of relations between the states and the Federal Government. He then examined the decree of the Circuit Court, observed that it "will destroy, not the property interests of the original stockholders of the constituent companies, but the power of the holding corporation," [8] and accordingly affirmed it. Justices Brown, McKenna, and Day concurred.

Harlan's opinion served for years as the great synthesis of all previous interpretations of the statute. The rule, as it now stood, was that "restraint of trade" meant any *direct* interference with *competition*.

[6] See above, pp. 178-80.

[7] 193 U.S. at 333 f.

[8] 193 U.S. at 357 f.

BREWER'S CONCURRING OPINION

The majority were joined by Justice Brewer, who however declined to concur in Harlan's opinion, and wrote a separate one of his own. He had been with the majority of the court in the *Trans-Missouri Freight, Joint Traffic, Addyston Pipe,* and *Montague v. Lowry* cases, Brewer said, and he continued to be convinced that those cases had been rightly decided, but he had come to believe that the interpretation advanced in those opinions—all, it should be noticed, composed by Peckham—was incorrect. "Instead of holding that the Anti-Trust Act included all contracts, reasonable or unreasonable, in restraint of interstate trade, the ruling should have been that the contracts there presented were unreasonable restraints of interstate trade, and as such within the scope of the act." Here, in short, was Brewer choosing an occasion to declare by *obiter dictum* that he too was defecting from Peckham's too simple, literal reading of the statute (as Peckham himself had earlier defected) and going over to the spirit of White's "rule of reason."[9] Another *obiter dictum* followed. The Sherman Act, Brewer asserted, could not prevent any single man—say, Mr. Hill—from buying control of both the Great Northern and Northern Pacific. This limitation on the scope of the Act, he said, proceeded from the constitutional, "inalienable" right of every citizen "to manage his own property and determine the place and manner of its investment." And Brewer buttressed this view by citing an older *obiter dictum,* in the *Pearsall* case—which involved the purchase of Northern Pacific stock by the Great Northern—where the Court had said in a perfectly hypothetical way: "Doubtless these stockholders [of the Great Northern] could lawfully acquire by individual purchases a majority, or even the whole of the stock of the reorganized [Northern Pacific] company. . . ."[1] Having said all this, Brewer turned to the Northern Securities case: as it involved an *unreasonable* restraint, exercised by a *combination* of individuals, he was satisfied that the Sherman Act could and did forbid the defendant's activities.[2]

[9] See above, pp. 170-71.

[1] 193 U.S. at 360-62.

[2] 193 U.S. at 362-64.

HOLMES'S DISSENT

From the standpoint of judicial literature, of course, the *Northern Securities* case is more memorable for its dissents than for its majority opinions. White wrote one, Holmes the other; Chief Justice Fuller, author of the *Knight* opinion, concurred in both of them, and so, most surprisingly, did Peckham. But Peckham was spared the need to subscribe to the "rule of reason," or even to give the impression that in endorsing White's opinion he might be subscribing to it, for White restricted himself largely to a single point. He set himself to denying that Congress had power to forbid the combination in this case. "The proposition upon which the case for the government depends then is that the ownership of stock in railroad corporations created by a State is interstate commerce, wherever the railroads engage in interstate commerce."[3] This proposition, White maintained at length, was contrary to the Constitution, to precedent, and long-continued practice; and the Government's bill should therefore have been dismissed.[4]

But even White's opinion, cogent and concentrated as it was, appears dim in the company of Holmes's opinion. It is one of Holmes's masterpieces, full of literary flourishes, intellectual forcefulness, and sophisticated political theory; in all these branches, and as a display of a vivid personality, it makes its counterparts look crude and unreflective. It also suffers from the defects of being malicious and unscholarly.

Consider, for instance, Holmes's famous preamble:

> Great cases like hard cases make bad law. For great cases are called great, not by reason of their real importance in shaping the law of the future, but because of some accident of immediate overwhelming interest which appeals to the feelings and distorts the judgment. These immediate interests exercise a kind of hydraulic pressure which makes what previously was clear seem doubtful, and before which even well settled principles of law will bend.[5]

The passage exhibits to great advantage Holmes's qualities as a thinker and writer; it is reflective and wise, clearly and strongly

[3] 193 U.S. at 367.
[4] 193 U.S. at 364-400.
[5] 193 U.S. at 400 f.

stated, and the slight imprecision of the metaphor of "hydraulic pressure" is amply redeemed by the opening—now classic—aphorism. But if one translates the passage from the abstract mode into the concrete, then clearly Holmes was saying that his brethren in the majority had allowed their feelings—perhaps their antipathy towards Morgan and Hill, or more probably their fears of Progress and of its offshoot, Big Business—to distort their judgment. They had let their feelings bend "well settled principles of law," they had interpreted the law to suit their feelings—they had, in short, enforced their prejudices. Seen for what it was in context, Holmes's preamble is something less than generous.

Nor did Holmes hold himself bound by the implications of his own logic. The preamble might lead one to expect that he would take it on himself to reassert the "well settled principles of law" so that even though the Court had forgotten them in the present circumstances they might be reminded of them later on. Dissent—which, curiously enough, Holmes said he considered "useless and undesirable, as a rule, to express"—might thus serve, as the tables of Moses, to remind sinners of the well-settled rules. But instead of going immediately to state the principles, Holmes passed on to a prescription of method that is, on the face of it, at odds with his opening. "What we have to do in this case," he said, "is to find the meaning of some not very difficult words." When the task of judges "is to interpret and apply the words of a statute, their function is merely academic to begin with—to read English intelligently. . . ." The emphasis he put on the *words* of the statute makes it appear that Holmes had shifted ground: he was no longer concerned with "well settled principles," that is, rules established by the interpretations offered in the precedents; instead he was advocating that the statute be newly interpreted by returning to the plain meaning of its words. As the early Protestants returned to the text of the Bible and the American Revolutionaries to Magna Carta, so Holmes was returning to the Sherman Act, in order to tear away the false interpretations in which it had gradually become enveloped.

A sample of the method of interpretation that Holmes seemed to be advocating is offered in the few sentences in which he analyzed the scope of the antitrust act.

It hits "every" contract or combination of the prohibited sort, great or small, and "every" person who shall monopolize or attempt to monopolize, in the sense of the act, "any part" of the trade or commerce among the several States. There is a natural inclination to assume that it was directed against certain great combinations and to read it in that light. It does not say so. On the contrary, it says "every," and "any part."

To this the majority might have answered that the Supreme Court, at least, had never experienced the presumed "natural inclination" to treat the Act as though it were directed against "certain great combinations." The Sugar Trust, which was, if anything was, one of those "certain great combinations," had escaped unscathed by the Court, whereas two minute and local combinations, those in the *Addyston Pipe* case and in *Montague v. Lowry*,[6] had been roundly condemned by the Court. The majority might with justice have answered further that in every one of the leading cases Peckham had made much of the term "every,"[7] and that Harlan in his opinion for the majority had just finished saying that the Act declared illegal "every contract, combination or conspiracy, in whatever form, of whatever nature, and whoever may be parties to it . . ." that imposed a direct restraint on interstate commerce.[8] At whom, then, was Holmes directing his criticism? Was it the public at large, was it Roosevelt and Knox, or was it the wild antitrust Democrats who were "naturally inclined" to misread "every"? Did Holmes have any warrant, whatever the object of his criticism, for returning at this late date to the plain words of the statute, and disposing of the "well established principles of law" by arguing that the statute "does not say so"?

Again Holmes spoke in the tones of a prophet recalling his people to the sacred text, again unfairly, when he proceeded to analyze the language of the first section of the Act. It says "every contract, combination in the form of trust or otherwise, or conspiracy in restraint of trade or commerce among the several States, or with foreign nations" is illegal. Said Holmes:

Much trouble is made by substituting other phrases assumed to be equivalent, which then are reasoned from as if they were in the act.

[6] 193 U.S. 38 (Feb. 23, 1904).
[7] See above, pp. 167-69.
[8] 193 U.S. at 331.

The court below argued as if maintaining competition were the expressed object of the act. The act says nothing about competition. I stick to the exact words used.[9]

But the court below had not *assumed* that "competition" was equivalent to "trade or commerce"; on the contrary, in equating them it was following a principle of law laid down by the Supreme Court. Had not Peckham declared in the Court's *Joint Traffic* decision, "An agreement of the nature of this one which directly and effectually stifles competition, must be regarded under the statute as one in restraint of trade . . ."?[1] The Circuit Court had cited that decision as its authority. Had not the majority of the Supreme Court just finished confirming that interpretation? For Holmes then to say that the Circuit Court "argued *as if* maintaining competition was the *expressed* object of the act" was deliberate misrepresentation. For Holmes to maintain that "the act says nothing about competition" was deliberate obscurantism, or disingenuousness, for he knew as well as anyone that the function of judges is to enable a statute to *mean* any number of things that it did not and could not *say*. To argue that judges have gone contrary to the spirit of a statute is fair comment; to argue that they have gone beyond the "exact words" is to voice the criticism of a child.[2]

Holmes, being no child, did not himself "stick to the exact words used." When he wanted to know what the statute *meant* by "contracts in restraint of trade" and "combinations in restraint of trade," he explicitly turned to the common law.[3] When he wanted to know what the statute meant by the words, "in the form of trust or otherwise," he referred, though implicitly, to the intent of the legislature, deducing it not from the words of the statute but from conditions existing when the statute was passed.[4]

But the conclusions he drew from both historical sources were

[9] 193 U.S. at 403.

[1] 171 U.S. at 577.

[2] Later in his opinion, Holmes produced a more reasoned basis for this view; see 193 U.S. at 410: "It is true that the suppression of competition was referred to in United States v. Trans-Missouri Freight Association . . . but. . . ."

[3] 193 U.S. at 403 f.

[4] 193 U.S. at 405: "The prohibition was suggested by the trusts. . . ."

strained, not to say seriously wrong. According to common law, he said, contracts in restraint of trade were "contracts with strangers to the contractor's business, and the trade restrained was the contractor's own." Combinations or conspiracies in restraint of trade were "combinations to keep strangers to the agreement out of the business." [5] The latter "definition" is utterly at odds with the precedents: in many or most of the common-law cases, the courts held that a combination was unlawful, whether it excluded others or did not exclude others, because it sought to control the prices at which *its own members* bought or sold goods, or the areas in which they sold them, or other terms on which they themselves did business.[6] It is all the more striking an error since Holmes cited not a single common-law case in support of his statement. And again, when he referred to the legislative history of the statute, he radically distorted the facts. The prohibition of the statute, he said, "was suggested by the trusts, the objection to which, as every one knows, was not the union of former competitors, but the sinister power exercised or supposed to be exercised by the combination in keeping rivals out of the business and ruining those who were already in. It was the ferocious extreme of competition with others, not the cessation of competition among the partners, that was the evil feared." [7] The legislative history of the Act shows that Holmes' summary, passed off with the phrase "as every one knows," is incorrect: the evils feared were "unfair competition" and the cessation of competition, both alike.[8]

As Holmes viewed the statutory meaning of "contracts" and "combinations" in restraint of trade, the defendants in the *Northern Securities* case fitted neither category. None of the parties, particularly neither railroad, had restricted itself as would a party to a "contract in restraint of trade." And the parties could not be said to have entered a "combination in restraint of trade" since they were not doing what was, as Holmes understood it, the essence of such a combination, that is, "keeping rivals out of the

[5] 193 U.S. at 404.

[6] See above, pp. 49, 80. Cf. Judge Jackson's view in the *Greene* case, above, pp. 148-49.

[7] 193 U.S. at 405.

[8] See above, pp. 96-97.

business" of railroading, in this instance, or "ruining those who were already in." [9] He concluded, therefore, that the decision should have gone for the defendants.

Holmes's opinion is great despite its flaws. Not the least of its greatness consists in his bringing so sharply into view the paradox inherent in the policy of the antitrust law. The paradox had been there from the beginning. Congress had wanted to do two things which, although not incompatible are not easily kept in tandem: to preserve the benefits of competition while enjoying the benefits of consolidation. Not knowing how to frame a statute that would even-handedly accomplish both these purposes, Congress had deliberately experimented, leaving it to the courts to serve as laboratory. A case had now come to court which raised the issue squarely. Holmes was the only judge to face it absolutely head-on. The statute, he argued, did not "require all existing competitions to be kept on foot, and . . . invalidate the continuance of old contracts by which former competitors united in the past." [1] The two railroads had been consolidated long since; was that "fusion" now to be dissolved on the principle that all past competitors should be kept competing forever? If so, the Act must destroy also "a partnership between two stage drivers who had been competitors in driving across a state line, or two merchants once engaged in rival commerce among the States whether made after or before the act, if now continued. . . ." [2] He was convinced, he concluded, that Congress had not intended to pass a law which "would make eternal the *bellum omnium contra omnes* and disintegrate society so far as it could into individual atoms." And he added, in a parting jibe at the narrowness of Harlan's victory, "I am happy to know that only a minority of my brethren adopt [such] an interpretation of the law. . . ." [3]

In private Holmes was a fairly stock Social Darwinist. His allusion, in the opinion, to Hobbesian chaos and atomistic competition, shows it. His total disdain for the Sherman Act shows it also. "Of course," he wrote Pollock, "I enforce whatever constitutional laws Congress or anybody else sees fit to pass—and do it in good faith to

[9] 193 U.S. at 405-10.
[1] 193 U.S. at 410.
[2] 193 U.S. at 410.
[3] 193 U.S. at 411.

the best of my ability—but I don't disguise my belief that the Sherman Act is a humbug based on economic ignorance and incompetence. . . ."[4] Yet despite this private view, or perhaps because of it, Holmes recognized more sharply than most that the Sherman Act embodied a combination of goals that could not be consistently achieved in practice by the rules of interpretation so far laid down. The narrowest rule, Jackson's, which Holmes himself followed, would give absolute latitude to any combination that consolidated itself by outright corporate merger—that went, in Holmes's term, into "fusion." The broadest rule, that now voiced by Harlan, would prohibit—if consistently applied—every effort to reduce competition. None of the other rules by then propounded, except White's rule of reason, could do better to achieve the compound intent of the Act.

It is one of the many ironies of the *Northern Securities* case that Holmes, who should have understood Roosevelt's desire to have a law that could distinguish "good trusts" from "bad trusts," who should have found utterly congenial to his own principles the Darwinian doctrine of "inevitable development" from which Roosevelt derived that aim, could never sympathize with Roosevelt's way of doing things. All the irritation that Holmes expressed in his opinion, although it cut innocent bystanders, was almost certainly incited by Roosevelt's manner and the tactics of his antitrust campaign. It was a clash of temperaments, and, more important, of attitudes toward politics. Holmes's side of the affair is on record in a letter to Pollock.

> Of course I pretty well made up my package about him a good while ago, and I don't think I was too much disturbed by what you admit to and what was formulated by a Senator in his day, thus: "What the boys like about Roosevelt is that he doesn't care a damn for the law." It broke up our incipient friendship, however, as he looked on my dissent to the *Northern Securities case* as a political departure (or, I suspect, more truly, couldn't forgive anyone who stood in his way). We talked freely later but it never was the same after that, and if he had not been restrained by his friends, I am told that he would have made a fool of himself and would have excluded me from the White House—and as in his case about the law, so in mine about that, I never

[4] Letter from Holmes to Pollock, Apr. 23, 1910, in *Holmes-Pollock Letters,* I, 163 (1941).

cared a damn whether I went there or not. He was very likeable, a big figure, a rather ordinary intellect, with extraordinary gifts, a shrewd and I think pretty unscrupulous politician. He played all his cards—if not more. *R.i.p.*[5]

Roosevelt's reaction to Holmes's dissent is equally revealing. In the first place, Roosevelt had expressed his views on the political responsibility of justices in a letter to Henry Cabot Lodge, Holmes's sponsor for the Supreme Court appointment, a letter that Roosevelt invited Lodge to show Holmes.

In the ordinary and low sense which we attach to the words "partisan" and "politician," a judge of the Supreme Court should be neither. But in the higher sense, in the proper sense, he is not in my judgment fitted for the position unless he is a party man, a constructive statesman. . . . Now I should like to know that Judge Holmes was in entire sympathy with our views, that is with your views and mine and Judge Gray's, for instance . . . before I would feel justified in appointing him. . . .[6]

Presumably Roosevelt had been given the assurances he wanted. Holmes's dissent, coming so soon after, must have seemed to him a defection not only from his party's policy, but also from the statesmanship that he required of justices, as of all senior officers of government. On hearing of the dissent, Roosevelt is supposed to have exclaimed, "I could carve out of a banana a judge with more backbone than that!" And a few years later, Roosevelt was still calling Holmes "a bitter disappointment." [7]

In the larger view of the matter, the falling out of Holmes and Roosevelt was a small inconvenience. There were some other small inconveniences. During the congressional elections of 1902, Roosevelt feared that his forwardness in antitrust suits had dried up some sources of Republican campaign funds.[8] Worse was to come. The Northern Securities action, so Elihu Root reported early in 1904,

[5] Letter from Holmes to Pollock, Feb. 9, 1921, in *Holmes-Pollock Letters,* II, 63 f.

[6] Letter from Roosevelt to Lodge, July 10, 1902, in *Roosevelt Letters,* III, 289.

[7] Harbaugh, *Power and Responsibility* 162 (1961).

[8] Letter from Roosevelt to Winthrop M. Crane, Aug. 19, 1902, in *Roosevelt Letters,* III, 316 f.

was regarded by the gentlemen interested as a blow at corporate enterprises, and they set to work to prevent Roosevelt's renomination on the ground that he was not a safe man for the business interests of the country to have in the White House. This view . . . naturally met with the most general acceptance in New York City, where there had come to be a quite general feeling that the President was much more in sympathy with the labor people than he was with capital and that he must be distrusted on this account.[9]

Root himself managed to dispel this menace by a speech at the Union League Club—of which he had been president—in the course of which he proclaimed that Roosevelt was "the greatest conservative force for the protection of property and of capital in the city of Washington during the years that have elapsed since President McKinley's death."[1] Roosevelt's great gratitude for Root's endorsement makes it seem that he had regarded the liability that he had created by his antitrust activities as quite real.[2]

On the other hand, Roosevelt knew perfectly well that what might be an obstacle in capturing the nomination could be a huge asset in winning the election. He was persuaded that his antitrust record would play that role. So he said to Cortelyou, his campaign manager,

The Northern Securities suit is one of the great achievements of my administration. I look back upon it with great pride, for through it we emphasized in signal fashion, as in no other way could be emphasized, the fact that the most powerful men in this country were held to accountability before the law.[3]

And, at the level of policy rather than politics, the *Northern Securities* case was a clear gain for Roosevelt. It was a step in persuading the American people that "the control of corporations" —for this, rather than "antitrust," was the title under which Roosevelt preferred to discuss the issue—was the leading issue of domestic policy, and that Roosevelt recognized it as such.

[9] Letter from Root to J. St. Loe Strachey, Mar. 23, 1904, in Jessup, *Elihu Root,* I, 415 (1938).

[1] (Feb. 3, 1904), in Root, *Miscellaneous Addresses* 223 (1917).

[2] See, e.g., Letter from Roosevelt to Joseph B. Bishop, June 15, 1905, in *Roosevelt Letters,* IV, 1219 f.

[3] Letter from Roosevelt to Cortelyou, Aug. 11, 1904, in *Roosevelt Letters,* IV, 886.

CHAPTER SEVEN

REFORMING THE SHERMAN ACT

1905-1914

A statute that is simple and general does not commend itself to every taste. Many citizens dislike it, especially if their own conduct might be subject to it, because no man, they believe, ought to be left in any doubt about *exactly* where the line is drawn between lawful conduct and unlawful conduct. A law that does not tell them quite explicitly and concretely what they can safely get away with is, they feel, a law that exposes them to unwarranted risk. Further, they disapprove of a general statute because it seems to them to confer too much discretionary power—even absolute discretionary power—on judges. A law that does not instruct the judge quite exactly as to the decision he must reach in any conceivable case that might arise under it is, in the mind of such critics, a law that leaves the judge free to do whatever he pleases. And finally, they disapprove of a general statute because it seems to them to be the production of an irresponsible legislature, whose members are lazy, stupid, or corrupt. A law that does not tell the public exactly what it may do and does not tell judges exactly what they must do, owes its defects, in this view, only to the remissness of the legislators who wrote it.

The premise of this sort of criticism is that laws can catalogue exhaustively and precisely every specific action they command or prohibit. Only from this assumption does it follow that a simple and general law imposes deep injustice on the governed, grants intolerable powers to judges, and demonstrates a failure of the legislature to do its proper duty. A milder form of such criticism is of course sometimes justified: there are vague laws, poorly drafted, hence allowing too much judicial discretion and creating excessive uncertainty for the public. But a general and simple law is not the same thing as a vague law; it appears to be so only to men who suppose that it is possible to eliminate all risks from legal processes, who imagine that a legislator can foresee and predetermine every case that might arise under a statute, and who fail to recognize that although no judge can do any judging without exercising some discretion, any judge who respects the common-law tradition sets strict limits on the amount of discretion he allows himself or any subordinate judge to use. A perfectly precise law, made by omnipotent legislators and applied by impotent and otiose judges, is impossible. Yet this impossibility was in some degree desired by those who criticized the Sherman Act for its "generality."

The desire for an antitrust law more specific in its prohibitions, more discriminating in its application, and more continuous in its operation was expressed from the beginning of the Sherman Act's existence. Writers of all sorts objected to the Act, businessmen and labor leaders complained, dissident congressmen tabled bills of the most compendious intricacy. They did so throughout the 1890's, without success. But during the next decade, their criticisms began to be more effective. One proposal above all others began to gather popularity as a remedy for all the supposed failings in the Sherman Act. This was the proposal to establish an administrative commission, which would follow specific instructions written into its enabling statute. Being released from the rigors and artificial rituals of courts, it could decide cases quickly; being staffed by experts, it could decide correctly; being armed with quasi-legislative powers, it could create supplementary rules as soon as the need arose, thus constantly informing citizens of what they might and might not do; and being in constant session and having the power to command the appearance of parties, it could supervise business continuously rather than intermittently. By 1914, the proposal to establish such a body was realized in the passage of the Federal Trade Commission Act and the Clayton Antitrust Act.

First Steps Toward a Regulatory System

The first great sponsor of a system for regulating big business was Theodore Roosevelt. The persistence with which he sponsored such a system is somewhat obscured by the well-publicized vigor with which he prosecuted under the Sherman Act. His first term was marked by the brilliant defeat of the Northern Securities Company and by a most popular attack against the Beef Trust.[1] During his second term, between 1905 and 1909, the pace of antitrust prosecution was very much stepped up. It was remarkable that the Government started as many as thirty-seven cases; it was much more remarkable that a number of them were directed against the giants—Standard Oil, American Tobacco, DuPont, and the Union Pacific system. The Sherman Act was finally being used against trusts of the dimensions that had called it into being, and with enough energy to justify the boast that the President was using a Big Stick. Yet all the while, Roosevelt was urging that the Sherman Act be supplanted by a more discreet and discriminating method for regulating corporations.

THE BUREAU OF CORPORATIONS

The first step was the establishment in 1903 of the Bureau of Corporations, an agency of the newly formed Department of Commerce and Labor.[2] Its enabling act, which Roosevelt took immense trouble to get into the precise form he thought appropriate, put the Bureau in charge of that "publicity" which Roosevelt considered the essential of a correct antitrust policy. The act directed the Bureau to investigate corporations, to transmit its findings to the President, and to publish as much of them as the President directed. Some Democrats in Congress had been perturbed by the last provision because, as William Richardson of Alabama said, it would enable the President to "suppress all data, every scintilla of information. He can hold it secret and stand pat and say and do nothing, and no law can move him. Is that publicity?" [3] What they said Roosevelt wanted, and what later events proved he wanted, was publicity pliable enough to become an instrument of policy. Having repeatedly distinguished "good trusts" from "bad trusts," he wanted the power to publicize the activities of the latter alone—in other words, to use publicity as a punitive device. Moreover, he wanted the

[1] See below, pp. 241-44.

[2] Act of Feb. 14, 1903, 32 Stat. 827.

[3] 36 *Cong. Rec.* 2005 (Feb. 10, 1903).

power to use such publicity as a political tool in its broadest sense.

This became clear in the Bureau's first great inquiry, an investigation that began in 1904 of the "Beef Trust."

The Bureau's investigation came after a long prelude. Early in 1902 the House Committee on Judiciary had been investigating the Beef Trust, a combination alleged to supply 60 per cent of the fresh meat entering interstate commerce,[4] and on April 12, its chairman asked the Attorney General whether he proposed to take action. Knox replied that he had directed an investigation to be made "some time ago"[5]—meaning, in fact, five days earlier.[6] In any event, once started, Knox moved fast; within a fortnight he was able to write to S. H. Bethea, the U. S. Attorney at Chicago, "I am satisfied that sufficient evidence is at hand upon which bills in equity for injunction may be framed to restrain the combination from further proceeding. . . ."[7] On May 10, Bethea filed the bill in the Circuit Court at Chicago, to the applause of persons as diverse as a Democratic congressman from Maryland, the Secretary of the Central Labor Union of Massachusetts, the Board of Aldermen of New York City, and the Live Stock Commission Merchants of Southern Ohio.[8] Within a year, and about a week after the Circuit Court had decided the *Northern Securities* case in the government's favor, Circuit Judge Grosscup at Chicago overruled the defendants' demurrer and issued a preliminary injunction.[9] An appeal being lodged, time passed, and the case was losing its publicity effect. The next spring, Roosevelt, denied action, asked for words. "Would it not be well," he wrote Knox in the spring of 1904, "to have some statement made as to what has been done about the beef trust, so that people will be advised? Sometimes things of this kind ought to be hammered in."[1] What the Department was doing about

[4] 122 Fed. at 529.

[5] 57th Cong. 1st Sess., H.R. Report 1614, p. 2 (Apr. 15, 1902).

[6] See Letter from Knox to S. H. Bethea (U. S. Att'y, Chicago), Apr. 24, 1902, in D.J. Instruction Bk. 159, p. 157.

[7] Letter from Knox to Bethea, Apr. 24, 1902, in D.J. Instruction Bk. 159, p. 157.

[8] D.J. File 6073-1902, nos. 6456-, 6837-, and 7600-1902.

[9] U.S. v. Swift, 122 Fed. 529 (Apr. 18, 1903).

[1] Letter from Roosevelt to Knox (Mar. 26, 1904); *Roosevelt Letters,* IV, 765.

the Beef Trust, in fact, was gathering evidence that the Trust had been systematically disregarding the injunction.[2]

At just this moment, the Bureau of Corporations made its entrance, having been invited to investigate by a resolution of the House of Representatives.[3] James A. Garfield, the Commissioner of Corporations, went off to Chicago in April and spent several days interviewing leading members of the Trust. He told them, by way of preface, that he would not use "detective methods," that he was not working with or for the Department of Justice, and that the Bureau's function was not to find violations of law, but to gather information to be used in framing new legislation.[4] On the strength of these assurances, the packing company officers answered Garfield's questions, and during the following year opened their books and files to the Bureau's investigators. On March 3, 1905, at the direction of the President, the Commissioner of Corporations published his report on the Beef Industry—a report which, however, excluded all information that the Bureau had gathered about the *combination* among the packers.[5]

The Department of Justice, meanwhile, had been carrying on its own investigations aimed at preparing a criminal prosecution under the Sherman Act, this form of action having been chosen because of ample hints, if not evidence, that the Beef Trust was blithely ignoring the injunction issued against it in *U.S. v. Swift.*[6] During 1903 and 1904, Bethea had been using special agents to investigate violations of the injunction—and among those agents, it appears, was an employee of the Bureau of Corporations.[7] In

[2] See below, pp. 242-43.

[3] *Report of the Commissioner of Corporations, 1904* (58th Cong. 3rd Sess., H.R. Doct. 165) 28.

[4] U.S. v. Armour, 142 Fed. 808, at 811 ff. Garfield wrote the same policy into his first annual report, 34 ff.

[5] Commissioner of Corporations, *Report . . . on the Beef Industry* (1905); *Annual Report* (1905), 4.

[6] See above, p. 241.

[7] Letter from Bethea to Att'y Gen., Sept. 22, 1903, in D.J. File 6073-1902, 14176-1903. Letter from Bethea to Att'y Gen., Sept. 28, 1903, in D.J. File 6073-1902, 14636-1903. Letter from Day to Bethea Oct. 1, 1903, in D.J. Instruction Bk. 185, p. 151: "Department of Commerce will furnish an agent to cooperate with Murphy." [F. T. Murphy, Bethea's special investigator.] Cf. also D.J. Instruction Bk. 188, pp. 432, 469, 470; and D.J. File 6073-1902, 19702-1903.

August 1904, Bethea asked for further help, and was assigned two Secret Service officers.[8] He also asked that the Commissioner of Corporations give him what information he had gathered and that the Commissioner's subordinates in Chicago be ordered to do the same.[9] Commissioner Garfield, after conferring with the Attorney General and the Solicitor General,[1] complied by handing over a list of thirty persons from whom Bethea might get statements.[2] This gesture of cooperation was carefully guarded, the Commissioner giving away no information of his own, but only mentioning *possible* sources of information. Garfield felt very strongly, as he said repeatedly, that it was not the function of the Bureau of Corporations to aid in enforcing the antitrust laws. Bethea, in Chicago, busy preparing a prosecution, renewed his request that the Bureau's men in Chicago deliver evidence to him, but the Secretary of Commerce flatly refused to allow it.[3] Knox, who felt just as strongly that the Bureau *should* help the Department of Justice, pressed the President for a decision. But for the time being, Roosevelt offered no help: "I do not wish as yet to commit myself on one side or the other of the proposition that incidentally to this main object [of publicity, the Bureau] may be able to secure information which will be of value in securing the better execution of the [antitrust] law through the Department of Justice."[4] The reason he did not wish to commit himself at just that time is easy enough to guess: the presidential election campaign was well under way.

Not long after the election, and not long before the U. S. Attorney at Chicago went before a grand jury to ask for an indictment of the Beef Trust, the President decided. He directed Garfield to turn over to the Attorney at Chicago all the relevant information.[5]

[8] D.J. File 6073-1902, 39965-, 40146-, and 40152-1904.

[9] Letter from Bethea to Att'y Gen., Aug. 16, 1904, in D.J. File 60-50-10, Sec. 6.

[1] 142 Fed. at 815.

[2] Letter from Garfield to Act'g Att'y Gen., Aug. 22, 1904, in D.J. File 6073-1902, 40189-1904; and D.J. File 60-50-10.

[3] Letter from Bethea to Att'y Gen., Aug. 26, 1904; Letter from Secy. of Commerce and Labor to Att'y Gen., Sept. 12, 1904; in D.J. File 6073-1902, 40430-, 41289-1904.

[4] Letter from Roosevelt to Garfield, Sept. 30, 1904; *Roosevelt Letters,* IV, 960 f. For the background of the letter, see Letter from Roosevelt to William Miller Collier, Sept. 26, 1904; *Roosevelt Letters,* IV, 953 f.

[5] Letter from Roosevelt to Garfield, Jan. 18, 1905, cited in Johnson,

Garfield did so, and the Attorney used the information in getting the indictment.

Unfortunately, this cooperation, so hard to secure, was the undoing of the Department's prosecution. The defendants argued that under the guarantee of the Fifth Amendment, the evidence they had given to Garfield could not be used against them. The court, sustaining their pleas of immunity—as to the natural and individual defendants, though not as to the corporate defendants—directed the jury to bring in a verdict in favor of the defendants.[6] "Publicity," in short, had vitiated enforcement.

The Bureau's unanticipated and unwanted power to grant "immunity baths" was soon corrected by the passing of an act which extended immunity to witnesses only if they had been formally subpoenaed and had given evidence under oath.[7] On this new basis, the Bureau went ahead in 1906, at the direction of Roosevelt, to investigate the Standard Oil Company, Roosevelt frankly intending to aid the Department of Justice in taking action under the antitrust law.[8] And so, until 1914, the Bureau continued working in its dual role, to provide publicity about certain businesses, and, progressively more important, to act as investigating auxiliary to the Department of Justice.

PRESIDENT ROOSEVELT'S POLICY

Roosevelt nevertheless continued to insist that the Federal system for control of business was radically incomplete. He kept reiterating his criticisms and proposals in every major public statement during his second term, varying the details from speech to speech according to his sensitive perception of political facts at the moment. Yet in each of these speeches, Roosevelt outlined the same doctrine, the doctrine which during his first term he had learned and adapted and finally made his own.

"Theodore Roosevelt and the Bureau of Corporations," *Miss. Valley Hist. Rev.*, XLV, 571, 580 (1959).

[6] U.S. v. Armour, 142 Fed. 808 (D.C., Ill.; Mar. 21, 1906); *nolle prosequi* entered Feb. 25, 1913 (1 *D. & J.* 687).

[7] 34 Stat. 798 (1906).

[8] Johnson, "Theodore Roosevelt and the Bureau of Corporations," *Miss. Valley Hist. Rev.*, XLV, 583 *et seq.* (1959). See also, Commissioner of Corporations, *Annual Report 1907* 3-4 (1908).

Roosevelt's matured doctrine began from the premise that industrial enterprises were becoming larger, not merely as a matter of convenience or choice, but as the result of natural forces. From this premise the briefest of steps carried him to the conclusion that the laws of man could not and should not attempt to stop the process. "As I have repeatedly said in messages to the Congress and elsewhere, experience has definitely shown not merely the unwisdom but the futility of endeavoring to put a stop to all business combinations. Modern industrial conditions are such that combination is not only necessary but inevitable." [9] As usual, the historicist prophet did not inform the audience what there was about "modern industrial conditions" that made the process of combination "inevitable"; the intellectual weight of the argument was carried by the belief that ripples of the recent past are impeccable evidence for inferring the wave of the future.

From this conclusion it followed obviously that the Sherman Act was disastrous, because what it did, according to Roosevelt, was to "forbid all combinations." [1] A law that laid down so impracticable a prohibition was worse than no law, because it inevitably led to hypocrisy and ultimately to disrespect for law in general. "It is a public evil to have on the statute-books a law incapable of full enforcement because both judges and juries realize that its full enforcement would destroy the business of the country. . . ." Moreover even if the Sherman Act did not aim at so wrong-headed a goal, it would still be defective because the action it gave rise to was much too cumbersome and expensive.

> The government must now submit to irksome and repeated delay before obtaining a final decision of the courts upon proceedings instituted, and even a favorable decree may mean an empty victory. Moreover, to attempt to control these corporations by lawsuits means to impose upon both the Department of Justice and the courts an impossible burden. . . .[2]

These defects in the policy and practice of the Sherman Act made it clear, Roosevelt argued, that the system of prohibition en-

[9] Roosevelt, Seventh Annual Message (Dec. 3, 1907), in *Works,* XV, 416.

[1] Roosevelt, Sixth Annual Message (Dec. 3, 1906), quoted and endorsed in Seventh Annual Message; *Works,* XV, 367, 417.

[2] *Works,* XV, 420.

forced by the courts should give way to a system of regulation "administered by an executive body."

The first requirement in establishing the new system was to amend the Sherman Act so "as to forbid only the kind of combination which does harm to the general public," specifically exempting those that do no harm and especially those that are beneficial. The *quid pro quo* for this amendment would be a "grant of supervisory power to the government over these big concerns engaged in interstate business." The supervision, aiming to nip monopolistic abuses in the bud, would of course need to be carried out by "an executive body, and not merely by means of lawsuits." [3] The reason, as it appeared from a slightly later statement, was not only that lawsuits were costly and slow, but also that "no judicial tribunal has the knowledge or the experience to determine in the first place whether a given combination is advisable or necessary in the interest of the public." [4] An expert commission, on the other hand, could operate a supervision analogous to that already exercised over the national banks by the Comptroller of the Currency and over public carriers by the Interstate Commerce Commission; the agency obviously destined for the purpose was the Bureau of Corporations.[5]

This general plan was embellished by a motif that became much stronger during Roosevelt's Progressive years. As a matter of fairness to businessmen, Roosevelt said, the policy of the amended act and of the regulatory agency should be declared with utter precision. "The law should make its prohibitions and permissions as clear and definite as possible, leaving the least possible room for arbitrary action, or allegation of such action, on the part of the Executive, or of divergent interpretations by the courts." This clarity could be achieved by specifically prohibiting such practices as "unhealthy competition" (instanced by cut-throat pricing), stock-watering, and exclusive dealing arrangements. It could be achieved also by specifying that "reasonable agreements between, or combination of, corporations should be permitted, provided they are submitted to and approved by some appropriate govern-

[3] Works, XV, 420-21.

[4] Roosevelt, Special Message to Congress (Apr. 27, 1908), p. 7.

[5] Roosevelt, Seventh Annual Message, 1907; *Works*, XV, 420-22.

ment body."[6] In short, businessmen should be told in detail what they were not allowed to do, and should be given explicit license to do all other things.

Not surprisingly, the Commissioner of Corporations had been campaigning, ever since the Bureau was established, for the same goal. In 1908, Herbert Knox Smith, then Commissioner, summed up the Administration's views succinctly.

> There is an irresistible movement toward concentration in business. We must definitely recognize this as an inevitable economic law. We must also recognize the fact that industrial concentration is already largely accomplished, in spite of general statutory prohibition.
>
> Recognizing these facts, the aim of new legislation should be to regulate, rather than to prohibit, combination. It is an obvious absurdity to attempt to do both at the same time, and prohibition has practically failed. Our present law, forbidding all combination, therefore needs adaptation to the actual facts. It is now inflexible and indiscriminate. It takes no account of the intent, methods, and results of combination. . . .
>
> . . . we must recognize concentration, supervise it, and regulate it. We must do this positively, through an active federal agency, and not merely by the negative prohibitions of penal law.[7]

It was a view echoed throughout the Administration, and endorsed by many of its supporters.

THE HEPBURN BILL, 1908

Widespread as was the view that the antitrust law should be revised, there was still so much disagreement about the practical details of revision that a draft of an amending act which might get broad support could not easily be drawn up. During Roosevelt's term of office only one serious attempt was made. Its vehicle, the Hepburn bill, introduced only six months before the presidential election of 1908, soon encountered obstacles and was lost from sight in the turmoil of the campaign.

That single effort grew out of a national conference held at Chicago in October 1907 under the auspices of the National Civic Federation, an organization founded in 1896 in the hope of achiev-

[6] *Works,* XV, 421.

[7] Commissioner of Corporations, *Annual Report 1908,* p. 5.

ing industrial peace by bringing together leaders of business, labor, and agriculture in the soothing presence of public officials, lawyers, and economists. The Chicago meeting was convened in order to find an antitrust policy that would be congenial to all these groups. And, indeed, many of them had grievances. Businessmen objected to the uncertainties of the Sherman Act as administered by the Attorney General and interpreted by the courts; they objected even more to the harshness of an act that had already suppressed peaceable combinations and would probably suppress mere trade associations as well. Labor leaders, spoken for by Samuel Gompers, decried the use that had been made of the Sherman Act to break strikes and unions. Economists, among them Frank Taussig and Jeremiah Jenks, reiterating the standing view of their American colleagues,[8] criticized the Sherman Act for its failure to concede the intrinsic defects and inevitable decline of competition. And lawyers considered the Sherman Act technically awkward, holding that it had abandoned the common-law distinction between "reasonable" and "unreasonable" restraints of trade and that it had thereby become too blunt an instrument. The Conference agreed to recommend that the Act be revised.[9]

The leaders of the Civic Federation soon went further; and after consulting with the President, the Commissioner of Corporations, and many others, drew up a proposed statute.[1] It was introduced in the House on March 23, 1908, by Congressman William Hepburn of the Committee on Interstate Commerce.[2] The bill provided that corporations might, at their option, register with the Commissioner of Corporations. To qualify for registration they must make full disclosure of their financial conditions and business methods. Once registered they could at any time file with the Commissioner copies of contracts or agreements in restraint of trade to which they had become parties. The Commissioner could, at his discretion, enter an order declaring the agreement to be an

[8] See above, pp. 73-77.

[9] *Proceedings of the National Conference on Trusts and Combinations under the auspices of the National Civic Federation, Chicago, October 22-25, 1907* (1908). See also Johnson, "Antitrust Policy in Transition, 1908," *Miss. Valley Hist. Rev.*, XLVIII, 415 (1961).

[1] Johnson, "Antitrust Policy in Transition, 1908," *Miss Valley Hist. Rev.*, XLVIII, 425.

[2] 60th Cong. 1st Sess., H.R. 19745.

unreasonable restraint of trade; however, if he did not do so within thirty days, the Government forfeited its right to attack the agreement thereafter. This rule was somewhat qualified by the proviso that the foreclosure of suit by the Government would not operate if the agreement in question were "in unreasonable restraint of trade"; but the intent of the bill, if not the clear meaning of its language, was that any agreement in restraint declared by the Commissioner to be "reasonable" would thereby become immune from attack by the Government.

To this licensing power, the essence of the Hepburn bill, were attached several lesser proposals. The section of the Sherman Act providing for triple damages in private suits was to be amended so that the plaintiff could recover to the extent of his damages only. The bill provided further that no public or private suits could henceforth attack agreements by registered corporations, made prior to 1908. Finally, the bill declared that the Sherman Act was not to restrict the right of employees to strike or combine, the right of employers to discharge their employees, or the right of employers to combine with each other in the hiring of labor—a section especially welcome to the trade unions as an antidote to the recent Danbury Hatters' decision,[8] but also repugnant to them insofar as it offered equal immunity to employers' blacklists and yellow-dog contracts. In short, the Hepburn bill offered concessions to a great variety of opinions—to those who wanted publicity, registration of corporations, supervision of corporations, reduced litigation, discrimination between reasonable and unreasonable restraints, an end to the restoring of "all past competitions," and a specific exemption for labor unions.

But the sponsors and draftsmen of the bill had not yet satisfied their backers. In particular, they felt impelled by pressure from certain businessmen to suggest revisions that would reduce the powers granted the Commissioner of Corporations. In doing so they sacrificed the support of Roosevelt, who had begun by calling it "a very good bill" and congratulating Seth Low, chairman of the Civic Federation, for having done "admirable work for the public." But he threatened to veto the bill if it were passed in the revised form and, on recognizing how ready Low and his collaborators

[8] Loewe v. Lawlor, 208 U.S. 274 (Feb. 3, 1908).

were to vacillate, finally withdrew his support.[4] Indeed, under the influence of Charles Bonaparte, then his Attorney General, Roosevelt condemned any bill that would restrict the operation of antitrust laws to "unreasonable" combinations only.[5]

The Hepburn bill, in its original form, was therefore sent to committees of both houses, which submitted it to long hearings. Its originators and others testified in its favor. Attorney General Bonaparte refused to testify, on the pretext of much work and "a slight indisposition." [6] Herbert Knox Smith, the Commissioner of Corporations, testified in favor of the bill, but in such a way as to insure its defeat. Among other things, he was forced to confess that he—the official whom the bill would charge with determining whether combinations were reasonable or unreasonable—knew no clear and objective way to tell reasonable from unreasonable, no way more precise, at least, than the common-law rules that the courts were already applying.[7] Finally, the very sponsors of the bill, businessmen and labor leaders alike, began objecting to it because it did not give each of them enough of what he wanted. The Senate committee then condemned the bill to death, declaring with great relish that the "dispensing power, a power of granting immunity" which the bill conferred "on a mere bureau head," would do violence to due process of law, and taking the opportunity to praise the Sherman Act as "clear, comprehensive, certain, and highly remedial." [8] So ended the first serious attempt to establish a regulatory commission for antitrust affairs.

PRESIDENT TAFT'S POLICY

That the principle of regulation, and its corollary of Federal registration, had by this time come to be widely held was demonstrated

[4] Letters from Roosevelt to Low, Mar. 28, Apr. 1, Apr. 9, 1908; *Roosevelt Letters,* VI, 984, 986, 997. See also Roosevelt, *Autobiography* 470 ff. (1913).

[5] Letter from Roosevelt to Low, Apr. 9, 1908; *Roosevelt Letters,* VI, 997. Cf. statement by Roosevelt quoted in Chicago *Inter Ocean* (Apr. 28, 1908), cited by Johnson, *Miss. Valley Hist. Rev.*, XLVIII, 427-28.

[6] Johnson, *Miss. Valley Hist. Rev.,* XLVIII, 430.

[7] Johnson, *Miss. Valley Hist. Rev.,* XLVIII, 430 f.

[8] 60th Cong. 2nd Sess., Sen. Report 848. Judiciary Committee, *Report on S. 6440* (Jan. 26, 1909); quoted in 43 *Cong. Rec.* 2321 (Feb. 13, 1909).

in the party platforms of 1908. They were, as always, imperfect forecasts of what the parties would do during the next four years. Yet, as always, they were the best available estimates of what voters thought they wanted done.

The Democrats, after endorsing the Sherman Act and demanding vigorous enforcement, asked for additional legislation. They gave three instances of additional remedies: to prohibit interlocking directorships, to prohibit discriminatory pricing, and to establish a Federal licensing system. The last-named, surprisingly, would make it necessary for a corporation in interstate commerce "to take out a Federal license before it shall be permitted to control as much as twenty-five per cent of the product in which it deals, the license to protect the public from watered stock and to prohibit the control by such corporation of more than fifty per cent of the total amount of any product consumed in the United States."[9] It was one of the more bizarre schemes in a field where imagination had always been fecund.

The Republican campaign plank was much less detailed, simply repeating that the Sherman Act, a wholesome Republican product, could be strengthened by giving the Government greater powers to supervise, control, and publicize "that class of corporations engaged in interstate commerce having power and opportunity to effect monopolies."[1] The last clause implied a shift from the criterion of "good and bad" to the very different criterion of "large and small"—but this appears to have been no more than a vagary of platform drafting.

In the event, however, Roosevelt's distinction between good trusts and bad trusts was quickly jettisoned by his former protégé, now his successor, William Howard Taft. In his first, long statement to Congress on antitrust matters, President Taft demonstrated the independence of his views, not to mention the clarity of his mind. Relying not at all on the mystique of historical inevitability, Taft asserted that some combinations were formed chiefly to achieve the economies of production on a large scale, whereas others were aimed directly at establishing monopoly control. Then, reviewing the effect of the Sherman Act on these two classes—and reviewing it with the skill of the judge who had written the *Addys-*

[9] Porter and Johnson, *National Party Platforms* 146 (1961 ed.).
[1] Porter and Johnson, *National Party Platforms* 159.

ton Pipe opinion[2]—he proceeded to show that despite the emphasis that Peckham's early decisions had put on the word "every," the more recent emphasis on "direct restraints" meant that the courts were now adequately distinguishing between combinations whose main purpose was to restrict competition and those that restricted competition only incidentally to the main purpose of achieving efficiency in production. And this judicial process of making the distinction, he argued, was the best that could be accomplished within the Sherman Act. He particularly paused to disillusion those who had "cherished a hope and a belief that in some way or other a line may be drawn between 'good trusts' and 'bad trusts' "; it was not practicable to introduce that distinction into the statute. Neither, he added, was it useful to insert the word "reasonable" into the Sherman Act, thus conferring on the courts power to say what was a reasonable restraint or a reasonable monopoly. "It is to thrust upon the courts a burden that they have no precedents to enable them to carry, and to give them a power approaching the arbitrary, the abuse of which might involve our whole judicial system in disaster." [3]

What Taft proposed, as the only possible way of augmenting the effect of the Sherman Act, was a conciliatory means of influencing the managers of large corporations to abandon the exercise of such monopoly power as they might have and to forego aggressive practices, thus bringing them back into "the zone of lawfulness without losing to the country the economy of [large-scale] management . . ." The means he suggested was a system for compulsory Federal incorporation of businesses engaged in interstate trade. The scheme would assign certain regulatory powers to the Department of Commerce, though what these powers would be Taft did not clearly say, except to instance that they would be used to prevent the corporations from issuing watered stock and from buying stocks in other corporations.[4]

This message to Congress was clear evidence that Taft did not share strongly the feeling that a regulatory system was needed as a replacement for, or even as an essential prop to, the Sherman

[2] See above, pp. 172 ff.

[3] Special Message (Jan. 7, 1910), in Taft, *Presidential Addresses and State Papers,* I, 524-32 (1910).

[4] Taft, *Presidential Addresses and State Papers,* I, 532 ff.

Act. It was only one of the many ways in which Taft sharply dissented from the views that most other political men regarded as the premises of current politics.

The Standard Oil *Decision*

Suddenly, in 1911, the terms of the discussion were radically altered by the Supreme Court's opinion in the *Standard Oil* case. The opinion, written by Chief Justice White, announced that the Sherman Act always had been interpreted—implicitly—by the "rule of reason" and would henceforth be consciously interpreted as though the word "reasonable" had been written into it. The opinion, thus, did by way of judicial interpretation what many people wanted done and had hoped to do by way of legislative amendment; moreover, it did what President Taft had just finished saying ought on no account to be done. Because the opinion aligned the Court with one side of an active controversy, it gave rise to a crisis of public opinion such as only a handful of the Court's decisions have provoked.

The suit had been initiated during Roosevelt's second term as a showcase piece—Morgan having fallen, Rockefeller was the next Goliath to take on. The groundwork of the assault had been laid by the Bureau of Corporations, which prepared a report of unparalleled detail. The case was the beginning of modern antitrust actions, the judges being for the first time presented with a record filling over a score of volumes and running near to five million words. In handling a case of this magnitude, the Department of Justice had conservatively and cleverly decided to follow a proven model, the *Northern Securities* suit. Accordingly, it once again invoked the Expediting Act of 1903 to bring the case speedily before a court of four Circuit judges. Luckily finding—or seeing to it—that one of the defendants, albeit a very minor one, was incorporated in Minnesota, the Department was enabled to sue in the same Circuit Court that had decided the *Northern Securities* case. And the Government imitated the model also in the relief it asked for: an injunction to prevent the Standard Oil Company from controlling or drawing dividends from its subsidiaries, obstacles which would force the empire to dissolve itself.

Presented with an issue similar in so many ways to the *Northern Securities* case, the Circuit judges behaved according to the Government's fondest hopes, delivering an opinion that followed the *Northern Securities* opinion in all but detail. A few new points of interest were raised by differences between the facts in the two cases, differences that led the Government to introduce some minor innovations into its tactics, differences that the defense fastened on as grounds for distinguishing its case from the presumptive precedent.

The defense, for instance, made much of the fact that the Standard Oil subsidiaries had ceased being competitors when the combination was first formed in 1879, almost forty years before the suit began. In putting forward this argument, the defense was seizing on a logical weakness in the Circuit Court's opinion in the *Northern Securities* case, and trying to exploit the counter-argument suggested by Justice Holmes: that the Sherman Act did not require all who had ever competed in the distant past to be kept eternally in competition or restored to it.[5] But the Circuit Court refused to honor this distinction, falling back on its previous argument—which had by now been endorsed by the Supreme Court—that as the companies were "natural and potential competitors," the defendants violated the Sherman Act by holding "the power to prevent them from actively competing."[6]

Another issue of great interest that the form of the Government's bill put before the court was the nature of monopolization. The Government alleged that the defendants had violated not only the first section of the Act but also the second, which declares unlawful any combination "to monopolize any part of trade or commerce among the several states." The Government invoked this section because the Bureau of Corporations had amassed much evidence that the defendants had engaged in all sorts of unsavory activities, using tactics that the Government might have described, had it chosen to do so, as "predatory," "abusive," or "unfair": such tactics as taking preferential rebates from shippers, representing their subsidiaries to be independent firms, employing commercial spies, and setting cutthroat prices. These tactics, coupled with the proven fact that the defendants had secured "a very substantial

[5] See above, pp. 221-24, 234.
[6] U.S. v. Standard Oil, 173 Fed. 177, at 186 f. (Nov. 20, 1909).

part" of the interstate trade in petroleum, were enough—in the Government's view—to satisfy the rule, as set forth by Judge Jackson,[7] that "to monopolize" meant *forcibly* to exclude competitors from the market.

The defendants implicitly conceded this rule of interpretation, and argued that such instances of aggressive behavior as could be proven were merely occasional and unauthorized actions of the defendants' agents.[8] But they put their heaviest emphasis on the proposition that even if they were found to have monopolized, the court's power was limited to enjoining "the use of continuing or threatened unlawful means and their like which have a direct and substantial effect to continue the illegal monopoly." An injunction founded on this theory would have commanded the defendants to do no spying, do not unlawful price cutting, take no rebates, and so forth—but it would have left intact the organizational structure of the Standard Oil complex.

Like the Government and the defendants, the court too accepted the view that illegal monopolization—in the sense of Section 2—took place only if the defendants had used illegal means to get control of a large share of the market. But, said the court, the use of illegal means was amply established by the proof that the defendants had joined in a combination in restraint of trade of the sort declared illegal by Section 1 of the Act. In this manner—by holding that persons who violated Section 1, and who thereby acquired a substantial part of interstate commerce in a given article, violated Section 2 automatically—the court could justify an injunction to dissolve the combination among the defendants. This mode of reasoning carried with it a huge collateral benefit: the court was able to set aside as moot the question "whether or not the charges in the bill that other unlawful means were or are employed are true," thus greatly abbreviating the task of dealing with an unwieldy record.[9]

These minor additions to received doctrine evoked little interest at the time; what stood out was that the Circuit Court had followed its *Northern Securities* doctrine almost to the letter.

[7] See above, p. 147.

[8] See Supreme Court opinion, 221 U.S. at 48: "It is not denied that in the enormous volume of proof. . . ."

[9] 173 Fed. at 190 ff.

WHITE'S RULE OF REASON

The great shock came two years later when the Supreme Court issued its decision. The Court's opinion, which ushered in the rule of reason, was written by Edward White, whom Taft had raised to Chief Justice in 1910. This curious appointment, breaking with the tradition that the new Chief Justice should be chosen from outside the Court, has been explained in many ways, one being that the Justices called on Taft in a body to request that he make White their chief, because they so greatly admired his personal qualities. However, his literary qualities were far from admirable; indeed, it has been said that his opinions were "models of what judicial opinions ought not to be";[1] his favorite mode of thought and expression was so intricate and elusive that his arguments have wrongly, though understandably, been called "sophistical." These defects of style badly mar his *Standard Oil* opinion, make his ideas difficult to apprehend, and create, superficially, the impression that he is resting his entire position on cheap debater's tricks. But examined patiently, his theory of the Act turns out to be as serious and cogent as any, and despite the frequent allegation that he deliberately amended the Sherman Act, his theory of the judge's function turns out to be not less conservative than that of his colleagues on the Court.

The thesis that White maintained is clear and unmistakable. It is that when the Sherman Act prohibits "every contract in restraint of trade" the words must be understood to mean "every contract that *unreasonably* (or *unduly*) restrains trade."

The main outline of the argument is also clear and unmistakable, though its articulation is often obscure, and it is expressed in sentences sometimes nearly impenetrable. White opened his argument on this central issue with the proposition that "restraint of trade" and "monopolize" took their meaning originally from English common law. This meaning White explored, somewhat summarily, by "a very brief reference to the elementary and indisputable conceptions of both the English and American law" before 1890.

At common law, long ago, "contract in restraint of trade" meant

[1] *DAB.*

a voluntary restraint on an individual's right to pursue his calling; it was considered illegal because it was thought to injure the public and also the individual who restrained himself. But later, "in the interest of the freedom of individuals to contract," the old rule was revised so as to permit such contracts to stand if they were partial —applying to less than the whole of England—and "otherwise reasonable." [2]

At common law, White continued, monopoly was defined as the exclusive power to make or sell something, the power being conferred by royal grant. The English public objected to monopoly because the monopolist could raise the prices of his goods while reducing their output and worsening their quality; the crown was therefore denied the power to make such grants. Since it was thought that engrossers, regraters, and forestallers could by their own efforts achieve the same result of raising prices, those activities came to be considered as "one and the same thing" with monopoly, and were accordingly prohibited—that is:

> prohibitions were placed upon the power of individuals to deal under such circumstances and conditions as, according to the conception of the times, created a presumption that the dealings were not simply the honest exertion of one's right to contract for his own benefit unaccompanied by a wrongful motive to injure others, but were the consequence of a contract or course of dealing of such a character as to give rise to the presumption of an intent to injure others through the means, for instance, of a monopolistic increase of prices.

And just as forestalling, engrossing, and regrating were assimilated to monopoly because they had similar effects, so monopoly was assimilated to "restraint of trade" because the monopolist restrained others from pursuing their trades.[3]

When White now "generalized" these brief historical remarks, a bit more "unreasonableness" crept into his generalizations. The injury that the common law deemed would result from monopoly, which White had hitherto expressed in the unqualified phrase "enhancement of the price," now became "*undue* enhancement of price." And the common-law rule on contracts in restraint of trade too, White now expressed more pointedly as the voiding of

[2] 221 U.S. at 51. See above, pp. 42-43.

[3] 221 U.S. at 51-54.

any contract by which an individual "put an *unreasonable* restraint upon himself." [4]

At this point in the opinion occurs one of those summarizing passages which, while lacking something in clarity, was a fundamental step in White's argument.

> From the review just made it clearly results that outside of the restrictions resulting from the want of power in an individual to voluntarily and unreasonably restrain his right to carry on his trade or business and outside of the want of right to restrain the free course of trade by contracts or acts which implied a wrongful purpose, freedom to contract and to abstain from contracting and to exercise every reasonable right incident thereto became the rule in the English law.[5]

White seems to be saying that freedom to contract became a fundamental rule of common law, every man's freedom to make contracts being qualified in three ways only: he could not contract unreasonably to restrain himself from practicing his own trade; he could not "wrongfully" restrain "the free course of trade" of others; and he could not exercise unreasonable rights incidental to contracts. What White was leading up to was the conclusion that the Sherman Act embodied this fundamental rule of common law, and therefore that the twofold essence of the Sherman Act was to affirm freedom of contract and to prohibit only "unreasonable" exercises of that freedom.

White observed in the development of American common law this same tendency to classify as "restraint of trade" and "monopolizing"—and thus to classify as illegal—any actions considered "to unduly diminish competition and hence to enhance prices." [6]

And the Sherman Act merely formulated this broad conception of restraint and the illegality attached to it as a rule for interstate commerce. The Act used broad terms—"an all-embracing enumeration"—to make sure that none of the new *monopolistic* devices then being invented would escape it. But in using such broad terms it

> evidenced the intent not to restrain the right to make and enforce contracts, whether resulting from combination or otherwise, which did not unduly restrain interstate or foreign commerce, but to protect that

[4] 221 U.S. at 54. Emphasis added.
[5] 221 U.S. at 56.
[6] 221 U.S. at 56 ff.

commerce from being restrained by methods, whether old or new, which would constitute an interference that is an undue restraint.

The Sherman Act used broad terms, in other words, so that no offending person could escape; but in using broad terms, it implied that the courts would need to exercise judgment in applying those terms; the courts' judgment would need to be guided by a standard, and "it follows . . . that the standard of reason which had been applied at the common law and in this country . . . was intended to be the measure. . . ."[7]

This view was buttressed in White's mind by the fact that the Sherman Act did not prohibit "monopoly" but "monopolizing"; it did not prohibit anyone from making or selling all of any given product; it did prohibit everyone from using means to exclude others from making the same commodity. The point is set forth in one of those sentences of White's that richly deserve paragraphs of exegesis:

> And it is worthy of observation . . . that although the statute . . . makes it certain that its purpose was to prevent undue restraints of every kind or nature, nevertheless by the omission of any direct prohibition against monopoly in the concrete [i.e., control of 100 per cent of the market] it indicates a consciousness that the freedom of the individual right to contract [—] when not unduly or improperly exercised [—] was the most efficient means for the prevention of monopoly [in the concrete], since the operation of the centrifugal and centripetal forces resulting from the right to freely contract was the means by which monopoly [in the concrete] would be inevitably prevented[,] if no extraneous or sovereign power imposed it and no right to make unlawful contracts having a monopolistic tendency were permitted. In other words that freedom to contract was the essence of freedom from undue restraint on the right to contract.[8]

In other words, free competition is the "most efficient" and, indeed, an "inevitably" efficient way to prevent anyone from becoming or remaining the sole seller of any good. The Sherman Act embodies this theory, as is shown by the fact that it does not prohibit anyone from being a sole seller. But free competition cannot take place if the government bars it, or if potential competitors have agreed by contract not to compete, or if potential competitors are

[7] 221 U.S. at 59-60.
[8] 221 U.S. at 62.

excluded from competition by acts of a successful or would-be monopolist—that is, a monopolizer; and on this account, the Sherman Act prohibits contracts or any other actions that exclude competitors from competition. In interpreting the Sherman Act, therefore, judges must remember that its purpose was not to limit the freedom to contract but rather to broaden it; that the means it uses to broaden that freedom is to prohibit only those contracts or acts that narrow or restrain one's own freedom or the freedom of others to contract; and that in judging any particular contract or action the judge must use discretion (or "reason") to determine whether it was a contract or action that unduly limited the rights of others to make future contracts or whether it was not, holding the former unreasonable and illegal and the latter reasonable and legal.

Having thus established his own view of the matter, White turned now to rebut the interpretation of the Act advanced by the Government, the interpretation that had been endorsed by the Circuit Court. It was a delicate task, for it required that he either reverse the Supreme Court's position in the Peckham opinions and the *Northern Securities* opinion—that is, to reverse an interpretation that had been growing up over a course of fifteen years —or to show how his interpretation could be reconciled with the precedents, which, as many thought, insisted on an interpretation exactly opposite to his own.

The Government, White said, stood on the thesis that the text of the Sherman Act "leaves no room for the exercise of judgment, but simply imposes the plain duty of applying its prohibitions to every case within its literal language." This White denied outright, on the ground that since the Act used general words—neither "specifically enumerating" nor "defining" the things prohibited—the use of judgment was inevitable. White could, one may suppose, have insisted that in the application of *any* statute to *any* case, judgment was inescapably required. Instead, White resorted to one of his favorite forms of argument, a dilemma—though in stating the dilemma with utmost force, White overstated it. The dilemma White proposed was this: if judges were not allowed reasonable discretion in applying generic terms to specific cases, then either they must condemn all actions that could conceivably be called in restraint of trade or they could not be allowed to condemn any. In his own words, the dilemma was that if the power of judgment were denied to the judges, this

would require the conclusion either that every contract, act or combination of any kind or nature, *whether it operated a restraint on trade or not,* was within the statute, and thus the statute would be destructive of all right to contract or agree or combine in any respect whatever as to subjects embraced in interstate trade or commerce, or if this conclusion were not reached, then the contention would require it to be held that as the statute did not define the things to which it related and excluded resort to the only means by which the acts to which it relates could be ascertained—the light of reason—the enforcement of the statute was impossible because of its uncertainty.[9]

Unfortunately, White's dilemma failed altogether to meet the Government's position, the failure emerging most clearly in his statement that a literal reading of the statute would require the prohibition of every contract "whether it operated a restraint of trade or not." The Government's position, of course, was that a literal reading required the prohibition of every contract *in restraint of trade*—and then only if it were in *direct* restraint—but of *no* contract that was not in direct restraint of trade.

When, however, White left this level of high abstraction to reconcile his interpretation with the precedents, his argument was more to the point. First, however, came an infelicitous prelude in which he used a play on words—as in his *Trans-Missouri* dissent[1]—to show that the *Trans-Missouri* and *Joint Traffic* opinions must be interpreted after his fashion, even though, as he admitted in a backhanded concession, "general language was made use of, which, when separated from its context, would justify the conclusion that it was decided that reason could not be resorted to for the purpose of determining whether the acts complained of were within the statute." Then came the pun:

As the cases cannot by any possible conception be treated as authoritative without the certitude that reason was resorted to for the purpose of deciding them, it follows as a matter of course that it must have been held by the light of reason, since the conclusion could not have been otherwise reached, that the assailed contracts or agreements were

[9] 221 U.S. at 63. Emphasis added.

[1] See above, pp. 170-71.

within the general enumeration of the statute, and that their operation and effect brought about the restraint of trade which the statute prohibited.[2]

It was not a handsome way to dispose of a sober argument in a serious case, and if not intended to enrage those who thought otherwise, it none the less enraged them, as Harlan's dissent showed.

Yet in the passage immediately following, the most difficult and elusive passage in the opinion, White turned to his most delicate operation, the effort to state a fine distinction as to when discretion could and could not be used in judging a Sherman Act case. Reason, he said, *must* be used to determine whether any given contract was of the sort prohibited by the Act, that is, whether it was a contract that unduly restrained trade. But once the court had determined that a given contract was of that sort and was therefore prohibited by the Act, the court *must not* then reason itself into the conclusion that the contract ought nevertheless to be considered immune. That was the meaning of the true principle which, White said, could be recognized in the *Trans-Missouri* and *Joint Traffic* opinions:

That as considering the contracts or agreements, their necessary effect and the character of the parties by whom they were made, they were clearly restraints of trade within the purview of the statute, they could not be taken out of that category by indulging in general reasoning as to the expediency or non-expediency of having made the contracts or the wisdom or want of wisdom of the statute which prohibited their being made.[3]

In short, a restraint of trade once it was found to be unreasonable must not be exempted by judges on the ground that the restraint was reasonable in other senses—say, from the standpoint of the judges' view of proper public policy. This distinction was of a piece with White's effort to reconcile his rule of reason with the earlier view that the court's function was "the plain judicial duty of enforcing the law as it was made."

White then showed in another way that the rule of reason was fundamentally the same as the rule by which the Court had always

[2] 221 U.S. at 64 f.

[3] 221 U.S. at 65.

previously interpreted the Sherman Act. He pointed out that in every opinion after the *Trans-Missouri* decision—and especially in the *Hopkins* opinion, the next antitrust case to have been decided by the Supreme Court—the Court had qualified the rule of absolutely literal interpretation apparently announced in *Trans-Missouri,* by doing which the Court had revealed its conviction that the Act did not apply to *every* restraint but only to those that had some *direct* and *immediate* effect on interstate commerce. "[The] rule of reason . . . and the result of the test as to direct and indirect, in their ultimate aspect, come to one and the same thing. . . ."[4]

Finally, he capped his argument, that the rule of reason was consistent with the Court's previous rules for interpreting the Sherman Act, with a show of force. Insofar as the "general language" of the *Trans-Missouri* and *Joint Traffic* opinions, when read in isolation from the context of those cases, appeared to conflict with the rule of reason, White declared, the "general language" was now being "limited and qualified" to bring it into line with the many antitrust decisions since made by the Court.[5] No doubt was allowed to persist that the rule of reason was *now,* if not always before, the governing rule.

Applying the rule of reason to the facts of the *Standard Oil* case, White readily found the defendants to have engaged in an unreasonable restraint of trade. The combination had the "inevitable result" of giving Standard Oil unified "power and control over petroleum"; this created a "*prima facie* presumption of intent and purpose to maintain the dominancy over the oil industry," an intent that the defendants tried to realize not by "normal methods," but by means that aimed at "excluding others from the trade." This presumption was "made conclusive" by considering the evidence of the defendants' actual practice:

> The acquisition here and there . . . of every efficient means by which competition could have been asserted, the slow but resistless methods . . . by which means of transportation were absorbed and brought under control, the system of marketing . . . by which the country was divided into districts and the trade in each . . . was turned over

[4] 221 U.S. at 66.
[5] 221 U.S. at 67 f.

to a designated corporation within the combination and all others were excluded. . . .[6]

In short, the unreasonableness of the Standard Oil combination was established by a presumptive intent to exclude others, evidenced by the use of tactics to exclude others.

The Supreme Court accordingly affirmed in a slightly modified form the decree requiring dissolution of the Standard Oil Company. Justice Harlan, concurring in the decision, bitterly dissented from White's opinion. The pendulum had swung back. Harlan, sole dissenter in the *Knight* case sixteen years earlier, having since become the Court's spokesman in *Northern Securities,* now found himself again the lone dissenter. He could have taken comfort, if he chose, in the reflection that despite the "loose" construction to which he objected, the great trusts now stood in far greater danger of being destroyed by the Act than ever before.

A briefer and clearer statement of the rule of reason became available to the public two weeks after the *Standard Oil* opinion when the Court published its opinion in the *American Tobacco* case.[7] There White summarized the *Standard Oil* opinion in these words:

Applying the rule of reason to the construction of the statute, it was held . . . that as the words "restraint of trade" at common law . . . only embraced acts . . . which operated to the prejudice of the public interests by unduly restricting competition . . . or which, either because of their inherent nature or effect or because of the evident purpose of the acts . . . injuriously restrained trade [—] that the words as used in the statute were designed to have . . . a like significance. It was therefore pointed out that the statute did not forbid or restrain the power to make normal and usual contracts to further trade. . . . In other words, it was held, not that acts which the statute prohibited could be removed from the control of its prohibitions by a finding that they were reasonable, but that the duty to interpret [—] which inevitably arose from the general character of the term restraint of trade [—] required that the words restraint of trade should be given a meaning which would not destroy the individual right to contract and render difficult if not impossible any movement of trade in the channels of

[6] 221 U.S. at 75 ff.
[7] U.S. v. American Tobacco, 221 U.S. 106 (May 29, 1911).

interstate commerce—the free movement of which it was the purpose of the statute to protect.[8]

What readily escaped notice was that White had taken infinite trouble, when discussing the proper role of judicial discretion, to make certain nobody could think he was arguing that judges ought to have a wider scope for intruding their personal views of public policy. True enough, he did not follow Taft's interpretation of the common law, according to which any combination in restraint of trade—that is, any agreement to restrict competition that was *not* ancillary to a lawful contract of sale or apprenticeship—was automatically illegal. White differed from Taft to the extent of being prepared to endorse a pure combination of mere convenience to the parties, for instance, a combination by which they profited from economies of scale. But with this exception, White, and Taft, and Peckham (in his later posture), and almost Harlan too, would have come out—did, in the case of Harlan, come out—on the same side of any decision, albeit by different courses of reasoning, which would have made them write different opinions, but always opinions concurring in the decision. White, in short, left the Act largely unchanged in its practical effects, though he established a doctrine which somewhat stretched the precedents. That doctrine recognized, as none of the previous interpretations had recognized quite so clearly, the obvious fact that some or many combinations took place innocently, being aimed not at all at monopoly control—and coming nowhere near it—but aimed merely at achieving an economically efficient scale of production. White's was a conciliatory position, encompassing or at least consistent with the positions of many others; but his idiosyncratic use of the term "rule of reason" created the impression that in fact he and with him the Court had changed a great deal.

THE RECEPTION OF WHITE'S OPINION

The *Standard Oil* opinion immediately reawakened the great controversy about antitrust law revision that had been going on more or less vividly for ten years. The opinion had a distinctly par-

[8] 221 U.S. at 179 f.

tisan appearance. It fit very nicely into the position of Roosevelt, who was now beginning to prepare his campaign as the Progressive candidate in the presidential elections of 1912. Three years earlier, in his last great pronouncement as President on the antitrust problem, Roosevelt had said: "The law should correct that portion of the Sherman Act which prohibits all combinations . . . , whether they be reasonable or unreasonable; but this should be done only as part of a general scheme to provide for this effective and thoroughgoing supervision by the National Government of all the operations of the big interstate business concerns."[9] Now that the Supreme Court had taken the step to make the Sherman Act more discriminating, Roosevelt could devote himself to campaigning for the rest of the "general scheme" that fit into his Square Deal.

The reception of the *Standard Oil* opinion by Taft's Administration was warm. The opinion was bound to have pleased Secretary of State Knox who, while serving as Roosevelt's Attorney General, had recommended that the rule of reason—as announced by Justice White in his *Trans-Missouri* dissent—be written into the Sherman Act by an amendment.[1] It certainly pleased George Wickersham, Taft's Attorney General, who said of the opinion:

> The area of uncertainty in the law has been greatly narrowed and its scope and effect have been pretty clearly defined. The school of literal interpretation has been repudiated and the application of a rule of reasonable construction declared.[2]

Taft's own reaction might have been expected to be less cordial. In his *Addyston Pipe* opinion he had written that judges who assumed the power to say that a deliberate restraint of trade was in the public interest were setting "sail on a sea of doubt."[3] As President he had reiterated this view as an argument against inserting "reasonable" into the Sherman Act by legislative amendment.[4] The interpretation that Taft, when a judge, had given the antitrust law was now apparently overruled by the Chief Justice he himself had appointed—an irony that caused a certain amount of com-

[9] Special Message (Jan. 31, 1908); *Roosevelt Letters,* VI, 1577.
[1] Knox, *Commerce Clause of the Constitution* 40 [Oct. 14, 1902] (1902).
[2] Address of July 6, 1911, quoted in 47 *Cong. Rec.* 3537 f.
[3] 85 Fed. at 284 (1898).
[4] See above, p. 252.

ment.[5] But Taft did not interpret White's decision as overruling his own. Quite the contrary. He noticed that White tested the reasonableness of a combination by its necessary tendencies and effects, not by the tactfulness with which it administered its powers; if the combination had acquired the power to raise prices, it was an unreasonable combination, even though it might be using that power in a "reasonable" rather than a "greedy" fashion. Taft recognized that this rule corresponded in its main effects to his own. He therefore signified his total satisfaction with the *Standard Oil* decision.[6]

Among leaders of the Democratic Party, on the contrary, the decision provoked a good deal of sharp dissatisfaction. Seven Democratic congressmen immediately submitted bills to undo the rule of reason by adding to the Sherman Act words that would make it apply once more to every restraint of trade, "whether reasonable or unreasonable." [7] A year later the Democratic platform of 1912 showed that they and their associates still felt much the same way:

> We regret that the Sherman anti-trust law has received a judicial construction depriving it of much of its efficiency and we favor the enactment of legislation which will restore to the statute the strength of which it has been deprived by such interpretation.[8]

The view of Democratic leaders, that by adopting the rule of reason the Court had made it imperative for Congress to enact additional legislation, was presented again and at length by Senator Albert Cummins early in 1913. The Interstate Commerce Committee of the Senate, of which Cummins was chairman, was reporting on its inquiry into the whole of antitrust law, an inquiry whose hearings had lasted from November of 1911 into the following spring. Lengthy testimony had been taken from over one hundred witnesses, among them promient businessmen—especially the great steel tycoons, E. H. Gary, Andrew Carnegie, and James A. Farrell; prominent lawyers—Francis Lynde Stetson (Morgan's counsel in

[5] See the remark of Senator Nelson (Jun. 15, 1911), in 47 *Cong. Rec.* 2070.

[6] Taft, Annual Message (Dec. 1911).

[7] 62nd Cong. 1st Sess., S. 2374 (May 17, 1911), S. 2375 (May 17), S. 2433 (May 18), H.R. 10508 (May 23), H.R. 11855 (Jun. 19), H.R. 13004 (Jul. 27). Only one such bill was introduced by a Republican, S. 2370 (May 17). The bills are gathered in House Committee on the Judiciary, 3 *Bills and Debates in Congress relating to Trusts* 2412 *et seq.* (1914).

[8] Porter and Johnson, *National Party Platforms* 169 (1961 ed.).

the *Northern Securities* case), Victor Morawetz, and Louis D. Brandeis; eminent economists—J. B. Clark and J. Lawrence Laughlin; and men as famed in public affairs as George Perkins, Samuel Gompers, Lyman Abbott, and Seth Low. Had all the witnesses appeared simultaneously, the assembly would have resembled closely the Chicago convention of 1907 called by the National Civic Federation. From these men the Senate Committee had taken testimony on all the many particular proposals for amending the antitrust law. It had heard suggestions ranging from the total abandonment of the Sherman Act to the strengthening of the Act by attaching to it long lists of prohibited practices and long glossaries defining for the courts its essential terms. Above all, it heard spates of argument about the need for a regulatory commission and the powers that ought to be assigned to it. Not a few of the witnesses urged that the commission be authorized to set the prices at which big corporations could sell their goods: this was a natural conclusion to derive from the widespread belief that a trade commission should be to business firms what the Interstate Commerce Commission was or might become to the railroads. Still other witnesses, conceding something to the clamorous objection that government price-fixing would be unconstitutional, recommended instead that the commission be authorized to approve price-fixing agreements that businessmen initiated of their own accord—thus prefiguring the NRA codes. And much more was suggested.[9]

The Committee's report, written by Senator Cummins, did not pretend to summarize the testimony or even to represent the consensus of the Committee. Cummins' four Democratic colleagues each wrote a statement of "additional views," in which they showed complete disagreement among themselves on everything but general principles, and the four Republican members, while commending "certain features of the report," refused to approve the whole. Nevertheless Cummins' statement, although expressing his own private position on details of antitrust revision, is interesting in its broadest outline as showing the preconceptions with which the new Democratic Administration of President Wilson approached

[9] 62nd Cong. 3rd Sess., Sen. Report 1326. Senate Committee on Interstate Commerce. *Report . . . pursuant to S. Res. 98* (Feb. 26, 1913). A useful key to the *Report* is given in Clark, *Federal Trust Policy* 149-59 (1931).

the problem. The first of these premises, as stated by Cummins, was that the Sherman Act should constitute the nucleus of all antitrust policy, with which all supplementary statutes should harmonize. The second premise was that the project for Federal incorporation should be abandoned—a conclusion not surprising in view of Democratic principles of states' rights. The third premise was that supplementary antitrust legislation must be enacted.[1]

Now in saying that supplementary legislation was necessary, Cummins was not making a partisan statement, but one that had been endorsed on all sides for a decade. However during the campaign of 1912 the issue, previously confused, had been sharpened by party slogan makers. Brandeis, who had become Wilson's mainstay on antitrust policy, had invented the happy formula that Roosevelt planned to "regulate monopoly" whereas Wilson aimed to "regulate competition." There was truth behind the gibe. Roosevelt believed that modern industrial conditions made competition impossible and, therefore, that the industrial giants inevitably being created ought to be acknowledged as legal, but that they ought to be prevented by a regulatory agency from using their power mischievously. Wilson, on the contrary—especially under Brandeis' tutelage—held that despite the economic incentives to form very large firms, competition could and would prevail, and would provide the greatest possible economic efficiency; it was only necessary that the predatory techniques by which some businessmen tried to destroy competition should be stopped by statutory prohibitions and by a regulatory agency.[2] To this formulation of the problem Senator Cummins turned, bluntly stating that any supplementary antitrust legislation must be conceived in the spirit of a system of regulated competition, not regulated monopoly.[3]

The need for supplementary legislation, said Cummins, had been aggravated by the installation of the rule of reason, which reposed in the courts "the vast and undefined power" to decide which restraints were reasonable and which unreasonable. To establish rules of this breadth was, Cummins maintained, the proper func-

[1] 62nd Cong. 3rd Sess., Sen. Report 1326, I, iii.

[2] Mason, *Brandeis* 378 ff. (1946). Diamond, *Economic Thought of Woodrow Wilson* 105-10 (1943). Link, *Woodrow Wilson and the Progressive Era* 18-22 (1954).

[3] 62nd Cong. 3rd Sess., Sen. Report 1326, I, v.

tion of the legislature, not the court, and the legislature should instantly assert its power. The Committee was not prepared to propose specific legislation; indeed, it noted the difficulty of reaching agreement on details of legislation. Cummins therefore went no further than to explain why a regulatory commission was necessary, to outline its possible work, and to urge that some sort of supplementary legislation be enacted making the antitrust prohibitions more explicit.[4]

Among the four concurring statements made by the other Democrats on the Committee, the most interesting was that by Senator Benjamin Tillman of South Carolina. He too objected to the "preposterous and dangerous judicial discretion" that the Court had assumed, and agreed that Congress should destroy it. But he wondered whether a regulatory commission was the answer. He "is inclined to believe that we have too many commissions now, composed largely of so-called 'lame ducks,' both Democrats and Republicans, who have been defeated at the polls and are given these places mainly as a compensation and means of support." It was a refreshing remark in the midst of so many pious affirmations that a regulatory commission, unlike Congress or the courts, would consist of men who were great experts on business; it was and has remained a realistic remark. After registering several other exceptions to Cummins' views, Tillman ended by saying that he preferred "to wait and to listen to the recommendations of the incoming President of the United States."[5]

The New Laws

The story of how the new antitrust laws were passed is in large measure the story of how Woodrow Wilson decided what they should be. By force of the large Democratic majority in Congress—over which, during his magically successful first year in office, Wilson exercised the stern discipline of a headmaster—and with the aid of a cooperative or complaisant minority, Wilson was able to have his way in the main policy of those acts. But the actual effect of a statute, especially if it is long and detailed, may depend as

[4] 62nd Cong. 3rd Sess., Sen. Report 1326, I, v-xii.
[5] 62nd Cong. 3rd Sess., Sen, Report 1326, I, xiv.

much of its exact words as on the main policy of its makers; and the members of the 63rd Congress, though amenable to party discipline, had very clear and divergent views on just how the new statutes should go about accomplishing the hoped-for goal. From these similar but different ideas were distilled a pair of statutes which, in practice, fell far short of having the knifelike edge that was one of the chief arguments for their existence.

PRESIDENT WILSON'S POLICY

Having managed within six months of becoming President to enact a tariff reform and to launch the Federal Reserve Bank bill, Wilson turned his attention to the trust question. Late in November 1913, he began conferring with leaders of the Democratic contingent in Congress in order to design the Administration's proposals. A too ample supply of possibilities was provided when Congress convened in December, for, sensing that some action would at last be taken, congressmen refurbished all the sovereign remedies that had been concocted and refined during the past twenty-five years. But Wilson had not yet decided. In his annual message[6] he therefore called in broad terms for supplementary legislation. The Sherman Act should stand unaltered "with its debatable ground about it," but the area of that debatable ground should be reduced by "further and more explicit legislation," which would reduce the discretion of the courts and dispel the uncertainties of businessmen. Having nothing more specific to offer at the moment, Wilson went South to spend the Christmas holidays pondering matters.[7]

At the beginning of 1914, he explained before a joint session of Congress the conclusions he had reached.[8] His recommendations fell into the two classes that had become standard in the discussion: he proposed a statute that would define more explicitly than did the Sherman Act the conduct that should be prohibited, and another statute that would establish a trade commission. The first of these laws, he argued, Congress was by now perfectly prepared to

[6] (Dec. 2, 1913); 51 *Cong. Rec.* 44.
[7] Link, *Woodrow Wilson and the Progressive Era* 67 f.
[8] 51 *Cong. Rec.* 1962 ff. (Jan. 20, 1914).

draw up and the nation to accept. "Surely we are sufficiently familiar with the actual processes and methods of monopoly and of the many hurtful restraints of trade. . . . These practices, being now abundantly disclosed, can be explicitly and item by item forbidden by statute in such terms as will practically eliminate uncertainty. . . ."[9] Among the practices that he proceeded especially to note was the interlocking directorship, a technique which the Pujo Committee's investigation of the Money Trust had alleged to be one of Morgan's favorite ways of establishing a "community of interests" among erstwhile competitors.[1] After cataloguing other abominable devices, and suggesting that private plaintiffs be authorized to use as *prima facie* evidence in their antitrust suits the decisions in suits initiated by the Government, Wilson moved on to the second branch of his program. A trade commission should be established to serve two chief purposes: it would be an "indispensable instrument of information and publicity"; and it would be assigned the expert work of drawing up dissolution decrees in antitrust suits, a job too involved in masses of detail about business conditions to be left to lawyers and judges.

Both of these functions had been projected for the commission by Senator Cummins in his report of the previous year; but what stood out was that Wilson declined to allow the commission the third power that Cummins had wanted it to have, the power to approve or disapprove *before the event* proposed changes in business organization. This was the power not merely to give a purely advisory opinion on the legality of some proposed arrangement—for this the Department of Justice could do, and had done under Roosevelt's orders in the celebrated case of the Tennessee Coal and Iron Company, though not without setting off a violent storm[2]—but rather to reach a decision permanently binding on the Government. The virtue of this plan, Cummins had maintained, was that a commission, "which though administrative in its character" sometimes exercised "quasi-judicial functions," could make legislative policy "vastly more effectually" than could the courts, "which in

[9] 51 *Cong. Rec.* 1963.

[1] 62nd Cong. 3rd Sess., H.R. Report 1593. House Committee on Banking and Currency, 3 *Investigation of Financial and Monetary Conditions* 129 and *passim* (1913).

[2] Bishop, *Theodore Roosevelt and His Time*, II, 54-59 (1920). Mowry, *Theodore Roosevelt and the Progressive Movement* 189-92 (1947).

most cases will take no cognizance of violations of the law for months or years after the violations occurred and when the difficulty of awarding reparation for the wrong is almost insurmountable."[3] What Wilson very likely objected to in this proposal was, first of all, the peculiar constitutional status of a body that would be at once legislative, judicial, and executive; and second, the impression the plan might create that he had gone back on his word and was now endorsing the very system he had accused Roosevelt of advocating, a system that would put government into "partnership" with the trusts. Wilson would have none of it. And so, in his special message, he said that though "the opinion of the country" was all in favor of a commission, "it would not wish to see it empowered to make terms with monopoly or in any sort to assume control of business, as if the government made itself responsible."[4] Wilson, in short, came out for a weak commission, with about the same powers and responsibilities as the Bureau of Corporations.

THE CLAYTON ACT

Within weeks, Wilson's views were embodied in a set of bills prepared by Henry Clayton of Alabama, chairman of the House Judiciary Committee. A number of these proposals formed the core of what eventually became the Clayton Antitrust Act. As put before the House by the Judiciary Committee,[5] the bill prohibited any seller from discriminating in the prices he offered different buyers, from requiring buyers who bought one thing from him to buy other things as well, and from insisting that any buyers who bought from him must not buy from his competitors. To these basic provisions—prohibitions against discriminatory pricing, tie-in selling, and exclusive dealing—were added new rules about the rights of plaintiffs in private antitrust suits, the status of labor unions under antitrust law, the powers of corporations to merge, and interlocking directorates—not to mention a host of procedural rules. As early as this stage, the table of contents of the Clayton Act was thus fixed, but the substance and flavor of this early draft came under violent and long attack. On the one hand, congressmen of all parties and

[3] 62nd Cong. 3rd Sess., Sen. Report 1326, I, xii.
[4] 51 *Cong. Rec.* 1963.
[5] 63rd Cong. 2d Sess., H.R. Report 627, Part I, pp. 1 ff. (May 6, 1914).

persuasions argued that the list of prohibited practices should be much longer, indeed that it should be a detailed and comprehensive catalogue of both prohibited and pretermitted practices. On the other hand, some congressmen insisted that as no *complete* catalogue of good and bad practices could possibly be constructed, general language should be included to guide the courts and the regulatory commission in dealing with the specific and unpredictable circumstances of future cases. All of these groups ultimately had their desires partially fulfilled.

In the Clayton Act as finally passed there were accordingly three families of provisions: those expressing Wilson's original proposals, others added at the instance of congressmen who wanted to make antitrust law more explicit and precise, and still others added in the interest of generality.

In the first class were the proscriptions of discriminatory pricing, exclusive dealing arrangements, and interlocking directorates, as well as the rule that judgments in any antitrust case could be used as *prima facie* evidence against the same defendants in later antitrust cases.

The second class, providing for greater specificity, included, first of all, the sections dealing with labor unions. What the labor unions and their supporters had long been asking for was a specific and total exemption from the antitrust law. Having supported Wilson in 1912, the labor leaders hoped that their moment at last had come, but found that the Democratic leaders refused to concede the whole of what they wanted.[6] The compromise for which they had to settle was a declaratory section which, after reciting that "the labor of a human being is not a commodity or article of commerce," went on to say that the antitrust laws should not be construed as forbidding the existence of labor unions.[7] The practical importance of this concession was not great, as the rule had long been established in American common law that a labor union did not, merely by existing, constitute an illegal combination in restraint of trade; and this principle did not appear to have been questioned in antitrust cases involving unions, even in so disastrous a defeat for the unions as the *Danbury Hatters'* case.[8] Somewhat more to the unions'

[6] Link, *Woodrow Wilson and the Progressive Era* 69 f.
[7] Sec. 6.
[8] Loewe v. Lawlor, 208 U.S. 274 (1908).

purpose was a further section of the Clayton Act[9] which provided that no injunctions should be issued in labor cases; though this safeguard—being hedged in by the qualification, "unless [the injunction be] necessary to prevent irreparable injury to property"—was not in fact very different from the rule that had long governed the issue of injunctions by any court of equity in any suit whatsoever. The strongest concession made to the labor unions was a subsequent paragraph declaring that peaceful strikes and peaceful boycotts were not to be considered in violation of any Federal laws. None of these provisions, however, was sufficient to render unions immune from attack by Federal injunctions.[1]

Another provision inserted in the Clayton Act to make antitrust law more specific, and in this instance more rigorous, was the antimerger section.[2] It prohibited any corporation from acquiring the stock of other corporations. This prohibition fit into the purpose of the bill, which—according to the Senate Judiciary Committee—was "to arrest the creation of trusts . . . in their incipiency and before consummation." [3] The particular point of the attack, reported the Judiciary Committees of both houses, was to destroy the monopolistic holding company, "a common and favorite method of promoting monopoly," "an abomination and in our judgment . . . a mere incorporated form of the old-fashioned trust." [4] It was curious that after the signal successes of the Sherman Act against such holding companies as the Northern Securities Company and the Standard Oil Company, Congress should have thought it useful specifically to outlaw holding companies. It was more curious that having reached that decision, Congress saw fit to outlaw the acquisition of *stock* in another corporation, but not of another corporation's *assets*. The reasons for this distinction were the particular aversion that had grown up to holding companies, and the old and somewhat superstitious desire to abolish secretive monopolizing, which many considered more reprehensible than open monopolizing. Thus, as Senator Cummins said in debate, "wherever the law permits the sale of the business then it ought . . . not to acquire

[9] Sec. 20.

[1] Cummings and McFarland, *Federal Justice* 445-62.

[2] Sec. 7. See Martin, *Mergers and the Clayton Act* (1959).

[3] 63rd Cong. 2d Sess., S. Report 698 . . . to accompany H.R. 15657, p. 1 (July 22, 1914).

[4] 63rd Cong. 2d Sess., S. Report 698, p. 13; H.R. Report 627, Part I, p. 17.

control of a business simply through the purchase of the stock of a company which continues under its own name and, so far as the public knows, is independent in its management." [5] The effect of the "assets loophole," as it came to be called, was that Section 7 of the Clayton Act, whether it did or did not discourage the formation of holding companies, proved thoroughly ineffective in stopping corporate mergers.[6]

But in addition to the impulse for specificity, which led to including in the Clayton Act prohibitions of particular practices, another impulse led to the inclusion in the Act of the third class of provisions. Few if any of the particular practices were clearly monopolistic or even deleterious under all conceivable circumstances; nor could the circumstances be catalogued under which they would certainly be inimical. It was therefore necessary to allow discretion to judges or to the officers of the Federal Trade Commission charged with responsibility for enforcing the statute. Consequently, a series of restrictive clauses were written into this Act, clauses expressed necessarily in most general language. For instance, price discrimination and exclusive selling were outlawed only where their effects "may be to substantially lessen competition or tend to create a monopoly in any line of commerce." An almost identical clause limited the anti-merger provision. The critical words—"may be," "substantially," "tend," and "monopoly"—being about as general as those that set the tone of the Sherman Act, the newly extended body of antitrust law could not do much—indeed, has not done much—to help judges interpret the law uniformly or to help businessmen understand its provisions exactly.

THE FEDERAL TRADE COMMISSION ACT

The Federal Trade Commission Act had in some ways an easier passage through Congress. The original bill prepared by Clayton would have converted the Bureau of Corporations into a trade commission armed with roughly the same powers as its predecessor;

[5] 51 *Cong. Rec.* 14316 (Aug. 27, 1914); cf. 14312 ff. and 15818 ff. for similar statements by others.

[6] See, for instance, F.T.C. v. Western Meat, 272 U.S. 554 (1926), and Arrow-Hart v. F.T.C., 291 U.S. 587 (1934).

Wilson recommended it as a "safe and sensible" move.[7] But there were many who wished to see a much stronger measure passed, one that would empower the commission to carry on positive and continuous regulation. Among this group was Brandeis, and during the spring of 1914 he persuaded Wilson to support the stronger measure that he had helped to draft. Despite some opposition, that bill was quickly floored and fairly easily passed by Congress.[8]

The Federal Trade Commission Act makes many procedural arrangements. It establishes the Commission; it authorizes the Commission to carry out certain investigations; it empowers the Commission to issue cease and desist orders; and it subjects the Commission's orders to judicial review. On the other hand, it contains one and only one substantive provision, which is expressed in a single sentence: "That unfair methods of competition in [interstate] commerce are hereby declared unlawful."[9] The conference committee of both houses which put the bill into its final form explained why these terms were used.

> It is now generally recognized that the only effective means of establishing and maintaining monopoly, where there is no control of a natural resource as of transportation, is the use of unfair competition. The most certain way to stop monopoly at the threshold is to prevent unfair competition.

But the committee went on to explain why the terms could not be made any more specific:

> It is impossible to frame definitions which embrace all unfair practices. There is no limit to human inventiveness in this field. . . . If Congress were to adopt the method of definition, it would undertake an endless task.[1]

Congress did not undertake the task. Having declared a general rule, it left the interpretation of the rule to the Federal Trade Commission. But it did not tell the Commission how to assign meaning to the critical phrase. And no businessman reading the Act would come any closer to finding the line between lawful and unlawful conduct.

[7] Link, *Woodrow Wilson and the Progressive Era* 68.
[8] Link, *Woodrow Wilson and the Progressive Era* 71 f.
[9] 38 Stat. 717, Sec. 5.
[1] 63rd Cong. 2d Sess., H.R. Report 1142, pp. 18-19 (Sept. 4, 1914).

. . .

Both of the supplementary antitrust laws of 1914, therefore, defeated the hopes of those who wanted *statutes* that would clarify, in practical terms and easily understood terms, the principle of the Sherman Act. The Clayton Act, by making its prohibitions pivot on so general a formula as "to substantially lessen competition or tend to create a monopoly," put a heavy burden of interpretation and judgment on the Federal Trade Commission and the courts. The Federal Trade Commission Act, by prohibiting "unfair methods of competition," added another burden.

In twenty-five years, antitrust law had come full circle. The old, simple, and general prohibition of the Sherman Act had been augmented by new, simple, and general prohibitions. The courts, whose discretion so many critics had sought to limit, were now augmented by a commission authorized to use much more ample discretion. But everything in the situation made it natural and reasonable that some discretion be allowed to those who decided cases. Given the complexity of economic organization, the scrupulous character of the American legal process, and the diversity of opinion and ideals in the American public, no ultimately precise and fully detailed law could have been drawn up.

CHAPTER EIGHT

CONCLUSION

As the supposedly excessive uncertainty of the Sherman Act has often been blamed on the supposed vagueness of its language, which presumably gives judges too much leeway to intrude personal opinion into their interpretations, the remedies that have been suggested fall into two classes.

One of the suggested remedies would make the Sherman Act less vague and more precise by passing explanatory statutes, which prohibit objectionable activities that judges have declared immune from the Sherman Act or exempt innocent activities that judges have held to violate the Sherman Act.

In principle nobody ought to object if the people and Congress try to make the law correspond more closely to their desires. But there is real danger if they do so by constructing a patchwork of very specific rules. It is the danger of legislative adjudication, comparable with the fault of judicial legislation. A judge ought not, we say, to change the law very much—though inevitably he changes it a little—when he interprets it. To change the law is not his function; when he does it he arrogates to himself the prerogatives of the sovereign. But, similarly, the legislature should not, in the guise of passing legislation, try to decide concrete cases. When Congress amends a general statute so as to reverse an unpopular decision of the courts, it is within its rights and duties. When Congress adds hosts of amendments to a general statute in order to override unpopular decisions of the judges, it appears to be setting itself up as a sort of super-supreme court. If, after all, a general statute gives rise to hosts of unpopular decisions, it should be repealed and replaced by a different general statute. In any event, a general principle thickly plastered over with special exceptions is not likely to clarify anything; what it does instead is provoke an understandable demand for codification. When a set of statutes becomes too intricate to read through, much less to live by, one of the great virtues of statutes has been undermined.

The second chief device that has been proposed for making antitrust law more certain and predictable is to turn it over to a regulatory commission, thus by-passing the judges. Regulatory commissions have exercised a special fascination over American opinion for nearly a century. They are supposed to have great virtues. Their members may be or may become experts in their fields, unlike judges. Not being bound by the formalities of law courts, they need not sit idle waiting for a plaintiff to bring suit, but can call parties before them of their own motion. They can diverge from strict standards of evidence and proof. Not being strictly bound by precedent or usage, they can make up new rules as occasion calls for them. They can, in short, do everything that the legislature, executive, and judiciary can do, and more.

No doubt they can. Within its own domain, in fact, a regulatory commission is immune from the principle of separation of powers. Worse, within its own domain, a regulatory commission acts as plaintiff, prosecutor, and judge in its own case—a status not enjoyed elsewhere within the adversary system of justice.

And to these constitutional irregularities is added another weakness. Commissions are authorized to invent new rules of law whenever they see fit. To do so is one of their chief reasons for existing. Their expertise is supposed to qualify them for doing so. But no amount of expert knowledge can or, in a democracy, should qualify a few men to decide the rules by which the community shall live. If, then, Congress in establishing a commission tells it to go out and make rules, but does not carefully instruct the commission that its rules must aim at certain well-defined goals, Congress is establishing an irresponsible and arbitrary sub-legislature. If, on the other hand, Congress has set out well-defined goals for the commission, then the commission when it makes rules is in effect deducing corollaries from the general rule that Congress set forth as its guide. But deducing corollaries is precisely what any court does when it interprets a statute. One might wonder why it is useful to add to the judiciary a set of court-like bodies called by another name. Leaving that question to one side, it does seem certain that as the mental process by which a commission makes rules is identical in principle with the process by which the courts do so, the commission's rulings cannot lead to greater certainty or be made with any less discretion than the courts' decisions.

These arguments in principle, indicating that neither specific explanatory legislation nor regulation by commissions can reduce the uncertainties of the Sherman Act, seem to be confirmed by experience of the Clayton Act and the Federal Trade Commission.

All of the problems produced by the multiplicity of goals at which antitrust law aims and by the complexity of the legal process used to enforce it remain with us today and show no signs of abating. As one observer has recently complained, antitrust law, as now applied, tells "some businessmen that they must not cut prices, others that they must not raise prices, and still others that there is something evil in similar prices."

If, as it appears, antitrust law cannot fail to produce such inelegant results—results that appear at first glance to be erratic and inconsistent—ought we to consider repealing the antitrust law altogether?

It can be argued that repeal would not carry with it any undue risk of monopolies springing up everywhere and monopolists enjoying unlimited power over the public. This argument will be credited by anyone who is confident that high rates of profit attract competitors as infallibly as nectar attracts bees. If, then, monopoly were not forbidden by law, and a monopolist set prices so as to earn an unusually high rate of profit—so the argument goes—he would inevitably be inviting competition. The competition might appear in the form of new companies entering his industry, or in the form of goods serving as cheaper substitutes for his own and being produced by firms in other industries. If a monopolist, for instance, were to set the prices of glass bottles too high, he would sooner or later find new bottle makers springing up, or would find that he could not sell his glass bottles because of all the wax-paper bottles, plastic bottles, and aluminum cans that were being offered at lower prices. If, on the other hand, the monopolist were public-spirited or prudent, he would not set his prices so high as to earn very high profits; competitors would not be induced to enter, but this would not matter because consumers would be suffering little or no exploitation. This entire line of reasoning, needless to say, can be expanded at great length to cover many lesser but still serious questions.

One great assumption, however, which this argument treats casually is that competitors will be called in "sooner or later." It is a critical phrase. One can with some justice consider antitrust law as a device serving above all to *accelerate* the natural decay of monopoly power. To accelerate the breakdown is desirable, for the community is sooner enabled to benefit from lower prices. But, on the other hand, to accelerate the breakdown by government action is not altogether desirable, for the community suffers from higher taxes. Again, to accelerate the breakdown of monopoly is desirable because it destroys undue private power, but to do so by government action may contribute unduly to the power of government. One is left wondering, therefore, how to arrange matters so that the costs of the solution do not exceed the costs imposed by the unsolved problem.

In the end as in the beginning, the quandary of antitrust policy is that every way of dealing with it is uncertain and in some measure undesirable as well as desirable.

APPENDIX

The Sherman Antitrust Act

ACT OF JULY 2, 1890 (26 STAT., 209).

An act to protect trade and commerce against unlawful restraints and monopolies.

Be it enacted by the Senate and the House of Representatives of the United States of America in Congress assembled,

SECTION 1. Every contract, combination in the form of trust or otherwise, or conspiracy, in restraint of trade or commerce among the several States, or with foreign nations, is hereby declared to be illegal. Every person who shall make any such contract or engage in any such combination or conspiracy shall be deemed guilty of a misdemeanor, and, on conviction thereof, shall be punished by fine not exceeding five thousand dollars, or by imprisonment not exceeding one year, or by both said punishments, in the discretion of the court.

SECTION 2. Every person who shall monopolize, or attempt to monopolize, or combine or conspire with any other person or persons, to monopolize any part of the trade or commerce among the several States, or with foreign nations, shall be deemed guilty of a misdemeanor, and, on conviction thereof, shall be punished by fine not exceeding five thousand dollars, or by imprisonment not exceeding one year, or by both said punishments, in the discretion of the court.

SECTION 3. Every contract, combination in the form of trust or otherwise, or conspiracy, in restraint of trade or commerce in any Territory of the United States or of the District of Columbia, or in restraint of trade or commerce between any such Territory and another, and between any such Territory or Territories and any State or States or the District of Columbia, or with foreign nations, or between the District of Columbia and any State or States or foreign nations, is hereby declared illegal. Every person who shall make any such contract or engage in any such combination or conspiracy shall be deemed guilty of a misdemeanor, and, on conviction thereof, shall be punished by fine not exceeding five thousand dollars, or by imprisonment not exceeding one year, or by both said punishments, in the discretion of the court.

SECTION 4. The several circuit courts of the United States are hereby invested with jurisdiction to prevent and restrain violations of this Act; and it shall be the duty of the several district attorneys of the United States, in their respective districts, under the direction of the Attorney General, to institute proceedings in equity to prevent and restrain such violations. Such proceedings may be by way of petition setting forth the case and praying that such violation shall be enjoined or otherwise prohibited. When the parties complained of shall have been duly notified of such petition the court shall proceed, as soon as may be, to the hearing and determination of the case; and pending such petition and before final decree, the court may at any time make such temporary restraining order or prohibition as shall be deemed just in the premises.

SECTION 5. Whenever it shall appear to the court before which any proceeding under section four of this Act may be pending that the ends of justice require that other parties should be brought before the court, the court may cause them to be summoned, whether they reside in the district in which the court is held or not; and subpoenas to that end may be served in any district by the marshal thereof.

SECTION 6. Any property owned under any contract or by any combination, or pursuant to any conspiracy (and being the subject thereof) mentioned in section one of this Act, and being in the course of transportation from one State to another, or to a foreign country, shall be forfeited to the United States, and may be seized and condemned by like proceedings as those provided by law for the forfeiture, seizure, and condemnation of property imported into the United States contrary to law.

SECTION 7. Any person who shall be injured in his business or property by any other person or corporation, by reason of anything forbidden or declared to be unlawful by this Act, may sue therefor in any circuit court of the United States in the district in which the defendant resides or is found, without respect to the amount in controversy, and shall recover threefold the damages by him sustained, and the costs of suit, including a reasonable attorney's fee.

SECTION 8. That the word "person," or "persons," wherever used in this Act, shall be deemed to include corporations and associations existing under or authorized by the laws of either the United States, the laws of any of the Territories, the laws of any State, or the laws of any foreign country.

BIBLIOGRAPHY

Law cases mentioned in the text are listed in the Table of Cases, pp. 293-296. Most reports of English cases prior to 1865 are gathered in *English Reports, Full Reprint,* 176 vols. Certain early reports, such as the *Registrum Brevium* and the *Year Books,* as well as reports subsequent to 1865, can be identified fully by referring to Soule, Charles Carroll, *The Lawyer's Reference Manual,* 1883. For reports of American cases, a useful guide, in addition to Soule, is Pollack, Ervin H., *Fundamentals of Legal Research,* 1956. Reports of early antitrust cases are compiled in Attorney General, *Federal Anti-Trust Decisions* . . . (see below), and judicial orders in such cases are compiled in Attorney General, *Decrees and Judgments* . . . (see below).

Earlier English statutes, cited by the regnal year of the monarch (for instance 3 Jac. II, c.1), are gathered in *The Statutes of the Realm,* (1101-1713), 10 vols., 1810-22. The texts of royal proclamations referred to here are gathered in Steele, Robert Reynolds, ed., *Tudor and Stuart Proclamations,* 2 vols., 1910.

Statutes of the United States are gathered in *Revised Statutes of the United States,* 2 ed., 3 vols., 1878-1901, and *United States Code,* 5 vols., 1948. Public documents of governments in the United States, state and local as well as federal, can be traced by referring to the bibliography given in Handlin, Oscar, et al., *Harvard Guide to American History,* 1955, pp. 112-39.

Congressional debates on the trust problem between 1887 and 1914 are compiled in *Bills and Debates in Congress Relating to Trusts* . . . (see below), though this collection is not utterly complete.

Unpublished records of the Department of Justice referred to in the text are located in the National Archives in Washington.

Abbreviations used in the footnotes, except those which refer to reports of law cases and to statutes, can be identified by referring to the margin below.

Adams, Henry Carter, *Relation of the State to Industrial Action,* in *Publications of the American Economic Association,* vol. I, no. 6, 1887.

Adler, Cyrus, *Jacob H. Schiff,* 2 vols., 1928.

Adler, Edward A., "Monopolizing at Common Law and under Sec. II of the Sherman Antitrust Act," 31 *Harvard Law Review* 246, 1917.

Allen, Arthur M., "Criminal Conspiracies in Restraint of Trade at Common Law," 23 *Harvard Law Review* 531, 1910.

Allen, Frederick Lewis, *The Great Pierpont Morgan,* 1949.

Att'y Gen. Ann. Rep. Attorney General of the United States, *Annual Report.*

———, *Decrees and Judgments in Federal Antitrust Cases, July 2, 1890-Jan. 1, 1918,* 1918.

———, *Federal Anti-Trust Decisions, 1890-1912,* 4 vols., 1912; supplements to vol. 11, 1934.

1896 Appendix ———, *Annual Report 1896,* Appendix.

Barnes, Donald G., *History of the English Corn Laws,* 1930.

Bascom, John, "Social Harmony," *Independent,* XL, 419, 1888.

Bills and Debates *Bills and Debates in Congress relating to Trusts,* vol. I: 57th Cong., 2nd Sess., Sen. Doc. 147; 1903; vols. II, III: House Committee on the Judiciary, 1914.

Bishop, Joseph B., *Theodore Roosevelt and His Time,* 1920.

Bland, Thomas A., *The Reign of Monopoly,* 1881.

Boisot, Louis, "The Legality of Trust Combinations," 39 (N.S. 30) *American Law Register* 751, 1891.

Buck, Solon J., *The Granger Movement,* 1913.

Busbey, L. W., *Uncle Joe Cannon,* 1927.

Butt, Archibald W., *Taft and Roosevelt,* 2 vols., 1930.

Cadman, John William, *The Corporation in New Jersey,* 1949.

C.C.R. *Calendar of the Close Rolls.*

C.P.R. *Calendar of the Patent Rolls.*

Letter Book G, *Letter Book H* *Calendar of Letter Books of the City of London,* 1899-

Cheyney, Edward P., *History of England,* 2 vols., 1926.

Clark, John Bates, "The Limits of Competition," reprinted in Clark and Giddings, *The Modern Distributive Process* II, 1888.

———, "The 'Trust,'" *New Englander,* LII, 223, 1890.

Clark, John D., *Federal Trust Policy,* 1931.

Clarke, M. S., and Hall, D. A., *Legislative and Documentary History of the Bank of the United States,* 1832.

Clode, Charles M., *Merchant Taylors,* 2 vols., 1888.

Cloud, D. C., *Monopolies and the People,* 1873.

Cochran, Thomas C., and Miller, William, *The Age of Enterprise,* 1942.

Coke, Sir Edward, *Institutes of the Laws of England,* 1628-

Commerce Clearing House (CCH), *The Federal Antitrust Laws, with Summary of Cases . . . ,* 1952 ed.

Comm. & Fin. Chron. *Commercial and Financial Chronicle.*

Commissioner of Corporations, *Annual Report.*

———, *Report . . . on the Beef Industry,* 1905.

Conant, "Industrial Consolidations in the United States," *Publications of the American Statistical Association,* VII, 207, 1901.

Consitt, Frances, *The London Weavers' Company,* 1933.

Cook, William W., *Trusts,* 1888.

Coolidge, L. A., *An Old-Fashioned Senator: Orville H. Platt,* 1910.

Croly, Herbert D., *Marcus Alonzo Hanna,* 1912.

Crosskey, William, *Politics and the Constitution,* 1953.

Cummings, Homer S., and McFarland, Carl, *Federal Justice,* 1937.

Davies, D. S., "Further Light on the Case of Monopolies," 48 *Law Quarterly Review* 394, 1932.

Davis, Joseph S., *Earlier History of American Corporations,* 2 vols., 1917.

D. J. File — Department of Justice, Files (Manuscript, in National Archives).

D. J. Instr. Bk. — ———, Instruction Books (Manuscript, in National Archives).

D. J. Misc. Letter Bk. — ———, Miscellaneous Letter Books (Manuscript, in National Archives).

Dewey, Donald, "The Common-Law Background of Antitrust Policy," 41 *Virginia Law Review* 759, 1955.

———, *Monopoly in Economics and Law,* 1959.

Diamond, William, *Economic Thought of Woodrow Wilson,* 1943.

Dicey, Albert V., *Law and Opinion,* 1905 ed.

Dodd, Edwin M., *American Business Corporations until 1860,* 1954.

Dwight, Theodore W., "The Legality of 'Trusts,'" *Political Science Quarterly,* III, 592, 1888.

Eaton, A. M., "On Contracts in Restraint of Trade," 4 *Harvard Law Review* 128, 1890.

Elliot, Jonathan, ed., *Debates in the Several State Conventions . . .* , 2nd ed., 5 vols., 1861.

Ely, Richard T., "The Founding and Early History of the American Economic Association," *American Economic Review,* XXVI, Supp., 141, 1936.

———, *Ground Under Our Feet,* 1938.

———, "The Nature and Significance of Corporations," *Harper's Magazine,* LXXV, 71, 1887.

———, *Problems of Today,* 1890.

———, "Report on the Organization of the American Economic Association," *Publications of the American Economic Association,* Vol. I, No. I, 1886.

Evans, George H., *Business Incorporation in the United States,* 1948.

Firth, Charles H., and Rait, R. S., *Acts and Ordinances of the Interregnum,* 3 vols., 1911.

Fox. Harold G., *Monopolies and Patents,* 1947.

George, M. Dorothy, "The Combinations Laws," *Economic History Review,* VI, 172, 1935.

Gordon, John W., *Monopolies by Patents,* 1897.

Greenhood, Elisha, *The Doctrine of Public Policy in the Law of Contracts,* 1886.

Gresham, Matilda, *Life of Walter Quintin Gresham,* 2 vols., 1919.

Gunton, George, "The Economic and Social Aspects of Trusts," *Political Science Quarterly,* III, 385, 1888.

Hadley, Arthur T., "Private Monopolies and Public Rights," *Quarterly Journal of Economics,* I, 28, 1887.

Halsbury's Laws of England, Hailsham's 2nd ed., 1939.

Handlin, Oscar and M. F., *Commonwealth Massachusetts,* 1947.

Harbaugh, William H., *Power and Responsibility; the Life and Times of Theodore Roosevelt,* 1961.

Heinsheimer, N., "The Legal Status of Trusts," 2 *Columbia Law Times* 51, 1888.

Hill, Norman L., *Mr. Secretary of State,* 1963.

Hofstadter, Richard, *Social Darwinism in American Thought,* 1944.

Holdsworth, Sir William S., *History of English Law,* 15 vols., 1903-64.

Holmes, Oliver W., Jr., *Holmes-Pollock Letters,* Howe ed., 2 vols., 1941.

House of Commons Journal.

Howell's State Trials — Howell, Thomas Bayly, ed., *Cobbett's Complete Collection of State Trials . . . ,* 33 vols., 1809-26.

Illingworth, William, *An Inquiry into the Laws . . . Respecting Forestalling . . . ,* 1800.

Interstate Commerce Commission, *In the Matter of Consolidation and Combinations of Carriers,* 1902.

———, *Letter of the Chairman . . . Respecting an Agreement to Form a Joint Traffic Association,* 54th Cong., 1st Sess., 1895.

James, Henry, *Richard Olney and his Public Service,* 1923.

Jameson, John A., *The Grounds and Limits of Rightful Interference by Law with the Accumulation and Use of Capital,* 1882.

Jessup, Philip C., *Elihu Root,* 2 vols., 1938.

Johnson, Arthur M., "Antitrust Policy in Transition, 1908," *Mississippi Valley Historical Review,* XLVIII, 415, 1961.

———, "Theodore Roosevelt and the Bureau of Corporations," *Mississippi Valley Historical Review,* XLV, 571, 1959.

Kennan, George, *E. H. Harriman,* 2 vols., 1922.

Kerr, James M., "Contracts in Restraint of Trade," 22 *American Law Review* 873, 1888.

Knox, J. J., *History of Banking in the United States,* 1903.

Knox, Philander C., *The Commerce Clause of the Constitution and the Trusts:* An Address . . . on October 14, 1902, 1902.

Letwin, William, *Documentary History of American Economic Policy,* 1961.

Lewis, Benjamin B., *A Talk About "Trusts,"* 1889.

Lindsey, Almont, *The Pullman Strike,* 1942.

Link, A. S., *Woodrow Wilson and the Progressive Era,* 1954.

Liber Albus London Corporation, *Munimenta Gildhallae Londoniensis: Liber Albus* . . . , Riley, H. T., ed., 3 vols., 1859-62.

Longman, William, *Life and Times of Edward III,* 2 vols., 1869.

Mason, Alpheus T., *Brandeis,* 1946.

McKee, T. H., *National Conventions and Platforms,* 1904.

McMurray, D. L., *Coxey's Army,* 1929.

McQuillan, Eugene, "Validity of Contracts in Restraint of Trade," 33 (N.S. 24) *American Law Register* 217, 281, 1885.

Meyer, B. H., *History of the Northern Securities Case,* 1906.

Mickey, D. M., "Trusts," 22 *American Law Review* 538, 1888.

Mowry, G. E., *Theodore Roosevelt and the Progressive Movement,* 1947.

National Bureau of Economic Research, *Business Concentration and Price Policy,* 1955.

National Civic Federation, *Proceedings of the National Conference on Trusts and Combinations . . . Chicago, October 22-25, 1907,* 1908.

Nef, John U., *Rise of the British Coal Industry,* 1932.

Nelson, Ralph L., *Merger Movements in American Industry,* 1959.

Nevins, Allan, *Grover Cleveland,* 1932.

Olney, Richard, "Labor Unions and Politics," *The Inter-Nation,* 23, Dec., 1906.

———, "Modern Industrialism," *The Inter-Nation,* 29, Feb., 1907.

Patten, Simon N., *The Premises of Political Economy,* 1885.

———, *The Principles of Rational Taxation,* 1890.

Periam, Jonathan, *The Groundswell,* 1874.

Porter, Kirk Harold, and Johnson, D. B., *National Party Platforms,* 1961 ed.

Pringle, H. F., *Theodore Roosevelt,* 1931.

———, *The Life and Times of William Howard Taft,* 2 vols., 1939.

Pyle, J. G., *Life of James J. Hill,* 2 vols., 1917.

Ry. & Corp. L.J. *Railway and Corporation Law Journal.*

Reg. Brev. *Registrum Brevium.*

Richardson, J. D., ed., *Messages and Papers of the Presidents,* 10 vols., 1907.

Richardson, Leon Burr, *William E. Chandler, Republican,* 1940.

Riley, Henry T., *Memorials of London . . . ,* 1868.

Robbins, Lionel, *The Theory of Economic Policy, 1952.*

Roosevelt, Theodore, *Autobiography,* 1913.

Roosevelt Letters ———, *Letters,* E. E. Morison, ed., 8 vols., 1951-54.

———, *Works,* National ed., 24 vols., 1923-26.

Root, Elihu, *Miscellaneous Addresses,* 1917.

Rot. Parl. *Rotuli Parliamentorum,* 6 vols., 1767-77.

Sanderson, William A., *Restraint of Trade in English Law,* 1926.

Schlesinger, Arthur J., Jr., *Age of Jackson,* 1945.

[Sedgwick, Theodore], *What Is a Monopoly?,* 1835.

Seligman, E. R. A., "Railway Tariffs and the Interstate Commerce Law," *Political Science Quarterly,* II, 374, 1887.

Sherman, John, *Recollections of Forty Years . . . ,* 1895.

Sherman Letters Sherman, John and W. T., *Letters,* 1894.

Stephenson, N. W., *Nelson W. Aldrich,* 1930.

Stimson, F. J., "Trusts," 1 *Harvard Law Review* 132, 1887.

Sumner, William Graham, "Trusts and Trade Unions," *Independent,* XL, 482, 1888.

Swisher, Carl B., *Roger B. Taney,* 1935.

Taft, William Howard, *The Anti-Trust Act and the Supreme Court,* 1914.

———, *Presidential Addresses and State Papers,* 1910.

Tawney, R. H., and Power, Eileen, *Tudor Economy Documents,* 3 vols., 1924.

Thorelli, Hans B., *Federal Antitrust Policy,* 1955.

Trevelyan, George M., *England in the Age of Wycliffe,* 1915 ed.

U. S. Congress, *Hearing in Relation to the Agreement of the Joint Traffic Association,* 55th Cong., 1st Sess., 1897.

———, *Hearings before Senate Committee on Interstate Commerce, pursuant to Sen. Res. 98,* 62nd Cong., 1st Sess., 1912.

———, Senate Committee on the Judiciary, Minute Book 226 (March 31, 1890) (Ms. in U. S. Archives).

Unwin, George, ed., *Finance and Trade under Edward III,* 1918.

———, *The Gilds and Companies of London,* 1938.

———, *Industrial Organization in the 16th and 17th Centuries,* 1904.

Wagner, Donald O., "Coke and the Rise of Economic Liberalism," *Economic History Review,* VI, 30, 1935.

———, "The Common Law and Free Enterprise: An Early Case of Monopoly," *Economic History Review,* VII, 217, 1936.

Walker, Albert Henry, *History of the Sherman Law* . . . , 1910.

———, "Who Wrote the Sherman Law?," 73 *Central Law Journal* 257, 1911.

Washburn, Charles, G., *History of a Statute: Sherman Antitrust Act* . . . , 1927.

Wells, David Ames, *Recent Economic Changes,* 1889.

Wiener, Philip Paul, *Evolution and the Founders of Pragmatism,* 1949.

Williston, Samuel, "History of the Law of Business Corporations before 1860," 3 *Select Essays on Anglo-American Legal History,* 1909.

Winfield, Percy Henry, *The Chief Sources of English Legal History,* 1925.

———, *The History of Conspiracy and Abuse of Legal Procedure,* 1921.

Wollman, H., "The Mortality of Trusts," 67 *Albany Law Journal* 227, 1905.

TABLE OF CASES

INDEX

For references to specific cases, see Table of Cases, pp. 293-296.